Drs. Tom & Maureen Anderson

A *Marriage* BEYOND THE *Dream*

D1736243

More than you could dream, hope or imagine.

Phoenix, Arizona

FIRST EDITION

Published by **Word for Winners Publishing**
3520 E. Brown Road, Mesa, AZ 85213
(480) 964-4GOD

ISBN 978-1-58588-987-7
True Romance: *A Marriage Beyond the Dream*

Office number for book orders:

1-888-4WORDTV (1-888-496-7388)

Printed in the United States

Editors: Becky Gilbert and Tammy Zubeck

Dedication

This is dedicated to "the one I love, Maureen."

Dedication and love do not do justice to the fullness in my heart of the depth of love and appreciation I have for the girl I fell in love with when she was 15 and I was 17. She is my inspiration. She's my life. Without her I would not be who I have become, and I will forever be grateful for the investment of love and life she has made in me.

This book reveals the path our lives, love, and marriage has taken. It is a surreal relationship most do not understand and in some cases, believe, but it is available to all who are willing to travel the path and experience *A Marriage Beyond the Dream.*

Table of Contents

Introduction

Marriage was designed by God to be a portrait of His love for the world to see. In the marriage relationship, we should be able to gaze upon the remarkable relationship that exists between Christ and His Bride, the Church. Yet in many marriages, it seems the world is instead witnessing a skewed image of the love God has for His people. With divorce rates in the Church rivaling secular statistics, the true nature of God and His wonderful plan for man have been obscured from the eyes of many.

Marriage is so much more important than we've perhaps realized. A great marriage can promote success in the workplace, a sense of health and well-being in the home, and the assurance of happy marriages for our children and future generations. A marriage that portrays "Heaven on earth" is a godly witness to our children, our families, our friends, and the world. When others see how much a believing husband and wife love each other, they can draw closer to the Master Designer and Architect of marriage and have hope for the future.

Understanding God's intention and design for marriage, it's no wonder that Satan seeks to destroy individual marriages and, indeed, the very institution of marriage as we've understood it. Every Christian divorce is a broken canvas where God intended a masterpiece.

In *True Romance — A Marriage Beyond the Dream*, we have endeavored to share the insights we've gleaned over the years from God's Word and from our own life's experiences. Whether you're a husband, a wife, or someone who desires to marry, please read each chapter with an open heart, even those chapters designated specifically for men or for women. Anyone can benefit from the life-giving truth of God's Word and the insights He has graciously given us to share that have strengthened our own marriage and will be certain to strengthen yours.

We are truly "living the dream" in our marriage, but we didn't begin married life so enriched! In fact, when we began our lives together more than forty years ago, we were just in the babyhood stage of learning. We knew only that we loved each other and that we desired to build a life together that would stand the test of time. Having both come from a broken home, we wanted more for our own marriage.

After we became born again, our desire to build a happy, successful marriage grew even greater. We wanted to bless our children and honor the Lord with our marriage relationship. Still, our early years were fraught with mistakes you'd typically expect a young couple to make. But we were committed to our on-the-job training! We purposed unswervingly to succeed and to build a godly marriage and a legacy of honor and blessing for our children and the generations that would follow.

Since those early days, we've not only learned what makes marriage work, we've discovered what makes it work *well*. And the Lord has equipped us along the way to help others build healthy, happy marriages that last.

No matter where you are in your own marriage, God can work miracles in your life. Whether you simply want to improve a marriage that's good — or you need to rebuild one that's been devastated — there is hope and help in the Lord. All it takes is a heart to glorify God and to pay the price to make your marriage the picture of Christ and the Church that He intends.

It seems that married couples that are living the dream get so much attention because they are a rarity in our society today. But it's not God's will that these "Heaven-on-earth" marriages be so few and far between! Marriages thrive and are a breath of fresh air because of what each person has invested in the relationship and because of the godly patterns that were established over time. In other words, those marriages didn't happen by accident. They happened on purpose because those couples esteemed their relationship as valuable and precious and chose to honor God with the gift of marriage they'd been given.

To be truly successful in marriage and in life, you must value what God values and demonstrate honor for what He honors, not just by your words, but also by your life. What you value in life will always increase in worth because of the great respect with which you treat it. What you value, you will protect and go to great lengths to ensure its preservation. So will be the state of your marriage. When you value your relationship with your spouse, you will protect and keep it, and it will increase in value over time.

God bless you as you read.

Living the dream for His glory,
Drs. Tom and Maureen

1

The Purpose of Genders

Dr. Tom Anderson

God Himself designed the genders; He created us "male and female" (Genesis 1:27; 5:2). Our design is connected to our purpose and value. In other words, when we understand His design for the genders, we'll understand His purpose for the genders. And in gaining new understanding of our purposes, we'll learn to value the opposite sex, especially our spouse.

> *Husbands, likewise, dwell with them with understanding, giving honor to the wife, as to the weaker vessel, and as being heirs together of the grace of life, that your prayers may not be hindered.* (1 Peter 3:7)

We often laugh about our seeming inability to understand the opposite sex. It seems that men especially just accept and resign themselves to the fact that they'll never understand their wife. It reminds me of the following story.

> A guy walks along a California beach, where he finds a small bottle. He rubs the bottle, and a genie appears before him. The genie says, "You can have anything you'd like; I'll grant you one wish."
>
> The man thinks for a moment and answers, "Well, I've always wanted to see the beaches of Hawaii, but I'm afraid to travel by boat or plane. If you could create a road from here to Hawaii, I could drive over and see the beaches."

The genie responds, "That's a tall order that would require a tremendous amount of power and resources to make happen. Isn't there anything else you'd like?"

After a long moment of silence, the man finally says, "Well, there is one other thing that's really important to me, and that is, I would really like to understand my wife."

The genie replies, "Would you like one lane or two?"

Husbands often make jokes about their inability to understand their wife. But it really isn't funny in light of the fact that the Bible commands us as husbands to understand her. Since God says, "Live with her with understanding," that means we can do it. Likewise, it is within a woman's grasp to understand the man in her life.

For years, I'd heard, read, believed, and even joked about the fact that it is impossible for a man to understand a woman. Because the design of men and women is so different, I actually thought that having this understanding wasn't possible and that it wasn't supposed to be possible. But because the Word of God is my standard in what I believe, live, and teach, I have changed my mind on this matter. It is possible for a husband to understand his wife, because the Bible says it is!

Then what has been the problem between the sexes? In counseling couples, it seems one of the complaints I hear most often is, "I just don't understand her!" or, "I don't get where he's coming from!" But the Bible says it's possible for us to gain this understanding. And in honoring each other for our differences instead of criticizing each other, blessings can begin to flow in our marriages where strife once ruled and reigned.

The key to experiencing this level of blessing is application — or applying the truth we know. I'm not saying that you'll have empathy with your spouse because once you understand his or her uniqueness, you'll experience all the same emotions and think the way he or she thinks. I'm simply saying that you can understand the emotions and the thoughts and change the way you respond to them.

'His' and 'Hers' Brains

In recent years, medical science has discovered much concerning the dramatic chemical, hormonal, and even physical differences between "his" brain and "her" brain. We now understand that these physiological differences impact thoughts, emotions, and virtually every area of human behavior.

The Purpose of Genders

What is the bottom line? Men and women are not the same! By God's design, they are uniquely different from one another. So in understanding some of the physical and emotional differences between the genders, we are better able to understand the God-given, God-ordained purpose for those differences.

Let's start at the beginning of a person's life. Men and women are created different from conception. In other words, there are no such things as unisex brains in babies, children, or adults. From our beginnings, we were wired "boy" or "girl" with vital differences that are unique to our gender.

Some "progressive"-minded people accuse traditional society (as if it were a criminal activity) of conditioning boys to be boys and girls to be girls. But these differences between the genders are not nurtured as much as they're natured. Association and environment can play a role in the development of the genders; how-

It is possible for a husband to understand his wife, because the Bible says it is!

ever, the inherent differences are strongly "nature" and God-ordained: A person is either a boy or a girl.

Hormones play the largest role in the development of the male and female brains. At conception, the embryo possesses chromosomes that have determined the gender of the child. However, the embryo does not distinguish gender until about six weeks into gestation. Until that time, the human brain is a basic female brain, because, in simple terms, the egg, or ovum, in a woman is strictly female-produced — then it is fertilized by the male sperm.

If the child is a boy, the hormone testosterone becomes the messenger to the brain, and the network of connections between the right and left sides of the brain diminishes. On the other hand, the female brain — untouched by testosterone — grows even more connections between the two sides of the brain.

What all this means in laymen's terms is that girls mentally have greater processing power than boys — that's why a man will never win an argument with a woman!

The following are some additional facts about the male and female brains:

- The male brain is about ten percent larger than the female brain, which should make him smarter, right? Wrong. Women score consistently equal to men in all intelligence testing.

- Men have 6.5 times more gray matter in the brain (the thinking matter) than women, and women have 9.5 times more white matter (the processing matter) than men. Women have multiplied more connectors between the left (analytical) and right (creative) parts of the brain.
- One third of the male brain is sexual-oriented, while the female's sexual part of the brain is about the size of an almond. Yet one third of her brain is communication-oriented, while his communication part is almond-sized.

Men and women are different, and we shouldn't try to make them alike. Have you ever heard a husband or wife complain about a spouse, "I wish she [he] were more like me"? Have you ever said it yourself? We shouldn't try to make men more like women or women more like men, because it doesn't work. To attempt to "combine" the design of the sexes creates dysfunction and chaos. That is not God's will or design.

The Best Marriage Advice on the Planet: Find Your Spouse's Need and Meet It!

As we've seen, "different" is God's design for the genders. And since men and women are different, their needs in relationships are also different (remember the disparities in the sexual parts and the communication parts of the brain between the genders?). Those "different" needs between the genders must be met if their relationships are to succeed and thrive.

This is usually where the problems begin. In general, we don't want to meet each other's needs! We simply want to ensure that our own needs are met. But that is not God's will. Selfishness won't create a Kingdom marriage, or a marriage that's "Heaven on earth." A Kingdom marriage is established and brings blessing to both people in the marriage when each one learns to die to self and give.

How different are a man's needs and a woman's needs? They are as different as the "his" and "her" brains they were created with!

The following is a general list of gender-specific needs — in order of importance — based on various studies. These needs may not match yours perfectly, but you should be able to recognize and identify with many items on the list. They will help you understand the vast differences between your needs and your spouse's needs.

MALE NEEDS:
1. sex
2. ego affirmation
3. physical touch
4. acts of service
5. security
6. unconditional love
7. trust

FEMALE NEEDS:
1. unconditional love
2. trust
3. communication
4. emotional connection
5. protection
6. security
7. provision
8. affirmation
9. quality time
10. acts of service
11. romance

Some of these needs "overlap" between the genders. Others are altogether exclusive. But whatever the case, in order for love to be true love, both the husband and wife must work to meet the other's needs.

For example, men must learn to love unconditionally. We must purpose to be trustworthy. We must learn to communicate and to be in touch with our emotions and our wife's emotions. We must be the strength in the relationship, offer companionship, and protect, provide for, affirm, serve, and romance.

Women must learn to have and enjoy sex! They must learn to speak sweetly and to affirm, to touch and to allow physical touch, to serve, to be trustworthy, and to love unconditionally.

However, as I said, meeting one another's needs in marriage has historically posed problems. So many needs have gone unmet due to ignorance, selfishness, and indifference.

When a husband and wife's needs are met in their marriage, a remarkable transformation takes place in the marriage and in the man and woman who make up that union. There remains no need to be met by children, workplace or careers, or friends. A happy, fulfilled marriage produces happy, fulfilled lives.

So let's pursue understanding each other's differences as "male and female" so we can understand how to best meet each other's needs.

Created in God's Image

Understanding our spouse is the first key to meeting his or her needs; therefore, it is crucial that we understand our differences as "male and female." We looked at the difference between the genders from conception. Now let's go back even further — to our beginnings in Creation, in God's creation of the first man and woman on the earth.

I believe that everything in God's creation relates to one another — and that there is something we can learn about God by studying or observing His creation (see Romans 1:20). Therefore, if we will pay attention to the creation of man and woman, we will better understand God since we are created in His image and likeness (Genesis 1:26-27). But we will also better understand each other as male and female.

The Bible says that God created both male and female in His own image.

> *Then God said, "Let Us make man in Our image, according to Our likeness; let them have dominion over the fish of the sea, over the birds of the air, and over the cattle, over all the earth and over every creeping thing that creeps on the earth." So God created man in His own image; in the image of God He created him; MALE and FEMALE He created them.* (Genesis 1:26-27)

It is important to note that God is Spirit (John 4:24) and therefore neither male nor female in a human sense. Remember, this passage says that God created both male and female in His image.

The Father, Son, and Holy Spirit were all present in Creation. We've heard so much teaching about God the Father and Jesus the Son. But we haven't heard as much in-depth teaching about the Holy Spirit, who is often represented as the "feminine" side of God. We know that the Creation relates directly to Jesus, the Word that was "made flesh and dwelt among us." Nothing was created except by the Word of God. (See John 1:1-3,14.) But let's look at the Holy Spirit's role in Creation.

Genesis 1:2 says, "The earth was without form, and void; and darkness was on the face of the deep…." Then it says, "…And the Spirit of God was hovering over the face of the waters." So the Holy Spirit was brooding over the waters. Yet nothing happened until God spoke.

Then God said, "Let there be light"; and there was light.
(Genesis 1:3)

When God gave the word, the Holy Spirit brought forth that word in power and gave life and substance to that spoken word. The following pages will reveal how this function of the Holy Spirit relates to the design of the genders, especially the woman.

The 'Wombed Man' —
Comparable But Different

Genesis 2:18 says, "And the Lord God said, 'It is not good that man should be alone; I will make him a helper comparable to him.'" You can read the recorded account of God's creation of woman in Genesis chapter 2. God put Adam to sleep and took from him a rib. From that, he fashioned woman — "comparable" but different. She came from man, but she was noticeably different.

God made Adam a helper — woman — in part, to carry Adam's seed and to bring forth life. I don't need to give you an anatomy lesson to simply tell you that woman was made with reproductive organs distinctly differently from man's. She is a "wombed man," if you will, with the ability to receive seed and to hold, incubate, nurture, and grow that seed until it is brought forth as new life.

This aspect of woman's design was no accident; it was a purposeful, deliberate act of the Creator. Remember, in Genesis 1:27, it says, "…God created man in His own image…male and female…." At that point, there was just Adam. Then in creating Eve (Genesis 2:18-23), God separated the "male and female" in Adam so that there was now man and woman — two genders, each with a distinct design and a distinct purpose.

Weakness or Design?

What is the purpose of a man and a woman, especially as it pertains to marriage? Very simply, men are by design sowers and initiators, and women are by design receivers and responders. Besides the obvious fact that a wife receives "seed" from her husband in pro-creation in order to bring forth new life, she receives what he sows into her heart and mind, and she "incubates" that until it, too, comes to life. In other words, she is an especially good "meditator" of the words and actions of her husband! This is not her weakness; it's her design, as we will see.

If you as a husband want to have a good relationship with your wife, you're going to have to sow the right kind of seed. The right words get the right reaction, and the right seed gets the right harvest. As I said, man is a sower by nature; woman is an "incubator" by nature, or a meditator. What does she incubate? Words. This is who she is by design, not by weakness. It's her design by God.

Have you ever noticed that a woman can tell you the same story four times and use different words each time? There's a reason for that. She has meditated on that story over and over again — and when she tells it to you, she's meditating on it again.

This irritates a lot of men, but, frankly, men have to hear a story four times before they'll remember just a part of it! A wife will say something to her husband, and he'll think, Didn't we talk about this yesterday? I don't remember for certain. Did we? She's simply trying to get something across to him, and her attitude is, if she says it enough, maybe some of it will "stick"!

Women are by nature great meditators and great communicators. What does it mean "to meditate"? It means to imagine, muse, devise, study, mutter, utter, talk, speak, roar, and groan. This word also portrays the idea of a person chewing something — as a cow chews its cud — and digesting it until it becomes a part of him.

Meditating in the Word of God is something we are all called to do as believers (see Joshua 1:8). But women by design are especially good meditators. They are brooders, so to speak, and will brood over words in much the same way a hen will brood over the life that's in the egg until it is finally brought forth.

A woman can give life to everything that is communicated to her — every thought, word, and deed, including body language and tones. She can meditate on it and incubate it until those thoughts, words, or deeds are given life.

Sowing and Reaping in Marriage

One of the most basic things every husband should know about his wife is that every seed he plants into her life is going to produce after its own kind.

For example, the Bible says, "Husbands, love your wives and do not be harsh with them" (Colossians 3:19 NIV). I have searched the Scripture over and over to find where God says, "Wives, do not be harsh with your husbands." But it's not in there. That doesn't mean that it's okay for a wife to be harsh toward her husband, because it certainly isn't okay. However, God specifically addresses husbands about loving their wife and not being harsh toward her. A man must sow love, peace, patience, gentleness, and kindness into the life of his bride.

What often happens, however, is a man gets caught up in his worka-day world dealing with frustrations on the job — and then he brings that attitude home to his wife. He sows harshness into her life in his tone of voice and body language, and perhaps even his words.

Well, she'll meditate on that. After all, she's been working hard too. She's trying to serve her husband, take care of the kids, and perform other tasks in the home. So she begins brooding. He's fussing, and she's fuming. While he's taking his frustrations out on her, she's in deep thought: *I married this guy and gave my life to him. I pledged to honor him, and he's treating me harshly. Okay then, I'll show him harsh!* And his harvest begins to be multiplied back to him.

Some men don't want to hear that, but it's the truth, anyway. Every seed that he plants into his wife's life is going to produce after its own kind! In fact, everything he sows into his marriage, he's going to reap as a multiplied harvest. It's scriptural, and it's absolutely true.

In light of this truth, how foolish would it be for a husband to sow harshness toward his wife? On the other hand, how wise would it be to sow love, peace, patience, gentleness, and kindness? As a husband, when you truly understand the design and purpose of the genders and the law of sowing and reaping in marriage, you will wisely and earnestly sow into your wife what God says you should sow.

In Ephesians 5:21-33, the Lord compares the relationship between a husband and wife to the relationship between Christ and the Church. Christ is the picture of the husband in marriage, and the Church — the Bride of Christ — is the picture of the wife. And just as we, the Bride of Christ, are to receive the Word of God and meditate on it until we bear fruit — or produce life — a woman will meditate on the words her husband speaks and bring life to those words.

When we as believers receive God's Word into our heart, we be-come "impregnated" by that Word and life is formed. That word becomes programmed into our actions and then surfaces in our circumstances. We become recipients of the divine life that's contained in the Word.

For instance, when you heard and received the Word concerning sal-vation, you became "impregnated" with salvation, and new life in Christ was brought forth; you became a child of God. That happened because of the completed picture: God the Father, Jesus the Word, and the Holy Spirit, who is the agent of the godhead that brings forth the life.

The Heart of a Woman

Proverbs 4:23 says, "Keep your heart with all diligence, for out of it spring the issues of life." The heart is a powerful spiritual force in bringing forth new life in the earth. This is especially true concerning women. As I said, women are programmed to meditate on and incubate words until those words bring forth life.

Mary the mother of Jesus was a great example of a woman who incubated words, meditating on and pondering them in her heart.

> *And they [the shepherds] came with haste and found Mary and Joseph, and the Babe lying in a manger. Now when they had seen Him, they made widely known the saying which was told them concerning this Child. And all those who heard it marveled at those things which were told them by the shepherds. BUT MARY KEPT ALL THESE THINGS AND PONDERED THEM IN HER HEART.* (Luke 2:16-19)

In the same chapter, we read again that Mary pondered and held close in her heart the words that were spoken to her. The fact that Mary pondered and meditated on the words she'd heard is important.

> *His [Jesus'] parents went to Jerusalem every year at the Feast of the Passover. And when He was twelve years old, they went up to Jerusalem according to the custom of the feast. When they had finished the days, as they returned, the Boy Jesus lingered behind in Jerusalem. And Joseph and His mother did not know it; but supposing Him to have been in the company, they went a day's journey, and sought Him among their relatives and acquaintances. So when they did not find Him, they returned to Jerusalem, seeking Him. Now so it was that after three days they found Him in the temple, sitting in the midst of the teachers, both listening to them and asking them questions. And all who heard Him were astonished at His understanding and answers. So when they saw Him, they were amazed; and His mother said*

to Him, "Son, why have You done this to us? Look, Your father
and I have sought You anxiously." And He said to them, "Why
did you seek Me? Did you not know that I must be about My
Father's business?" But they did not understand the statement
which He spoke to them. Then He went down with them and came
to Nazareth, and was subject to them, BUT HIS MOTHER KEPT
ALL THESE THINGS IN HER HEART. (Luke 2:41-51)

From what we know about Mary from Scripture, it's safe to say
that she was a meditator, holding God's words in her heart and pondering them. Mary is typical of most women today. Just as women bring
forth natural life, they also bring forth "life" from the words they ponder,
whether good or bad. Women are incubators of all things: A good word
spoken to a woman's heart will produce a good thing; a bad word spoken
will produce a bad thing.

Bearing fruit and bringing forth life from God's Word is a picture
of the Church. The Body of Christ can learn something from its female
members about pondering and bringing forth life from words.

Of course, we know that a woman who has been treated poorly by
her husband must walk in love and forgiveness just as any other believer
must walk in love. In other words, the commandment of God to walk in
love is given to the woman as well as to the man. And when God says
to meditate on things that are "true, noble, just, pure, lovely, and of good
report" (Philippians 4:8), He's talking to both men and women. Women
are responsible to take wrong thoughts captive and not dwell on them (2
Corinthians 10:5) just as men are responsible to take wrong thoughts captive and not dwell on them.

In my many years of performing marriage counseling, I've made some
observations over the years that corroborate what I'm saying to you now
from Scripture. (I don't perform marriage counseling for church members
anymore, because it robs me of my ability to yield to the Holy Spirit from
the pulpit and minister in the area of marriage. For example, I might say
something in a church setting by the unction of the Holy Spirit that coin-
cides with something someone has said to me in a counseling session. I
don't want that person to think I'm talking about him or her publicly, so
I've assigned many of those counseling responsibilities to my staff.)

Back when I did perform marriage counseling, this was a common
scenario: A husband and wife who were separated would come into my

office. They'd been married for years, but then the wife had given him the boot, so to speak. I would address the wife first, because in most cases, the husband was clueless. He thought everything was fine until his wife threw him out. He had a wife and kids, a job, a house, a car, so his attitude was, We're doing fine. What's the problem? But for years, he'd been sowing the wrong things into his wife.

If a man sows bitterness into his wife, it may take ten, fifteen, twenty years, or even more — but eventually there will be the birth of a "baby" called bitterness. And it will be a living thing that will likely destroy that relationship. In other words, once it happens, it's tough to restore what's been lost.

The heart is like a womb in that whatever grows there will produce something. The heart will give life and substance to what was planted there. And it never just gives back just the seed that was sown; it gives back a multiplied harvest on that seed.

This is especially true of women in marriage. Naturally speaking, if you give a woman a seed, she'll give you a baby. If you give a woman a house, she'll give you a home. If you give her a smile, she may give you her heart. A husband will always receive a multiplied harvest on the seed he sows into the life of his wife.

Women were created to multiply fruit and life from seed. They are gifted at turning something small into something large or significant. For instance, Jesus had one conversation with the woman at the well in Samaria (see John 4:4-26), and she turned it into an evangelistic crusade. She multiplied the word of the Lord that was sown into her life.

The Wonder of Pregnancy and Birth

Just as a woman receives "seed" from the man and conceives a baby, we as the Bride of Christ receive the seed of God's Word, hiding it in our heart where that seed grows and produces life. We read, study, meditate on, and talk about the Word until it has "conceived" in our heart and begins to grow. Then we expect a manifestation of what has been conceived, because we've entered into the "rest" of faith wherein we know that we know that we actually have what we've conceived although we do not as yet see it.

For instance, if you've meditated on God's Word concerning healing, and you believe you've received healing while you're still experiencing symptoms, you are "pregnant" with God's Word. You're expecting a "baby" — a manifestation of God's Word in the form of healing. And you'll begin making preparations for that "baby" to come forth!

In other words, the Word of God hidden and nurtured in a person's heart creates life, but it also creates expectancy. There's an air of excitement surrounding a person of genuine faith in God's Word.

Similarly, when a woman is pregnant, she usually knows it! And when a woman knows she's pregnant, no one can talk her out of the fact that she's going to have a baby. She'll decorate a nursery and obtain diapers, blankets, and other items to prepare for the arrival of that baby.

Similarly, when you're in faith about something, you know it. When you're believing God for something, you're expecting to see it show up at any time.

I'm using the analogy of pregnancy to explain God's design of a woman and why she is so significant. Women are incubators of words, and the best illustration of that process is pregnancy. Yet this process of bringing forth life from seed is a reality concerning every member of the Body of Christ.

To illustrate this point, in a physical pregnancy, one of the first things that happens in the woman is, her womb begins to thicken. That's like our heart when we receive the Word of God; it "thickens" so that we can hold on to that Word until the answer is brought forth. So when the enemy comes to steal the Word, that Word is guarded and protected in our heart.

When God's Word enters your heart, you have to toughen up. If you want to hold on to what you've received and see it grow and mature in your spirit so that it produces something visible, you have to be "thick-skinned." In other words, you can't waver every time a circumstance comes at you to tell you that God's Word isn't true or that you're never going to see what you're believing in your heart. If you ever want to see it, you have to be tough.

Some people don't like hearing that. They'll say, "I just can't walk by faith; it's too hard."

But you can be as strong as you need to be. You can be strong in the Lord and the power of His might (Ephesians 6:10). So you need to say, "Yes, I can endure because God says I can. He planted this Word in my heart — and I'm holding on to it! There's going to be a baby soon. Devil, you get out of here! I've received the Word, and you can't have it!"

In a pregnancy, after the womb thickens, hormonal changes also begin to take place. In part, these chemical changes are designed to prevent miscarriage. Similarly, that's what teaching does for the Bride of Christ.

All Scripture is given by inspiration of God, and is profitable for doctrine, for reproof, for correction, for instruction in righteousness. (2 Timothy 3:16)

If we don't continue in the Word, or if we don't understand how to hold on to and nurture what we've received, we become in danger of losing it. That's where the teaching of the Word comes in, producing the changes necessary in the hearer so that he doesn't miscarry and lose what was conceived in his heart.

One way people miscarry the Word of God in their heart is through their wrong confession. For example, if they're speaking the Word that's in their heart one day, but the next day they're saying, "Things don't look any different. I'm not sure if this is coming to pass or not," they could miscarry the Word that's in their heart, making it unproductive in their life.

Most women who are pregnant will go to great measures to protect the life that's growing within them. They know that if they guard what's been conceived in their womb, in nine months, they'll be holding a baby.

After the thickening of the womb and the hormonal changes that take place in the body of a pregnant woman, there is a third change that takes place. Nutrients from all over her body begin to flow toward the life that's growing inside her. Nourishment goes first to the baby before providing nutrition to the mother's body.

Let's look at this from a spiritual viewpoint. A woman has a crisis of some kind that she needs to overcome. Like those nutrients in the body of a pregnant woman, all this woman's thoughts, emotions, and energies begin to flow toward that situation. She's endeavoring to bring something forth. Then she sees the answer in her mind's eye, and in her heart, and she begins to prepare for the manifestation of the answer she needs.

Another interesting thing happens in a woman's body when she's pregnant. Her center of gravity changes. In case you haven't noticed, a woman sits, stands, and walks a little differently when she's nine months pregnant than when she's only three months pregnant. As the baby within her grows, her stance becomes stronger and more balanced.

Similarly, when we're holding fast to God's Word in our hearts, we, too, must stand fast so that we will not be shaken or moved from our position or place. No matter what the circumstances, we will not back up or back off. We are determined to give birth to the dream God has placed in our heart.

I've shared this analogy so you can see that women by design are keepers of words. They hold words spoken to them until those words produce something. If only husbands would grasp this important truth! It would change their life and their marriage. So much of a husband's success or failure — his enjoyment or his "just enduring" — is determined by the seeds he sows into his marriage. A woman by nature will produce what a husband sows into her life.

Another unique facet of a woman's design that goes along with this is her persistence. I'll illustrate this from the following well-known passage.

> *...There was in a certain city a judge who did not fear God nor regard man. Now there was a widow in that city; and she came to him, saying, 'Get justice for me from my adversary.' And he would not for a while; but afterward he said within himself, 'Though I do not fear God nor regard man, yet because this widow troubles me I will avenge her, lest by her continual coming she weary me.'* (Luke 18:2-5 NKJV)

Verse 2 says, "There was in a certain city a judge who did not fear God nor regard man." In other words, he just didn't care. But notice that didn't stop this woman. In other words, she came to get something, and she wasn't leaving without it!

A woman will stick with the program, so to speak, until the job is done. Just as a pregnant woman will not let go of the life that's developing within her, a woman is persistent and enduring by design. And her God-given design should teach all of us that once we've conceived the Word of God in our heart, we must never let go of that Word. We must stay with it until there is a birth. Whether it takes six months, nine months, or even years, if you know that Word has been conceived in your heart, you must persist and never change your mind about the outcome.

Very simply, a woman who's pregnant knows she has a baby coming. She can't see the baby yet, but you can't talk her out of her belief that a baby is on the way! We all can learn something from that.

So women are not only great incubators of life — they are also gifted at bringing forth that life. They are meditators and communicators of life!

Do you know why did Jesus waited for a woman to come by the tomb after His resurrection? He knew that if He told a woman that He had risen from the dead, she would recognize the significance and wouldn't forget it! She would communicate it immediately to everyone she knew. That's not her fault or weakness; it's her design.

Many have seen this strength as a flaw and have not valued it properly or as God requires. Think about it. John and Peter were both at the tomb, but after they discovered that it was empty, there's no record of them telling anyone about it. It's as if one turned to the other and said, "Hey, you wanna go fishing?"

Jesus trusted a woman with the revelation of His ascension from death and the grave. He knew that she would carry that Gospel to every person who would listen. She would disseminate and communicate life. That's part of her design — and it's a strength, not a weakness.

If you as a husband will recognize the design, purpose, and value of your wife — and sow the right things into her and into your marriage, you will reap a marriage that's Heaven on earth. If you sow peace, you'll reap peace. If you sow gentleness, you'll get gentleness. If you sow love, you'll get love — and you'll always get a multiplied harvest on your seed. You'll receive a lot more peace, gentleness, and love.

If you get hold of this secret, you've gotten hold of the secret of life, because your wife will bring forth life from what you've planted into her. And she'll do it by the design and purpose of God.

2
The Motivated Marriage: What Makes You 'Tick'?

Dr. Maureen Anderson

Every person on earth has a basic need to feel loved. And marriage is a relationship in which both parties especially need to experience feelings of love, contentment, and well-being. When both a husband and wife feel happy and loved in their marriage, they create a happy home environment in which their children are raised experiencing those same feelings. The children's basic need for love is met in an atmosphere where their parents' marriage is healthy and thriving.

To be loved unconditionally is the cry of each person's heart. But everyone receives love differently. There are three components to a great marriage: (1) the physical; (2) the relational; and (3) the familial. And although all three elements of physical intimacy, relational intimacy, and familial intimacy must be present in a successful marriage, one of these elements will have a higher priority for each one of us.

In other words, each spouse will feel most happy in the marriage when he or she is being fulfilled in one of these areas — physical intimacy, relational intimacy, or familial intimacy.

Sex, Friendship, and Feelings of 'Happily Ever After': God's Complete Picture for Marriage

Certainly, a marriage needs all three of those things to survive: (1) sex, or the physical aspect of marriage; (2) friendship, or the relational aspect; and (3) commitment, or the familial aspect of marriage. But for every married person, one of these elements will be more meaningful to him or her than the other two.

Physical Intimacy in Marriage

God created sex for the marriage. Sex is a gift from God to you to be enjoyed in marriage beginning on your wedding day. God intended sex for pleasure and pro-creation, but it's also a symbol of the covenant between you and your spouse to remain through life as "one flesh" (Genesis 2:24; Ephesians 5:31).

People who lean toward this aspect of marriage more than the other two are most interested in the physical part of the relationship. Because of the various brain chemicals that are released during sexual intercourse, they feel almost "high" from the feelings of intimacy they derive from a healthy, satisfying sex life. The levels of certain hormones in their bodies are higher than in others. Sex is very important to them (and it should be important to every married couple). They are fulfilled by the feelings of love they receive when they enjoy physical intimacy with their spouse.

Friendship in Marriage

People who favor this aspect of the marriage place a huge amount of importance on personality and on emotional and intellectual compatibility. They view their spouse as their best friend and thrive on participating in hobbies and activities they can do together. They feel most loved when they are spending quality time with their spouse — having long talks together, sharing their dreams, goals, and desires, or just being together.

Family and Commitment in Marriage

Although marriage is a "forever-after" commitment for every couple, some people place preeminence on that feeling of deep commitment from their spouse. They derive great fulfillment in the assurance that no matter what, there's no turning back in their commitment to each other.

People who value this quality above all else also value family relationships. Those who favor familial intimacy simply must have children because their lives are all about "family" and a sense of community. They are extremely family-oriented; everything revolves around family activities because family equals security. You usually find people like this with extended family that live nearby. They highly value having family close to them at all times.

Don't misunderstand me. Family is important no matter who you are, and marriage is a serious, sacred commitment of love "till death do us part." Friendship and emotional compatibility are crucial to the success of any marriage relationship — and sex and physical closeness are also vital to the life of a marriage. All three of these elements must be present in a truly successful marriage. However, since every one of us is different, one of these elements will have a higher priority in our heart than the other two. And that one element will be absolutely essential to our happiness in the marriage.

That's why it's so important to find out what pleases your spouse — and what makes him or her feel the most loved — and then strive to do that. Both people in a marriage must derive happiness and fulfillment from the relationship in order for that marriage to be completely successful.

Understanding What Makes You 'Tick'

I liken these three elements — physical intimacy, relational intimacy, and familial intimacy — to the main ingredients in a recipe. All three of them are needed to make the recipe work — just one missing item will cause the dish to flop. However, you might have a favorite ingredient! It doesn't mean your ingredient is more important than the others; it simply means it's most important to you.

Do you know your "ingredient"? Equally important, do you know your spouse's favorite ingredient for a great marriage?

If you don't know which element is most important to you, ask yourself the question, What says love to me like nothing else? Is it physical intimacy and closeness? Is it emotional intimacy — long con-

> *To be loved unconditionally is the cry of each person's heart.*

versations and time spent together doing everyday activities? Is it repeated expressions of long-term commitment in every season of life — and feelings of warmth that you feel when family is near?

Once you know what makes you "tick" in marriage, it's important to communicate that to your spouse and then find out which of these three elements he or she favors most. Even if it's not the thing that touches your heart the most, your willingness to meet that other person's need will make your marriage complete.

Great marriages are kept fresh and alive by remaining in a constant mode of discovery concerning your mate's likes and dislikes. People's needs can change over time, so it's important not to paint your spouse into a corner, so to speak, concerning his or her needs and desires in marriage. For example, sex and physical intimacy may be of foremost importance to you at one point in your marriage — yet later, commitment and family become the things you live for. So never assume you know everything about your spouse! Stay interested in learning his or her changing priorities and desires through every season of your lives together.

Now let's look in greater detail at the three elements that motivate people in marriage.

Physical Intimacy

A person whose priority is physical intimacy ranks sex and romance as the highest joy in their relationship with their spouse. They appreciate sex as a gift from God. And people in a highly physical relationship usually have a lot of energy or chemistry between one another. These are the people who feel just as in love with their spouse as the day they married, because they keep the thoughts and emotions of physical intimacy alive. As a result, the sexual attraction between them keeps growing, even as they grow older — not because of what's happening on the outside but because of what's happening on the inside, in their heart and emotions. (We'll look further at the physiological effects of these thoughts and emotions in Chapter 9.)

Let him kiss me with the kisses of his mouth — for your love is more delightful than wine. (Song of Solomon 1:2 NIV)

Sexually motivated people place a strong emphasis on great sex, and the act of lovemaking keeps their relationship close. They feel emotionally connected through sexual intercourse. Outside of the bedroom, a physical couple often engages in flirting with each other. They tease each other often, and there is sexual energy in the dynamics of their unique relationship.

In any marriage, sex deepens the bond of love between a husband and wife. One of the reasons for this is the releasing of certain chemicals by the brain during sex. Peptide oxytocin is the feel-good chemical produced during sex that causes us to feel good about the relationship, about ourselves, and about life in general. This chemical actually promotes deep bonding and encourages more affectionate behavior.

The body also releases endorphins when a couple engages in affectionate behavior. That's why affection promotes feelings of well-being. Endorphins produce energy and promote healing and have also been proven to act as natural pain-relievers in the body.

During sex, the chemicals that flood our body bring a deep sense of peace, calm, and well-being. Studies have shown that oxytocin actually blocks unpleasant memories in the brain. This sheds some light on why make-up sex is so popular! Plus, whatever it was we were so upset about, this chemical causes us to "forgive and forget"!

> *The body is absolutely amazingly put together by God, and science is catching up to understand just how it works. Just as our body releases chemicals during sex, it also releases chemicals when we argue or fight that can be detrimental to our health and well-being. That's one of the reasons why God commands us, "'Be angry, and do not sin': do not let the sun go down on your wrath"* (Ephesians 4:26).

It's crucial that we learn to forgive our spouse quickly and refuse to allow strife to interfere with our physical intimacy. If we've had an argument or disagreement, the act of sex can actually "wipe out" negative memories and provide us with a clean slate so that emotional intimacy and bonding can continue in the relationship.

Potential Problems in the Physical Marriage

Physically oriented people always feel "in love" because, whether they're consciously aware of it or not, they crave the emotional high that comes from the release of those feel-good chemicals during sex with their spouse. No matter where they are, when they think of their spouse, they are flooded with that desire for intimacy with him or her.

However, people who are motivated this way can confuse their emotions for true love — their emotions can bounce around from high to low. They need the stability that comes from a knowledge of God and His Word — so that when their emotions try to confuse them, they can stand steady in the godly character that's produced by a genuine relationship with God. (We'll talk more true love, sex, and the covenant of marriage in Chapters 11 and 15.)

Relational Intimacy

> *My dove in the clefts of the rock, in the hiding-places on the mountainside, show me your face, let me hear your voice; for*

*your voice is sweet, and your face is lovely.... His mouth is
sweetness itself; he is altogether lovely. This is my lover, this
my friend, O daughters of Jerusalem.*
(Song of Solomon 2:14, 5:16 NIV)

In these two verses, we have the perspective of the husband in his
attitude toward his wife — and then that of the wife toward her husband.
They highly value their time spent together, just noticing and admiring one
another. In these verses, we see two perspectives of a friendship relationship that's based on true love.

People who prize the relational facet of marriage need to regularly get
away with their spouse, free from the distractions of everyday life. They
enjoy focusing on activities they can do together, but they especially crave
spending quality time focusing just on each other. Just as those who value
physical intimacy need a fulfilling sex life to feel connected to their mate,
"relational" people need intimate, heartfelt conversation to feel connected
to their loved one.

Certainly, relational, or friendship relationships aren't limited to marriage. Yet in principle, friendships provide the model for the behavior in
marriage that a relational person desires.

We find this same principle of relational intimacy at work in Moses'
friendship with God.

> *As Moses went into the tent, the pillar of cloud would come
> down and stay at the entrance, while the Lord spoke with
> Moses.... The Lord would speak to Moses face to face, as a man
> speaks with his friend....* (Exodus 33:9-11 NIV)

Moses enjoyed face-to-face fellowship with God. Moses' relationship with God was anything but casual; it was an intimate friendship that
became the focus of Moses' life. Moses wanted to be God's friend, so he
built a tent to shield himself from distraction so that He could commune
with the Lord. That tent was the place where Moses would go to meet with
God face to face. Moses honored God in friendship, longing for God's
companionship and giving God his undivided attention on a consistent
basis. And Moses had great favor with God in return.

It has been said that the lifeline of true love is friendship. Friendship
connects you to your spouse because there's so much emotion involved in

the sharing of thoughts and feelings — communicating your dreams, goals, desires, ideas, your love for each other, and the things you care about and need. And the same way you connect with and develop your relationship with your spouse is very similar to the way you develop your relationship with God. When you read His Word, you hear His heart, and you better understand His character and nature.

Of course, God knows everything about you, but when you talk to Him, communing with Him from your heart, you form a greater bond. That bond affects everything about you — how you view others and how you react to the situations of life. You're always conscious and aware of His loving Presence in your life and His great love for you. Your friendship with God has a positive affect on your whole outlook on life. You are more confident and assured of your future when you're in close fellowship with God.

You and I can have many wonderful friendships in life — with fellow church members, co-workers, or even extended family. But intimate friendships, such as the one you have with God and with your spouse, are different. Those friendships go beyond the level of "small talk" and acquaintanceship. People in these kinds of relationships are very close. They share things with one another that they wouldn't share with anyone else. Trust and loyalty have been established and connection is easy, not forced.

Proverbs 18:24 says that a true friend sticks closer than a brother. In other words, intimate friendship takes you to another level. When other friendships have come and gone, a true, intimate friendship remains. This is the kind of friendship the relational-oriented person desires in marriage with his or her spouse.

Friendship Is About Connecting

In John chapter 15, Jesus talks about friendship and love. He addresses us as the branches and calls Himself the Vine. Then He says, "Apart from Me, you can do nothing" (see John 15:5). What was Jesus talking about? Vital connection and union.

Then after talking about the connection that happens between the Vine and the branch, Jesus goes on to call us His friends.

Greater love has no one than this, than to lay down one's life for his friends. You are My friends if you do whatever I command you. No longer do I call you servants, for a servant does not know what his master is doing; but I have called you friends, for all things that I heard from My Father I have made known to you. (John 15:13-15)

Jesus said, "Greater love has no one than this, than to lay down one's life for his friends" (v. 13). Isn't that how Christ loved us? He loved us by laying down His life, by giving it up for us.

Ephesians 5:25 says that men should love their wives in the same way Jesus loved us — by laying down his own life for his wife.

Husbands, love your wives, just as Christ loved the church and gave himself up for her (Ephesians 5:25 NIV)

God has called husbands to befriend their wife! That may not come naturally to some men, but if they're married, it's their calling as a husband, nevertheless.

In fact, if you're a husband, you need to know that your wife is to be your very best friend next to Jesus! God has called you to an intimate friendship with the wife He has given you, and the two of you are to be closer to each other than you are to your friends, co-workers, parents, children, or grandchildren. A relationship like this must be cultivated. It grows over time as trust is built — trust in the other person's character and in the love you consistently show one another.

As we've seen, friendship thrives when there's heart-to-heart, face-to-face communication. As hectic as our lives can get in this day and age, sometimes that means having to plan spending quality time with your spouse. You need time away from everyday life just to focus on each other and on your marriage.

People who most value friendship in marriage enjoy doing everyday activities as well as special activities, such as sports and other hobbies with their spouse. But for them, it's not just about the activities; it's about spending quality time with that other person with the goal in mind of connecting and remaining connected through relational bonding.

Tearing Down the Walls of Fear

Friendship in marriage also means you confide in each other as husband and wife; you don't keep secrets from one another. Friendship is a relationship in which you can make yourself vulnerable. You can be yourself and let the other person know who you are without fear. You can also be trusted with what your spouse shares with you, and you will always believe in your mate. When the relational aspect of your marriage is being nurtured, there is transparency. There is a feeling of safety and security in the relationship that make transparency possible.

In the Garden of Eden before the fall of man, Adam and Eve were "naked and not ashamed" (see Genesis 2:25). Similarly, in marriage today, we must be able to "bare" our thoughts and feelings with each other and not feel ashamed or threatened.

Yet so many people in marriage do feel intimidated about sharing their true feelings with their spouse. They're unwilling to make themselves vulnerable with that other person because trust has been broken, or trust has never been established to begin with. They keep up walls of separation to avoid being hurt by their spouse — the person they became "one flesh" with in marriage. Those walls are built on the foundation of fear. But if those marriages are to be truly successful, the walls of fear must come down, and a new foundation of love must be established.

Marriage should be a safe haven of trust, warmth, acceptance, and love. It should not be a place where we feel as if we must hide from our spouse!

'Talk to Me'

Communication is a must in a friendship relationship, especially in marriage. A couple must share with each other their dreams, desires, needs, and the things they care about. This is how this type of relationship develops and grows.

When Tom and I were first married, he was the tall, dark, handsome, silent type — a man of very few words. But I was a communicator. Tom saw right away my need for friendship, so he studied the subject of friendship and marriage. He literally studied to change. He fasted and prayed, seeking God about how to better communicate and connect with me on personal level. He knew that if he was going to be in my world, we needed to be friends!

Some people have trouble communicating on a personal level with others because they don't feel connected to themselves. And if they're not connected to themselves, they can't be connected to others. Someone who's disconnected isn't in touch with himself. You might ask him how he feels about something, and he often answers, "I dunno." And he really doesn't!

He is disconnected and out of touch with his own emotions, desires, and needs. That person must reconnect with himself before he can enjoy a close relationship with his spouse.

Sometimes people "disconnect" from themselves because to be in touch with their feelings would be too painful or unpleasant for them. Perhaps they were raised in a home where communication was discouraged. Some children are punished for expressing their likes or dislikes. This practice teaches them the lie that what they feel isn't important, and they subconsciously begin early in life the process of withdrawing into their emotional "shell" where it's safe.

Some people are disconnected simply because no one connected with them in their childhood, even in their own family. They were raised in a family in which connection was not valued. Consequently, they grew up knowing very little about the people in their own home! As a result, these are not usually the people who seek out emotional connection in marriage! In fact, connecting emotionally in marriage is a foreign concept to them.

Yet friendship and emotional intimacy are a vital part of marriage. So if emotional and relational intimacy challenges you, don't give up! The Holy Spirit can help you connect with your spouse on an emotional level and cause you to know joy and fulfillment in your marriage relationship in ways you never thought possible.

When you need to confide in someone or you need to be consoled — or you have some really exciting news to tell — who is the first person you turn to? If you can't honestly answer, "My spouse," you and your spouse need to make this a matter of heartfelt prayer to God.

Potential Problems in the Relational Marriage

With every strength in a marriage, there can be extreme behavior that is counterproductive or unhealthy to your relationship. For example, in a relational marriage that's based on friendship, the couple may enjoy each other's company so much that they neglect their other relationships. They don't spend adequate time developing friendships with other couples or even with their own children. When this happens, the strength in their marriage can become a weakness, so extremes must be guarded against.

Also, developing an intimate friendship with your spouse shouldn't take away from your individuality. A husband and wife are one flesh in marriage, but they're still two individuals with unique gifts and talents placed within them by God.

Connecting with your spouse in relational marriage can be compared to a precious jewel — it's a single bright, sparkling gem but with many facets! And since it's those unique facets that make up the whole, each facet must be valued and esteemed. Similarly, a person's individual "brilliance" should not be shrouded or diminished in his or her marriage relationship.

Familial Intimacy

For some, commitment and unconditional love are the lifeblood of their marriage. People who prize this aspect of marriage crave affirmations of commitment on a regular basis and the feelings of security that family brings. There is a humorous anecdote in which the husband proclaims to his wife, "I told you when I married you that that I love you — and once is enough. If I ever change my mind, I'll let you know." That kind of mentality doesn't work for the commitment- and family-oriented spouse!

Commitment is crucial in any marriage, because during the hard times when you might be tempted to throw in the towel, commitment will keep you in the marriage. You will fulfill the vow, or commitment, you made to God and to the other person. Your commitment overrides any temporary feelings of discouragement, frustration, or disillusionment and holds you steady and stable so that you can "stay the course" in your marriage.

Although this should hold true in the lives of any married couple, this understanding of commitment makes a familial person truly excited! A commitment-oriented person loves the institution of marriage. This person is thrilled with the idea of having one partner for the rest of his or her life.

People who value this element the most like being married because they love the institution of marriage. In other words, they don't like the idea of being single at all! And children are a must in their lives. Of course, every good parent will acknowledge that their children are gifts from God (see Psalm 127:3), but "commitment" people take this to heart more than anyone! Their entire lives revolve around their children and family. People who are motivated by familial intimacy also have a broad social circle and are usually very involved in their community — but only as long as their involvement pertains to family and family-related activities.

Potential Problems in the Familial Marriage

What are the potential weaknesses with familial people? They can be highly committed to the institution of marriage, but not to the actual relationship! In other words, they like the idea of having someone so that they're not alone, but they can be insensitive or clueless about the quality of the marriage. They don't always nurture the relationship. That means that they can be very weak in one or both of the other two areas of sex and friendship.

Commitment-oriented people are all about the family but not necessarily all about the relationships in that family. As a rule, they don't like change, so they can be resistant to notions that their marriage might be needy. They must differentiate between commitment to the institution of marriage and commitment to their spouse, their marriage, and the life that they are building together. God desires that a couple be committed to making the marriage what He intends — not just to have an "ever-after" marriage in which one or both parties is neglected or unfulfilled.

First Things First

Before we can work on our marriage, we need to work on our relationship with God. Certainly, our relationship with God is secure through the finished work of Christ. But besides just being saved, we need to desire God's matchless and unbroken fellowship and companionship. We must be wholeheartedly committed to Him, spending time in His Word — not just causally reading it but deeply meditating on it. It's when we draw near to God and abide in Him that His Word sinks deep into our heart and changes us (see John 15:7).

Another characteristic of being committed to the Lord is the willingness to allow Him to change us in whatever way we need to be changed. Some believers don't want this kind of commitment. For them, just to be in the family of God is enough; they don't want to go any deeper than that.

But just as God is completely committed to us, He requires that we be committed to Him. And concerning the institution of marriage, when we are surrendered to Him, it becomes easy to surrender ourselves to our spouse and to commit with all of our heart to making our marriage what He wants it to be. It becomes our highest joy to meet our spouse's needs in marriage and to make his or her priorities in the marriage our own priorities.

Many people feel frustrated in their marriage, and they don't know why. They don't understand that God made them to have certain needs and desires. God wants you be happy and delighted in marriage! You must begin by delighting yourself in Him and His Word and by daring to believe in His love and goodness toward you.

> *Delight yourself also in the Lord, And He shall give you the desires of your heart.* (Psalm 37:4)

Nothing is too hard for God. He wants give you the marriage of your dreams, and He already has a plan! So be willing to change and to understand what motivates your spouse and what makes him or her "tick." The Holy Spirit will not only reveal truth to you, but He will also show how to walk in the light of truth so that you and your spouse can experience the joy and contentment in marriage that every couple longs for and needs.

True Romance: A Marriage Beyond the Dream

3
Different Is Good!

Drs. Tom and Maureen Anderson

We've already seen that understanding our differences as men and women helps us better meet one another's needs in marriage. And when both people's needs are met in a marriage, that marriage will be happy and successful.

Yet so often, instead of seeking to understand one another's differences and to value the unique qualities between the genders, we tend to devalue those differences. But in this chapter, we're going to learn that different is good! After all, everything that God created, He "saw that it was good" (Genesis 1:10,12,18,21,25). And since we know that He created the genders "male and female" — separate and distinct in their design, purpose, and value — we know that our differences are good as well.

MAUREEN:

Once of the biggest differences between the genders — and, therefore, between a husband and wife — is the way in which they each bond with their spouse. Since "male and female" are unique, it stands to reason that their needs are unique too.

One of the greatest ways that I've found to meet Tom's needs in our marriage is to participate in activities and hobbies that he enjoys. Generally, men are physically active, and they bond through physical activity. So it's important that women participate in the sports or hobbies that their husband enjoys so that bonding can take place.

I play golf with Tom. Of course, I can only play about nine holes before I'm done, but we have a great time playing golf together. Once we played in Jamaica, where the course overlooked the ocean. It was a beautiful day that we will remember forever. In fact, we have made a lot of memories playing golf together. Although I don't enjoy the game as much as Tom does, I wouldn't trade those times together or those memories for anything.

As a woman, you might think, But it's just a game or silly hobby. But to a man, it's an activity that creates bonding with the woman in his life. I encourage you as a wife to look for an activity your husband likes that you can learn to do and perhaps even really enjoy. I'm not saying that you need to learn to play every sport your husband likes or take up every hobby he enjoys. But you can try to find at least one, because it's important to him.

Maybe your husband doesn't like to play sports, but he likes to watch sports or even old movies. You can find a way to "get into his world" by preparing popcorn, snacks, or finger-foods that he likes and by enjoying a football game or movie with him. He may not express it to you, but having you engage with him in activities that he enjoys is one of his most basic needs. Your companionship and your interest in things that interest him affirms him at the most basic level and communicates love, security, and trust.

Once you realize how important bonding through activity is to the man in your life, hopefully, you'll make the effort to engage in one or more of his favorite activities with him. I learned to play golf and to ski as an adult. In fact, I was forty-seven years old when I learned to ski! I did this for Tom, not for me, because I realized the value he placed on enjoying these things with me.

How Women Bond

As a woman, you might not understand bonding through activity, because women generally bond through communication. Obviously, the way men and women bond is different, yet neither is "right" or "wrong." The unique way men and women bond is a part of their individual makeup.

Because women bond through communication, men must make the effort to talk! In the early years of our marriage, Tom was not a communicator at all, and that bothered me a great deal. After we'd eat dinner, he'd get up from the table, but I was just warming up for some after-dinner conversation! He finally did make the necessary adjustment to accommodate me and has since developed into quite a communicator! Tom and

I would rather spend time engaged in conversation with each other than with anyone else on the planet.

It's so important to understand the differences between men and women and to appreciate those differences rather than criticize them. When you do that, you will learn to value and respect your spouse. Then when the two of you have disagreements, you can work them out together instead of fighting and storming off to separate rooms. In addition, your goals will change. Instead of fighting to see who wins and who loses, you'll see yourself as a team, and you'll desire to help and bless each other and strengthen the marriage so that it becomes everything God wants it to be.

Ready-Made or Built Over Time?

So many couples get married with the idea that they married the perfect mate. And that's what they're looking for: perfection in marriage. Then when they see imperfections in the other person and in the relationship (and they inevitably will), sadly, they often bolt to a divorce lawyer to dissolve a union that had all the potential of being "Heaven on earth."

Where did these couples miss it? In failing to realize that "perfect" or great marriages don't come ready-made; rather, they are built over time. In other words, you don't just get a great marriage; you make a great marriage. And that takes time.

As you know, marriage is a picture of Christ and the Church, Christ's Bride (Ephesians 5:25-32; Revelation 21:9). Well, when we're born again, our new relationship with Christ doesn't just stop there. No, we are to grow in our walk with the Lord. Similarly, the marriage relationship should grow and mature over time. A husband and wife should marry with the idea that they are building something together. It's a process that lasts a lifetime.

If more people took that attitude, there would be less bickering and criticizing going on and a lot more praying and godly communication! The groom should love his bride in much the same way that Christ loves the Church. And the bride should adore the groom in much the same way the Church adores Christ. Jesus laid His life down for the Church. He came not to be served, but to serve (see Mark 10:45). And that is the husband's position in the marriage. He is to be an example to his wife, his children, his extended family, his neighbors, and his co-workers of what a godly husband should be. The people in his life should know how much he loves his wife, his bride.

The Way We Think

We already read the verse, "Husbands, likewise, dwell with them with understanding, giving honor to the wife…" (1 Peter 3:7). Husbands as well as wives must understand the differences between the genders and walk in love instead of criticize their wife over those differences.

One of the biggest differences in men and women — besides the most obvious physical differences — is in the way we each process and communicate information. Men tend to major on majors; women tend to major on everything! A man needs to understand that about his wife so that when she's majoring on things that he doesn't think are as important, he won't put her down or criticize her. Instead, he'll realize she's not looking for detailed solutions to her problems as much as just a listening, sympathetic ear.

A husband should know that comfort goes a lot further than criticism in the marriage. So instead of criticizing his wife for over-focusing on something, he could very lovingly and gently comfort her and let her know that what she's so focused on at the moment is not a priority in terms of spending her time and energy thinking about it. In doing that, a husband is helping his wife instead of hurting her, and that goes a long way in building a marriage based on differences instead of tearing it down because of them.

vMen are headliners. Women want the whole story. Women also want to tell the story ten times! A husband needs to exercise patience in this area. When his wife repeats herself, she's not trying to annoy him — she's simply being a woman! He married a woman, and the woman in his life is probably going to act like one. So he needs to understand and value all the ways in which she is different from him. (The opposite is true too. A wife must value the differences she sees in her husband. He's not a woman, and she shouldn't want him to act like one!)

Logic and Emotions — Seeing
Past the Facts and Feelings

In processing information, men tend to be motivated more by logic, whereas women are more motivated by emotion. So men represent logic in the marriage relationship, and women represent emotion. That is simply the way God created us — and, remember, what God creates is good!

Some people think that it's wrong to have or show emotions. Emotions are not wrong. They become wrong when we allow them to run our lives — or our marriages! We must be moved by the Holy Spirit and the

Word of God, not by our feelings. And God has given us the power to take control of our emotions and not allow them to dictate our lives.

In itself, logic is not wrong, either. But it can become wrong when it is exalted over the Word and the Spirit of God. It seems the world has exalted logic over a belief in the existence of God. That is a tragic, costly mistake.

Celebrating the Differences

As I said, in many marriages, instead of celebrating each other's differences, those differences are often criticized or belittled. For example, when a husband criticizes the fact that his wife is emotional, he is, in effect, devaluing her. Similarly, if the wife criticizes a male trait in her husband, she is calling into question his worth too.

Marriage is most successful when it becomes about the other person and not about you. Marriage is about laying down your life for the other person — not being a doormat, but laying down your life in an attitude of love. I'm talking about the unconditional, God-kind of love.

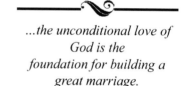

...the unconditional love of God is the foundation for building a great marriage.

And if you're a Christian, you can operate in that kind of love.

> *Now hope does not disappoint, because the love of God has been poured out in our hearts by the Holy Spirit who was given to us.* (Romans 5:5)

We have the outpouring of God's love in our life, so we are capable of showing forth that love. But we have to draw on it. Again, that takes effort; it's not something we're always going to automatically want to do. But the unconditional love of God is the foundation for building a great marriage.

In talking about unconditional love, people often get confused because they confuse love with a feeling. But love is not always a feeling; it is a choice. It may be accompanied by feelings, but often it's not. So there are times when you will need to choose to love your spouse. You can't wait for a feeling. If you do, your marriage could be destroyed while you're "waiting."

Love Begins at Home

Every day when I wake up, I embrace love. God is love, and I am His child. So that means I can walk in love. And I can love my husband the way he needs to be loved — the way he best receives it. Since that's different for everyone, that means I need to make the effort to understand Tom and then show him love in the way that he needs it, not the way that's easiest for me. That's what it means to lay down your life in marriage.

Have you ever heard the saying, "Love is not love until you give it away"? It's true. Love is an action, and it is expressed through giving. We see this in God's sending His Son Jesus to the earth as the Savior of mankind and Sacrifice for our sin.

> *For God so loved the world that He gave His only begotten Son, that whoever believes in Him should not perish but have everlasting life.* (John 3:16)

God loved the world — you and me — when we were dead in sin. And because He loved us, He gave of Himself in order to save us. In other words, He showed us His love in the Person of Jesus Christ.

> *And walk in love, as Christ also has loved us and given Himself for us, an offering and a sacrifice to God for a sweet-smelling aroma.* (Ephesians 5:2)

We are commanded as Christians to walk in love, but walking in love begins in the home. In other words, we should be thinking every day, How can I show my spouse love? We need to focus on what our spouse needs. If we don't love our husband or wife the way he or she needs to be loved, and then we go to church and show acts of love and kindness to others, our love is just "noise" (1 Corinthians 13:1), because love starts in the home.

Gary Chapman penned a book in which he categorized five love "languages."[1] In his book, he talks about the fact that each one of us speaks one of these languages better than the others. In other words, we each respond best to one of these five love languages: acts of service; quality time; words of affirmation; receiving of gifts; and physical touch. When our spouse fails to "speak" to us in our language, our "love tank" can be drained, and we begin to feel empty and unfulfilled in our marriage relationship. A healthy marriage results when both parties feel loved, cared for, and very secure in the relationship.

In my own words and in no particular order, I will briefly summarize a characteristic of each of these love languages, but I highly recommend that you read Dr. Chapman's book for yourself.

- Acts of Service – Receiving services rendered by a loved one.
- Quality Time – Spending quality, uninterrupted time focused just on each other and on communicating with one another — talking and listening.
- Words of Affirmation – Receiving words that affirm, express gratitude, and build up.
- Receiving of Gifts – Receiving gifts, big and small, as tokens of thoughtfulness and appreciation. These are simply "visual aids" that say, I love you.
- Physical Touch and Closeness – Receiving touch consistently from a loved one, such as a hug, a pat on the back, or a kiss on the cheek — and just being near each other.

My Own Story

When we were first married, Tom was very big into acts of service. That was the primary love language spoken in his home when he was growing up. His stepmother was from Norway and didn't speak English very well — but she knew how to show love through acts of service! At mealtimes, she hardly ever even sat down at the table; she was constantly waiting on everyone "hand and foot."

Tom enjoyed this expression of love, so you can understand why this was his primary love language. And his secondary love language was physical touch. Neither of those were my main love languages. My primary love language was quality time. I was big on communication, and it takes time, attention, and focus to really communicate with someone else. I came from a large family in which everyone did his own laundry and fended for himself. So there were not a lot of acts of service happening at my house! But among a family of seven, there was plenty of communication! We were all great communicators, so communication was what I liked.

When Tom would visit my family's house, he was amazed by all the communication that went on there! He was from a quiet home, so when everyone at my house would all talk at once, he almost couldn't stand it. Then when we got married, we both had to make some big adjustments in order to speak the right love language to each other — to show love to each other in the way we each needed to receive it.

We can understand from its simple definition that acts of service is manifested by performing tangible acts of meeting someone else's need, such as filling a water glass, doing a chore, or running an errand. Quality time is all about communicating — talking and listening. When you're spending quality time with someone, you're giving that other person your undivided attention. You're not clicking the remote and nodding your head every so often while your thoughts are somewhere else. When you're speaking the language of quality time, you stop what you're doing and look at that other person instead of staring at the TV or out into "space" while he or she is talking.

Now, let me show you from personal experience how the two love languages of acts of service and quality time can collide and leave behind a trail of hurt feelings. Just after Tom and I were married, I prepared a meal, and we were at the kitchen table enjoying that meal together. But then Tom made the statement, "I would like some ketchup."

At first, I honestly didn't understand why he would say such a thing! I remember thinking, Is he asking me for ketchup? So I responded by saying, "It's in the refrigerator." He got up and got his own ketchup, but I later learned that this instance and others like it affected his feelings of being loved by me. By failing to pick up on his cues that he desired help, I wasn't filling his "love tank."

After he ate his dinner that same night, Tom stood up from the table and walked away. He was ready to go on to the next thing, but his actions left my love tank leaking! I was sitting there thinking, Hey, we're supposed to sit here and talk, not eat and run!

That was early in our marriage. Tom wasn't a communicator, and I wasn't a server. In fact, I hated acts of service! When I first learned about the five love languages, I said, "Oh, God, why is he acts of service!"

So I had to change my attitude and my behavior, because acts of service was how Tom best received love. I eventually learned to love acts of service, but not before I made a wholehearted change in my willingness to show my husband love in the way he needed it most.

Acts of service was how Tom best received love in those days, but it was also how he showed love. Because he was responsible for our finances, he would often go grocery shopping with me to help me stay within our budget. But at first, I didn't know why he wanted to go to the store with me. In fact, the first time he said, "I'd like to go shopping with you," I thought, If he wants to go grocery shopping, why should I go too? Why waste the energy? I'll just let him do the shopping instead.

But eventually I learned to appreciate his love language. I needed to accompany him to the store, because he wanted me to do acts of service with him. And Tom learned to appreciate my love language. In fact, today Tom would say that his primary love language is affirmation, followed by physical touch and quality time. As anyone who knows him can tell you, he is an excellent communicator!

Since physical touch is also one of Tom's main love languages, I had other adjustments I needed to make in our marriage, because that wasn't one of my languages. In our early days together, Tom practically had to give me a "warning" before he hugged me! I got over that, and we are now a very affectionate couple, because I understood the value Tom placed on physical touch — and I also realized the important role that affection plays in a marriage. (We will talk about the subject of affection and physical intimacy in another chapter.)

Such a big part of having a successful marriage is learning to think about what the other person in that marriage needs and then being willing to meet that person where he or she is. When you meet someone else's "love need," it's amazing how your needs get met too.

Let's look at the negative side of this subject for a moment. What happens when a spouse is running on empty because that person isn't being loved the way he or she responds best? Insecurity, emotional pain, and feelings of rejection are usually the result. And if those feelings linger over a period of time, the marriage will not be in a good place. We all need to feel loved in our own unique way.

Love Must Give To Qualify as Love

Some people receive love best by the receiving of gifts or other tangible expressions of love. They need a visual aid that says, "I really do love you." To those motivated by this "language," you can say, "I love you," but you need to show them you love them, because they're motivated by tangible tokens of love and appreciation, not just by words.

The reason I recommend Gary Chapman's book, The Five Love Languages: How To Express Heartfelt Commitment to Your Mate, is that once you know your own love language and the love language of your spouse, you can go to work filling each other's love tank! Many couples go for years on end running on empty. It's no wonder that intimacy has been destroyed in those relationships.

The goal of every couple should be to build and maintain intimacy in the marriage. But you can't do that if you feel unloved as a husband or wife. Tom and I spent the first years of our life together learning these things about each other. We both came from dysfunctional families. In fact, we were first-generation Christians, so we had a lot to overcome. But we were committed to the marriage, and we persisted in our efforts to build a great marriage by understanding, valuing, and even celebrating our many differences. We learned the truth that "different" is good, and I can honestly say that today our marriage is Heaven on earth!

Tom:

Our differences as husband and wife are good, because our gifts and our very purposes are a result of our uniqueness and design. In other words, who we are inherently as "male and female" is what we bring to the table in marriage to foster, strengthen, and bless that union. In short, we need each other!

We've established the fact that women by design are incubators. They foster words and bring forth life from those words. In fact, the name of the first woman, Eve, means giver of life. Women tend to think about, meditate, and process in their minds the same thing over and over again — for long periods of time. They shouldn't be criticized or belittled for this because it's in their nature to do it. And a woman who's godly and who processes problems in the light of God's Word can bring forth wisdom and a godly solution to the dilemmas of life.

Men tend to make snap decisions when they're faced with a situation that needs their attention. Men have a gift for making decisions, but when those decisions are made in haste, oftentimes, they're not based on the wisdom of God.

I've made certain decisions in the past based on pure, simple logic — and that's a good thing — but at times I've inadvertently excluded the wisdom of God. Maureen has said to me, "I'm not sure we should do it that way," and she would tell me why. After I thought about it, in many cases, I concluded that she was right and that I was about to mess up if I continued with my original assessment. What happened? I had made a snap decision; she had given birth to truth.

I'm not saying a man can't walk in the wisdom of God. He certainly can and should do that. But a wise man will listen to the godly counsel of his wife.

There is another side to this process of decision-making that I want to reiterate. If I make my final decision based on input I received from my wife, the responsibility for that decision is mine, not hers. Ultimately, it is my responsibility to make the decision, so if something goes wrong, I can't lay the blame on her. I can't say, "I told you so! See what you've done!" No, I listen to Maureen, and I glean wisdom from her insight. But the ultimate decision is my responsibility. Therefore, I am responsible for the decision once it has been made.

There has been so much error involving this subject of a husband's headship in the home. But the truth is, marriage is a fifty-fifty partnership. Both parties have the potential to walk in the wisdom of God. If they're saved, both parties possess knowledge, understanding, and the power of God. As they learn to draw on each other and on their unique gifts as individuals, they will collectively meet with more and more success in the marriage. It's true that the husband must accept the ultimate responsibility for making decisions for the family, but that doesn't mean he's a "Lone Ranger," who doesn't value the gift of God in his partner and bride.

A Man Is a Protector and a Provider

In the last chapter, we learned the differences between the genders and the fact that there was a God-ordained purpose in our design and our differences. For example, men were designed to be faster and stronger. Does that mean that there's never been a woman who was faster or stronger than a man? No, of course not. The Bible says that men are to treat their wife as the weaker vessel (1 Peter 3:7). It doesn't say she is the weaker vessel; it simply says husbands are to treat her as the weaker vessel.

That might sound confusing to some people. Let me illustrate what I mean. When I'm with Maureen, I open the door to the car or to a building for her. That doesn't mean that she can't open a door by herself — she does it all the time when I'm not with her! But when I'm with her, I do that because I want to honor her as "the weaker vessel."

Have I always opened doors for my wife? No, she trained me to do it. She would just walk up to a door and stand there, cool and collected, until I opened it! So I was trained quickly to perform this act of chivalry for my wife.

The simple act of opening the door for my wife makes her feel cared for and protected. But I think it's courteous for men in general to open doors for women. Chivalry has been largely lost to this generation because parents haven't trained their children in this area. It's unfortunate because when a young man is groomed to behave biblically as a man, he creates the right atmosphere for success in his own home life, in his own marriage.

When I was growing up, we called our elders "ma'am" and "sir." You rarely hear that anymore. That's sad because those words carry with them tones of respect. And if we fail to teach our children respect, they'll grow up failing to respect themselves or anyone else as they should. We often see this in manifestation in the way young people treat property. They have no respect for property so they mishandle it. They weren't taught respect at home.

Man is a protector and a provider by nature. These traits were determined in his design. Sometimes these traits are misinterpreted as his being "macho." But, usually, a man who exhibits these qualities is only being true to his purpose.

I have been accused of being overprotective in my role as protector. For instance, I don't want Maureen to go out shopping at night by herself. So if she needs to go out at night, I'll offer to go along or even go to the store for her. I'm not babying her — I'm simply taking responsibility and being true to my nature. Just as a woman shouldn't be faulted for her design, a man shouldn't be faulted for his design. And a part of his makeup is to protect and provide.

I'm sure you know men who do not make an effort to provide for their families. They might be selfish, or they might be lazy. But a lazy man had to learn how to be lazy over time, because work is an integral part of his purpose. Perhaps something in his childhood "trained" him to be lazy and unmotivated. Maybe some outside influence impacted his life, because when a man is true to his design, he won't be lazy. He will work to provide for his family.

Unfortunately, many parents are raising children today to be unmotivated. I'm not saying they're doing it intentionally. But look around and you will find that motivated young workers are few and far between. Maybe as they were growing up, someone just handed them money to buy what they wanted instead of training them to work for it. Or maybe their home was cleaned by a cleaning service, and they were never required to learn these basic life skills for themselves. Failing to incorporate these basic values as children, young people grow up ill-equipped to thrive in a home of their own.

God knew what He was doing when He created the genders "male and female." He created them to look differently, act differently, and feel and think differently. We've seen that men are logical thinkers; they tend to think in terms of the "bottom line." They don't usually think as thoroughly as women do, and they are also emotionally disconnected from the thought process. Why? They're built that way so they can, for example, kill a deer, skin it, and provide food for their family. Or on the battlefield, they can kill an attacker when confronted in order to protect their family's freedom and well-being.

For the most part, women are not designed that way. They're both thinkers and feelers. But men make very few connections between the thinking and feeling parts of their brain. They have less connection between the hemispheres that, respectively, influence logic and emotion.

Emotion lives on the right side of the brain; logic lives on the left side. That's the way God created us. We've seen that in the womb, a male baby receives an infusion of testosterone in his brain that slows the growth of the emotional, right side of the brain so that the "logic side" grows a little bit faster. This doesn't mean that boys aren't emotional; it simply means they have less emotional feeling than girls do.

Generally speaking, men cannot do multiple tasks simultaneously. We like to do one thing at a time. So when a man says, "I'm listening dear — I'm just watching the game," he is probably lying about it no matter how good his intentions! He's only listening to one of those things — his wife or the game but probably not both.

On the other hand, women have the ability to do multiple things at once. Maureen can be listening to praise and worship and scriptures on CD at the same time she's doing Sudoku — and while she's doing that, she can even catch something she heard from another room on the evening news!

A Man and His 'Separate' Emotions

Men have difficulty thinking or feeling multiple things at the same time. We can think without feeling, and we can feel without thinking. Conversely, we can't think when we're feeling, and we can't feel when we're thinking! That's why we lose every argument with our wife!

A woman can get her husband over into the emotional realm in a conversation, where he can't even think straight. His brain is zeroed out! An hour later, he might think, Oh, I should have said this, this, and this. But at the moment, he couldn't think; he could only feel. That's part of what enables him to protect so well. That's just how he's made.

Men are able to set focused goals from which he can't be deterred. This is his strength. He has the ability to determine the shortest distance between two points, to gain momentum, and to maximize efficiencies.

To change a man's goals takes reprogramming and time. For example, if Maureen and I are set to go to a particular restaurant, I've already plotted the route I'm going to drive to get there, and I've already decided what I'm going to order off the menu! Then if Maureen suddenly says, "Let's go here instead," my brain has to reprogram. Suddenly, I'm dazed. Which way do I turn? What am I going to eat? Once I reprogram, I'm okay, but it takes a little bit of time and effort.

Men are protectors; women are nurturers. That's their design. Men and women can see the exact same thing and have two completely different thoughts about it. A woman can see a tree and think, How pretty. A man will see the same tree and think, I'll cut it down and build a house. Neither thought is wrong, necessarily. Each is different because different processes are taking place when the man and the woman look at the tree.

Women are emotional thinkers. They evaluate, incubate, and rehearse and review every possible scenario. A woman doesn't like it when a man solves a problem in one sentence, especially after she has thought on the whole picture for so long. Instead of trying to solve it in a sentence, he simply needs to listen to her as she continues to give birth to the answer by talking about it. She probably already knows, or think she knows, what she's going to do. The last thing she wants to hear from a man is, "That's easy; just do this."

Women see detail. They see everything going on around them, and they remember what they see and hear better than men do. They can remember who wore what or said what on what date, time, and location! We think back on certain events and have trouble even remembering the year it happened!

A woman can change a diaper, talk on the phone, and check homework! She can sense other people's feelings intuitively. She perceives, analyzes, and evaluates the status of relationships. She has insight about things that men don't have a clue about. It's because she can think and feel at the same time.

In order to separate the logic from the emotion, a woman must talk about a subject from every angle. Have you ever noticed that wives tell the same story over and over again, highlighting every angle — the left, the right, the middle, the top, and the bottom! And her husband is thinking, Okay, enough already! I got it! I got it! (Notice I said that he's only thinking these things. A smart man will never speak those words out loud, because he understands and appreciates his wife's differences.)

We Need Each Other

As differently as men and women think, perceive, process thoughts, and behave, the fact remains that men and women need each other.

Men need women to help them avoid the potholes of life. For instance, Abigail saved David from inflicting unnecessary harm to her wicked husband Nabal by intervening and feeding David and his starving troops (see First Samuel 25:2-42). She kept David from making a serious mistake — and later, when Nabal died, she became David's wife.

In the New Testament, Pilate's wife tried to influence her husband to have nothing to do with the crucifixion of Jesus. Finally, Pilate said to the Jews who were intent on killing the Savior, "I wash my hands of this Man's innocent blood. I find no fault in Him" (Matthew 27:24; Luke 23:4; John 18:38).

A woman needs her husband because of his ability to focus on a goal and make everything go in that direction. She needs him because he is the responsible party in the relationship. It is his God-ordained design to be the responsible party in the home — not a dominator but a partner who bears ultimate responsibility. A man and his wife are fifty-fifty partners, but, ultimately, he is responsible to protect and provide.

---

1   Gary Chapman, The Five Love Languages: How To Express Heartfelt Commitment to Your Mate, Northfield Publishing, Chicago, IL, 1992.

True Romance: A Marriage Beyond the Dream

4

Three Things That Drive a Successful Marriage

Drs. Tom and Maureen Anderson

It's been said that knowledge is power. And we certainly know from Scripture that people can be destroyed for a lack of knowledge (see Hosea 4:6). Many marriages have been destroyed because one or both parties in a marriage simply didn't know what else to do. Had they been equipped with knowledge and understanding from God's Word — or even with practical knowledge that had its basis in God's Word — many of these marriages could have been saved.

In this chapter, we're going to share some of that practical knowledge concerning the driving force behind every successful marriage. Certainly, God and His Word are number one. But connecting God and His Word to marriage requires understanding and effort. That's where prayer and seeking God come in — to give us the wisdom, understanding, and grace to apply His Word to the circumstances of our lives.

No Longer One, But Two — No Longer Two, But One

'And the two shall become one flesh'; so then they are no longer two, but one flesh. (Mark 10:8)

So far, we've addressed husbands and wives both separately and as couples. It's important to realize that while we each have our individual roles and parts to play in the relationship, marriage is indeed a partnership. We must work out our problems together, even if a particular problem is with only one spouse. If you're married, we encourage you never to allow that other person to go it alone when he or she is facing a difficulty or trial. You two are a team, and teams act together — in unison — toward a common goal.

It's been said that the happiest marriages consist of two of the best forgivers on earth! So whatever issues you may be facing, the first thing you need to do is to get past your hurt feelings quickly and join forces with your spouse to work through issues that ultimately affect you both.

MAUREEN:

I've discovered three specific keys to help you and your spouse achieve Heaven on earth in your marriage. In fact, they are the driving forces behind all successful marriages:

- Desire to please your spouse.
- Behave in a loving manner.
- Strive to meet your spouse's needs.

They may sound simple, but these are the elements that make a marriage happy and successful. When both the husband and wife buy into the truth marriage is about giving — not just receiving — both will be mutually fulfilled in the relationship.

Number One: Desire
To Please Your Spouse

The first driving force in a successful marriage is the desire to please your spouse. Do you know what pleases your spouse and makes him or her happy? Do you know the desire of his or her heart? Never allow yourself to become indifferent to the dreams in that other person's heart. Instead, take an active interest in those dreams.

As a husband or wife, we must know what makes our spouse "tick." We need to know what really makes that person happy and content in life. Whatever it is, we should want that for our spouse and should do whatever we can to please that other person.

How To Meet Your Spouse's Needs

Many people sincerely desire to meet their mate's needs, but they don't know where to begin. I have compiled the following list of helpful ways to discover and meet the needs of your spouse.

- Ask the Holy Spirit for help in discerning your spouse's needs. Sometimes we simply need help to stay sensitive to our spouse's changing needs. And who better knows our mate than his or her Creator?
- Spend quality time with your spouse communicating needs — talking and listening.
- Express your needs in love, not in accusing tones.
- Be flexible and willing to change if necessary.
- Accept each other's unique qualities and differences. It's difficult for someone to open up when he feels he might be ridiculed because of what he shares.
- Don't pressure the other person with "fairy tale" expectations. Put your faith in God first. Then realistically assess in your heart how your spouse can best meet your needs.
- Make the needs in your relationship a priority. Make no mistake — many activities will vie for your attention to distract you from the things that are most important: your relationships with God and with your spouse.
- Keep the goal of deeper intimacy ever before you. Remember the truth that meeting another's needs, big and small, creates emotional bonding.

TOM:

As Maureen said, there will always be things that will come to distract you from what's most important in life: your relationships — in particular, your family relationships and especially your relationship with your spouse. Most of those distractions will come in the form of activities and "obligations." I encourage you to be alert concerning the things you think you "must" do that take you away from your family, because Satan — the enemy of your soul and of your family — is very subtle in the way he presents some of these things.

The 'Parent Trap'

One huge way one or both spouses in a marriage can become distracted is by other loved ones, and I'm talking now about parents. Even the most well-intentioned parents can interfere in their children's marriages and cause great damage, even divorce. Although it's sad that many of these parents are blinded to Scripture regarding the type of relationship they're to have with their married children, it's up to that married couple — not the parents — to "draw the line" and set the boundaries where this type of interference is concerned.

> *Therefore a man shall leave his father and mother and be joined to his wife, and they shall become one flesh.*
> (Genesis 2:24)

We've been talking about the desire to please your spouse as one of the driving forces in a happy marriage. Pleasing your spouse can be a challenge when one or both of your parents are pressuring you to please them too. In that type of situation, you must focus on your priorities — on God first and on your mate second. And when you're putting the Lord first, His wisdom is going to dictate that you seek to please your spouse and that you say no to Mom and Dad!

Just Say 'No' to Mom and Dad

When a man and a woman say, "I do" and become joined in holy matrimony, they are becoming "one flesh" in the sight of God; they're not just making a connection in marriage. We've read Genesis 2:24, and we've thought it meant that a man leaves his family to get married, but it's okay for him and his wife to hang on to a dysfunctional, interfering relationship with their families. We've thought we could continue to have our families enmeshed in our lives and everything would be okay. It will not be okay! You cannot truly become one flesh in marriage if you still have the tentacles of your family's wishes, opinions, and desires woven into the fabric of your new life with your mate.

Genesis 2:24 says that a man shall "leave and cleave" in marriage — that he shall leave his parents and cleave or be joined to his wife. The word "leave" in that verse portrays a married person no longer controlled, obedient to, or submitted to his or her parents. With this verse as your standard of truth, it's easy to determine which behaviors from a married person's family are dysfunctional and distorted and which are normal and healthy.

A married man or woman can still love and respect his or her parents, but that husband or wife must not allow a parent to cross the boundary lines where God-ordained authority between the husband and wife is concerned. Too often, parents try to cross those lines, and one or both parties in the marriage allow those lines to be crossed. Once authority inside a marriage is yielded outside of the marriage — outside of God's will and established order — chaos and confusion will be the result.

When a man and woman become one flesh in marriage, a change must take place in the couple's relationship with their parents, siblings, grandparents, and so forth. Those relatives must take on new roles. They can continue as friends and advisors, but decisions concerning the new couple are ultimately theirs alone to make. That means that parents are not to try to control, manipulate, or stick their nose into the couple's business!

I'm not saying that a son or daughter can't seek and counsel wisdom from his or her parents and then take that advice back to the marriage. But that advice should not be taken back as a weapon to be used against his or her spouse! Ultimately, decisions come from inside the marriage, not from outside the marriage. If this principle is violated, it will be impossible to put your spouse first above all others, and this will not be pleasing to God or your mate.

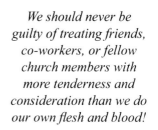

We should never be guilty of treating friends, co-workers, or fellow church members with more tenderness and consideration than we do our own flesh and blood!

Maureen:

From time to time, Tom and I will hear of a couple having marriage problems, and one of them has gone to a parent about the problem, often without talking about it first with the spouse. Fortunately, in some cases, a wise, godly parent encourages the person to go back and communicate with his or her spouse concerning the situation. But often the parent becomes hurt and angry instead, lashing out at the other spouse behind his or her back. Nothing is resolved — in fact, the fires of discord are only fanned until they become a raging inferno!

This reminds me of the sage counsel a respected minister once shared: "In every situation and circumstance, ask yourself, What does the Word of God say and what would love do?" Of course, love is the foundation for a great marriage. But remember, love is an action; it does something. It is a driving force in the success and well-being of a marriage.

Number Two: Behave in a Loving Manner

The first driving force in a happy marriage is the desire to please your spouse. The second driving force is closely connected to the first: We must behave in a loving manner at all times toward our spouse. Even if we have to address something in the marriage that could cause hurt feelings, we must do it in a loving way. We should never be guilty of treating friends, co-workers, or fellow church members with more tenderness and consideration than we do our own flesh and blood!

Also, behaving in a loving manner entails having insight into how our mate best receives love. For instance, we talked about the "love languages," and we discovered that in a marriage, one spouse might receive or respond to love differently than the other. Yet that doesn't make his or her way less valid or important. We must purpose in our heart to "wake up" to the needs and desires of our spouse — to allow our heart to become awakened to the beauty in that other person.

Real love — the God-kind of love — is about giving. That's the way God's Kingdom operates: in giving, not taking. Jesus came to give; the devil came to take (John 10:10). In so many marriages today, we see people entering the relationship for what they can get out of it, not for what they can contribute.

Love is about thinking of that other person and trusting that he or she is thinking of you. Marriage is two-sided. A marriage consisting only of one giver and one taker won't be successful. But a marriage in which both people are behaving in a loving manner will succeed and flourish.

How to Address a Lopsided Marriage

In any teaching on marriage, we invariably hear of situations in which one mate is giving, and the other simply takes with little or no regard for the needs of the other person. Well, that must be addressed, but it must be addressed in love! It can't be addressed in an emotional way, because that's usually when accusations begin to fly, and the "guilty" party starts throwing up walls and defenses. Then all attempts to resolve the problem become futile.

If you must address an issue of "lopsidedness" with your mate, address it first with the Lord. Go to Him in prayer and fasting. Seek His face and humbly and sincerely ask Him what to do. He may lead you to endure a season of sacrificial giving in love while He works in that other person's heart.

Then when the time is right, go to your spouse and say something positive first, such as, "I know that you're a kind person. I know you prob-ably don't realize it, but I'm feeling unfulfilled in certain areas, and I'd like to talk about it if it's okay with you."

Almost any marriage counselor will tell you to use "I" statements instead of "you" statements when confronting someone. In other words, instead of accusing the other person — saying things such as, "You always do this" or, "You never do that" —you're attesting to your own feelings, not in a whiny, complaining manner but as a matter of fact. You're being honest, but you're being loving, too. You're not getting into strife, saying and doing things that you'll later regret.

You Can Be Right and Still Be Wrong

Did you know that you can be right in a situation and still be wrong? You can be right in your argument but present it wrongly — outside the confines of God's love. Then you not only have the original problem to deal with, but you now also have your own misbehavior to address.

What happens most of the time in a lopsided marriage is, the person whose needs aren't being met just buries his or her feelings instead of communicating — or the spouse communicates in an unloving manner, and chaos ensues.

The need for change in such a marriage must be communicated, but it must be done in an attitude of prayer and forgiveness, not anger and resentment. Even then, things may not turn completely around overnight. But if the other person is open to God's dealings and is honest in his or her estimation of the problem, you will have taken a huge step toward a happy, rewarding marriage for both you and your spouse.

Number Three: Strive
To Meet Your Spouse's Needs

The third element of a successful marriage is striving to meet your spouse's needs. What are your spouse's needs? Needs change with the sea-sons of life. What your spouse needed last month might not be what he or she needs today. For example, if your spouse is working a lot of overtime at work, is there something you can do for him or her at home that will make life easier? Maybe you could double up on some of the responsibilities in the home on a temporary basis.

Your spouse's need might be anything from something tangible to a need for some extra quality time with you. You can train yourself to be more and more sensitive to your spouse's needs and then strive to meet them. That word "strive" implies expending effort and energy. In other words, it might not always be easy or convenient to meet your spouse's needs. That's why you must strive to do it!

How important is the effort you put forth to meet your spouse's needs? It's so important! It's the investment of a lifetime, and it will mean the difference between feelings of love that grow and flourish or feelings that weaken and wane over time.

Feelings of love are a response to having your needs met. In other words, when your needs are met, that's when you feel loved. For example, think of how loved you felt when God met your need for salvation. The moment you asked Jesus into your heart, you felt the weight of the world lift from you. And not only did God save you, He continues to meet your needs today, because He never changes; He's the same yesterday, today, and forever (Malachi 3:6; Hebrews 13:8).

> *And my God shall supply all your need according to His riches in glory by Christ Jesus.* (Philippians 4:19)

> *Let us therefore come boldly to the throne of grace, that we may obtain mercy and find grace to help in time of need.* (Hebrews 4:16)

Certainly, God doesn't expect you as a couple to take the place in each other's lives that only He can fill. You're not supposed to make your spouse a "god." But it is scriptural to meet your spouse's needs as much as you possibly can.

Even medical science has confirmed that when someone meets another's need, a special bond occurs between them. So a husband and wife should desire to meet each other's needs as much as possible! Feelings of pleasure, peace, and fondness grow in an atmosphere of having your needs met. A husband and wife who consistently meet each other's needs form a greater bond than those who don't.

Also, when your needs are being met, it creates within you a desire to meet the needs of others. But don't wait for your husband or wife to meet your needs first. Take the initiative to find his or her need and meet it. True love develops over a lifetime of putting each other first and meeting the other person's needs.

Science has also proven that when a person's needs consistently go unmet, chemicals are released in the body that cause negative emotions about the relationship to develop. The person becomes nagged by an overwhelming sense of disappointment, discouragement, frustration, dissatisfaction, and lack of connection or intimacy.

If those negative emotions are allowed to continue, a critical attitude usually begins to develop along with feelings of deep resentment and contempt. If this pattern is allowed to continue without acknowledging them and addressing them, the marriage will fall into deep trouble.

How does a marriage get to this place? Often it's the result of our hectic lifestyles — which is often the result of overvaluing material things and undervaluing our relationships. When we become too busy in our quest to obtain things, we gradually stop valuing our relationships. We stop valuing our marriage, and as a matter of course, we place less and less importance on pleasing our mate, walking in love, and looking for ways to meet our spouse's needs. Slowly and subtly, the marriage begins to erode. Dissatisfaction mounts until one day, suddenly, we're unhappy with the relationship, and the criticisms start to fly. We begin to devalue the other person, blaming each other for everything in the marriage that's wrong.

Happiness Is Found in People, Not in Things

Does this describe you or someone you know? If your marriage is in trouble, I encourage you to put your desire for material gain on hold to work on your marriage. Perhaps you'll need to get rid of some things that have become a "money pit" to maintain. Maybe you'll have to drive cars that are less than new for a while. Whatever you need to do to cut your budget so you can focus on what's important, you should do it as quickly as possible. You don't need more possessions, but you do need a happy marriage and a life of fulfillment, contentment, and effectiveness for the Kingdom of God. Happiness is found in relationships — relationships with God, your spouse, your children, and your family and friends — not in your possessions.

I'm not talking about something I read in a book. I've lived this. Tom and I didn't really begin prospering in life until we were in our forties. Our basic needs were met when we were in our twenties and thirties. Tom worked hard, but we didn't invest all of our time and energy into obtaining more things or bigger and better things. Instead, we invested in each other and in our relationship, and we were very happy and fulfilled.

It has been an investment that has paid off abundantly! Today we have material prosperity and possessions, but we know that those things can never fulfill us. We're happy in life, not because we have wealth, but because we have each other, and we have a happy, successful marriage that's Heaven on earth.

How to Make God Happy

God will give you and your spouse material things. He'll bless you and increase you when you put Him first, when you're chasing Him and His Kingdom and not the things.

But seek first the kingdom of God and His righteousness, and all these things shall be added to you. (Matthew 6:33)

Marriage is an institution created by God, and it is a picture of the relationship between Christ and the Church (Ephesians 5:21-33). When marriages thrive and succeed, God is honored. So part of "seeking first God's Kingdom" is honoring Him and His will in your marriage. When you pay the price to build your marriage according to His Word — and to endeavor to please your spouse — you're pleasing the Lord, too, and making Him happy.

5
Responsibility Before Authority — Don't Put the Cart Before the Horse

Dr. Tom Anderson

The roles and responsibilities in marriage have been so largely misunderstood over the years, and religion hasn't always helped. There have been many teachings on marriage in the Church that have hurt marriages more than helped them. But since God created the institution of marriage, His Word sheds light on the subject. God has established a divine order for the home, and following His design and order will cause a marriage to prosper and flourish beyond imagination.

Some traditional teachings have placed women in a hyper-submissive role to their husbands that is unreasonable and that reaches beyond the bounds of Scripture. In fact, some of it defies sound biblical doctrine! Some things that happen in the home in the name of religion do nothing more than bind up the spirit of a woman, making her a "shell" of a person, while giving her husband a free pass to do as he pleases, answering to no one.

Running With the Wrong Rule

What are the responsibilities of a man in marriage? Are we as husbands responsible to just sit on the couch and watch TV while our wife brings us our favorite cold drink or snack? Very often the picture of a husband is someone who lies on the sofa or recliner and hollers at his wife to toss him the remote — but she can't hear him because she's outside mowing the lawn!

I say that jokingly to make the point that the wife's role in the marriage is not servitude! That is a false concept that needs to be exposed and dealt with if a marriage is to be happy and thrive.

Yet many Christian men, and even whole denominations, tout the verses about men ruling over their wives and families (Genesis 3:16; 1 Timothy 3:5). They preach certain verses on rulership in the home and want to "run with it." The only problem is, they're running with the wrong rule!

Let's look at one of these verses on "ruling."

> *To the woman He said: "I will greatly multiply your sorrow and your conception; In pain you shall bring forth children; Your desire shall be for your husband, And he shall rule over you." (Genesis 3:16)*

After the Fall of man, God addressed the man and woman and then said to the woman, "Your desire shall be for your husband, and he shall rule over you." There have been so many misconceptions about that one statement!

What does that mean, "Your desire shall be for your husband"? That phrase actually means, "You'll desire to rule over your husband." And haven't we seen the battle of the sexes occur in every generation since God made that historic announcement?

This struggle for power was not something that God put on Adam and Eve; it was simply the result of sin. In other words, God didn't command the husband to rule over his wife; He simply related that a "power struggle" would ensue as a result of their sin. God said, in effect, "She will want to rule over him, and he will want to rule over her. They'll have to deal with it."

The result of the Fall was not a curse from God; it was simply a cause-and-effect outcome. Sin always has an outcome. The Bible says that although it may bring a sense of pleasure and satisfaction for awhile, it is only for awhile — for a season. Then the "wages" of sin are always some form of death. (See Hebrew 11:25; Romans 6:23.)

Christ has redeemed us from the curse of the Law (Galatians 3:13) and restored our position with the Father. It's a grace position. And under the New Testament in this era of grace, we are to operate under the law of love. We are commanded to love one another, even as Christ has loved us (John 13:34) — not vie for positions of authority and control!

In many marriages today, the wife does try to run the home, and there are several reasons for this. Perhaps the husband is lazy. Maybe he's passive, or he's ignorant and doesn't know what to do, so he does nothing; he becomes indifferent. Or perhaps he just doesn't want to do it. There's some selfishness on his part, and he simply doesn't want the responsibility that's involved in leading a family. She may also have some trust issues where men are concerned. Perhaps her own father wasn't responsible in her home when she was growing up.

At the other extreme, a woman finds herself in an abusive situation with an aggressive husband who has taken the "submission" verses out of context and is using them for his own ends.

> *Submitting to one another in the fear of God. Wives, submit to your own husbands, as to the Lord.* (Ephesians 5:21-22)

Most husbands who use this verse to rule over his wife with an iron hand miss the part of the verse that says "as to the Lord." The Lord Jesus is not abusive, harsh, cruel, or demanding. So these husbands are missing the point.

Something Every Woman Must Know
About God Before Submitting to Her Husband

Ephesians 5:22 says, "Wives, submit to your own husbands, as to the Lord." Let's look at that phrase, "as to the Lord," because this is where many people miss it concerning this verse. They either skip over it altogether or they misunderstand what it's actually saying. For example, if you have a wrong idea about God, you're going to misread this phrase. If you think God is the One who's making you sick, keeping you broke, and making your life miserable, you have the wrong attitude toward God — whether consciously or subconsciously, you believe that He is abusive.

Some people view God as a hard, cold judge who's just waiting for them to step out of line so He can rain judgment down on them. That's very sad, because if you don't see God as He really is — as a good God — you're probably going to submit to abuse in relationships (I'm especially talking about women, although men can be abused too). But if you see God as loving and good, and you understand that He has a good plan for your life, you will recognize abuse for what it is, and you won't accept it. You'll never accept that kind of behavior as normal because you know that the enemy, Satan, is the one who steals, kills, and destroys. You're vitally aware that Jesus is the Life-Bringer who came to bring you life "more abundantly" (see John 10:10).

In marriage, it's critical that a woman not submit to anything that trespasses the boundaries of God's love. Instead, she must encourage her husband to rise to the occasion and to become the loving leader that God intends. He is to portray the image or picture of Christ in the home — not the image of a harsh, tyrannical taskmaster.

Responsibility Before Authority

The husband and wife have the same value in the marriage, and neither one is to "rule over" the other. The husband has certain responsibilities where authority is concerned, and we're going to look at that. But his authority in the home extends only to the degree he's willing to take responsibility for his family. And he's to wield that authority in an attitude of love.

When a husband and wife are functioning in a marriage in an attitude of love and cooperation, it is amazing how problems get resolved, goals are reached, and the marriage is strengthened. When a husband and wife are submitting to each other "in the fear of God" (Ephesians 5:21), it transforms and blesses them, their marriage, and their children.

Working Together

Ephesians 5:21 (NIV) says, "Submit to one another out of reverence for Christ." It's important that the husband and wife submit to each other. In other words, they are to work together.

Yet much of the church world preaches, "Wives, submit to your husbands," and the attitude is conveyed that the wife is supposed to do any and every thing the husband says without questioning him. He's the king of his castle, and he has no queen! This mindset ignores the synergy that should and must exist between a husband and wife in marriage. The two are far more powerful working together than they are working separately. In fact, two people in agreement can do almost anything they set their hearts and minds to do!

If a husband and wife are in agreement and pulling together, they will be more successful and effective in every area of life. On the other hand, when a husband and wife aren't in agreement, everything in life becomes more difficult.

If a husband has one idea about how to raise children, and his wife has a completely different idea, that's going to have a negative effect on the children if those differences aren't discussed and resolved between both the husband and wife. They must work together to successfully raise a new generation.

A Side-by-Side Partnership

You've heard the saying, "Behind every great man is a great woman." But I will take that a step further and say, "Beside every great man is a great woman." She shouldn't be walking behind him through life; she should be walking beside him.

I'll also go so far as to say that every successful man on earth has been influenced by a woman who didn't "put up with" the things in his life that were unsavory or lacking in character. Instead, she submitted to God, prayed for the man in her life, and encouraged and helped him to grow and change.

I can honestly say that I am successful today because of God and my wife! Proverbs 27:17 (NIV) says, "As iron sharpens iron, so one man sharpens another." I am "sharp" today because of my wife. She is my equal and my partner in life and has played a vital, critical role in my growth and development as a man, a husband, a father, and a minister.

So much can be accomplished when a husband and wife working together, side by side, to build a marriage, a family, and a life together that will affect and bless future generations. Let me illustrate the power of this kind of unity from something I learned on my job as a young man. In those days, I cut timber for a living. I quickly discovered that if you had one horse, that one horse could pull one ton of logs out of the woods. It would logically stand to reason, then, that two horses could pull at least twice that amount of weight! Yet I discovered that if those two horses were not in stride together — working side by side — you could only pull half the amount of weight, or about half a ton, even though you had two horses! But together in unison, two horses could pull not just two tons, but as much as four tons of limber!

Similarly, if a husband and wife are not in unison, they shoot themselves in the foot, so to speak. Anything they try to accomplish is almost counterproductive. They aren't functioning at their optimum or highest potential, because they're not functioning side by side, in harmony and agreement.

Jesus said, "Take My yoke upon you and learn from Me…" (Matthew 11:29). Then He says, "For My yoke is easy and My burden is light" (v. 30). Jesus' yoke is easy, but the world's yoke is very heavy and difficult to be born; it's burdensome and wearisome. And if your family is in a situation in which you as the husband are being overbearing in the way you lead your family — or your wife is leading the family for some reason — you're wearing the world's yoke. Everything you do will take longer and be less than ideal. You'll have to work harder for fewer results.

I'm not saying this to condemn anyone whose marriage has slipped into a situation like this. I'm simply saying that when the "yoke" of responsibility in a marriage is taken up by both parties — and they walk side by side with that yoke — they can accomplish the miraculous!

> *Again, I tell you that if two of you on earth agree about anything you ask for, it will be done for you by my Father in heaven.* (Matthew 18:19 NIV)

Sadly, the opposite is true too. Prayers can be hindered and dreams and goals can "die on the vine" where a husband and wife disconnect by going in separate directions in marriage. Often one spouse has a vision for change, but the other does not. That can create a lot of tension because one is trying to pull for two, yet accomplishing only half the task!

A Scriptural Portrayal of the 'Ruling Male'

Too often in marriages, we see the self-centered attitude of the ruling man. But a man was not designed to be an egotistical dominator of his woman! He has been given dominion by His Creator, all right, but it's the same kind of dominion and spiritual authority that's been given to the woman. They were both created in the image and likeness of God (Genesis 1:26-27).

> *For the husband is head of the wife, as also Christ is head of the church; and He is the Savior of the body. Therefore, just as the church subject to Christ, so let the wives be to their own husbands in everything.* (Ephesians 5:23-24)

The man has been given headship in marriage. That's not the same as dominion as we know it or as it's been taught in some circles. As I said, so many men have confused authority with responsibility. They readily accept the idea of authority but aren't nearly as willing to take actual responsibility for the affairs of their home and family.

But the man has been given some weighty responsibilities in marriage. One of them includes the responsibility of making final decisions for the household. But a wise man will consult and confer with his wife, his partner given to him by God. Then he must prayerfully make the call based on what he senses the Lord leading him to do and on what he feels is best for his family, not what's best for him.

Let's look at a husband's responsibilities in marriage.

Number One: A Man Is Responsible To Know God

A man is responsible to seek out and discover the many facets of God's goodness and character — and then to duplicate those characteristics in his own life and display them toward his family. Well, how does God deal with things? Doesn't the Word says that it's His kindness that leads us to repentance (Romans 2:4) and that we should be gentle and speak the truth in love (Ephesians 4:15)?

Also, as a man, you must ask yourself, What is my process for making decisions? Am I willing to gamble or compromise the future success and prosperity of my family on my own intelligence and abilities — or am I willing to pray and seek the face of God?

> *...he must prayerfully make the call based on what he senses the Lord leading him to do and on what he feels is best for his family, not what's best for him.*

If any of you lacks wisdom, let him ask of God, who gives to all liberally and without reproach, and it will be given to him. (James 1:5)

When you as a husband make a decision, you must live conscious and aware of the fact that you're not making it just for yourself but for your family. When you live your life focused on God and your family and not on self, you build trust in your wife that you are indeed a godly leader — someone she can feel safe and secure in submitting to "as unto the Lord."

A family, especially children, looks to the man as the head of the family, and they're looking to see a picture of God. In fact, at a very young age, a child's entire perception of God comes from what he or she sees in Daddy. So a husband and father must constantly ask himself, What characteristics of the Heavenly Father am I displaying toward my loved ones? Do they see the Father in Me? Do they see Christ?

God is completely faithful as a Husband and Father. He will not leave us, nor will He forsake us. We never need to worry about Him betraying us or breaking our trust and confidence in Him and His Word.

Does your family have an unshakable trust in you as husband and father? Broken trust is devastating to a family and is very difficult to restore.

To illustrate how broken trust affects relationships, I'll use the example of a man's relationship with his stockbroker or financial advisor. Let's suppose, for example, that you had a financial advisor to whom you had entrusted your hard-earned money. That money represented your life because of the time you invested in earning it. Yet over time, you never earned a profit, and sometimes you even lost money, because that advisor was making decisions based on what was best for him, not you.

How long would it take you before you stopped giving that advisor your money? How long before you stopped trusting him completely! His selfish actions and disregard for your future welfare broke a relationship of trust.

That is exactly what happens when a man puts himself and his own interests above those of his family. No one wants to submit to a man like that because there's so much distrust and misgiving.

Most women have no problem submitting themselves to their husband when the husband is living in an attitude of love. When he loves his wife and family as Christ loves the Church (Ephesians 5:25), submission becomes almost an automatic response, because it's easy to trust someone you know won't ever hurt you or who has your best interests at heart.

Another way some men miss it is, they refuse to even listen to their wife. So when they make a decision, she doesn't wholly support it. When he neglects her ideas and her counsel, he sabotages his own success because he forfeits the support of his wife through his foolish behavior.

A wife who is required to submit to her husband's every decision without the ability to provide any input is in a "dictatorship" type of relationship, not a godly marriage.

Number Two: A Man Is Responsible
To Provide and Protect

For the husband is head of the wife, as also Christ is head of the church; and He is the Savior of the body. (Ephesians 5:23)

As I said, many people read, "For the husband is head of the wife…" and just stop there. They don't say much about the rest of the verse: "…as also Christ is head of the church; and He is the Savior of the body." It is a man's responsibility to be the head of his wife, but he is to do it as a covering for her. In other words, she is to come under the covering of her husband. And that's his duty, not just his privilege. This responsibility gives him orders from the throne room of Heaven to provide for her and protect her, not to boss her around!

Now, I understand that there are women, even some Christian women, who do not like the fact that their husband is a covering for them. They see it as an indictment that they are somehow inferior beings. But it's not at all that she is "less than." It's simply the way God set up the marriage relationship. He is a God of order, and everything He designs is created on a system of order. Marriage was set up by God as a 50-50 partnership, but the husband is the head — the covering, or protector, and provider — of his wife.

'I've Got You Covered'

And the Lord God commanded the man, saying, "Of every tree of the garden you may freely eat; but of the tree of the knowledge of good and evil you shall not eat, for in the day that you eat of it you shall surely die." (Genesis 2:16-17)

Before Eve ever arrived on the scene, God had presented Adam with responsibility and instruction. The Lord had ordered Adam to take care of the Garden and then commanded him concerning the tree of the knowledge of good and evil.

This is a picture of stewardship and of the man's responsibility to act as the "covering" in the home. The man covers his home as the responsible party for making sure his family is headed in the right direction spiritually.

Satan doesn't have the power to harm anyone. The only weapon he has is deception, and he uses that weapon to trick people into give him a place in their lives so he can work destruction in them. The enemy repeatedly spoke deception into Eve's life until deception finally took place in her heart (see Genesis 3:1-13). The deception occurred when, although she knew she shouldn't eat from the tree, she did it, anyway.

However, Adam was just as much at fault. His passivity in allowing her to eat as he stood by her side gave strength to her deception. Eve stepped out from underneath Adam's covering, and he allowed it without any apparent resistance on his part. By the time they realized their nakedness and knew there was a problem, it was too late.

Responsibility in the Fall seems to weigh very heavily upon Adam. As the authority figure and the one to whom God gave the initial instruction and warning, Adam could have and should have intervened. Notice that nothing happened after Eve ate of the forbidden tree. It was only after he ate that their nakedness was revealed. I wonder what would have happened if after she ate, Adam simply said, "Eve, ask God to forgive you and come on back under my covering"?

After the Fall of man when God revealed that there would be enmity between the devil's seed and the woman's seed, the husband's covering over his wife was still very important. When a husband is functioning properly in his role as head of his home, and his wife comes under that spiritual covering, then the enemy is unable to get to her emotions and wreak havoc in her thought life.

The enemy has continually attacked women in the area of the emotions. In fact, that's the tactic he used in the Garden to tempt Eve. But in order for him to get to the wife, he must go through the husband.

This duty to act as a covering for your family is not a light responsibility, and some men find it daunting and intimidating because their wives know more Scripture than they do. But if a man is born again and is willing to accept his role and responsibilities in the home as husband and father, he is anointed to do that job whether he knows one verse from the Bible or not!

The Covering Extends to Your Children
An elderly friend of mine, who founded counseling clinics all over the world, had a great impact on my life in this area of the "covering." He often related the story of a time when both of his daughters lived away from

home at two different college campuses. On one particular weekend, my friend's daughters, who were both engaged to be married, were planning a trip home to visit their parents.

On the Friday night before his daughters were to arrive, my friend was awakened in the middle of the night and began experiencing lustful thoughts that attacked his mind. He jumped out of bed, got on his knees, and began to pray until all those thoughts left him.

The following day, the man's daughters arrived with their fiancés. Both daughters had always enjoyed a very open and accepting relationship with their dad, and during that visit, each one shared with him separately that she and her fiancé had gotten involved in some heavy petting the previous night and had gone "a little too far." Both shared independently that as this was happening, suddenly, their attention was "arrested," and they abruptly stopped what they were doing.

What happened? The enemy was looking for an open door to gain an entrance into those girls' lives and their relationships. But because they were still submitted to their father as their covering, the enemy had to go through the father first. But my friend upheld the shield of his covering over his children in prayer, and he prayed the power of God into those situations before they had a chance to turn really bad.

Husbands and fathers have the responsibility to "cover" their family. Yes, the husband and wife have a 50-50 relationship because they were created as equal in God's sight. And when they come together in marriage, they become one. But someone has to bear responsibility in the partnership. Otherwise, there's no leadership. There's no forward progress, only wasted motion.

'The Buck Stops Here'

As I said before, acting as a leader in the home is not about authority as much as it it's about responsibility. That means "the buck stops here" with you, the husband. So when you have to make a tough decision, you can't go back in retrospect and blame your wife if you missed it and made the wrong decision. Even if you sought your wife's input, and you made a wrong decision based on her counsel, you have to own the mistake and bear responsibility for it.

In other words, you can't go back to your wife and say, "I knew you were wrong. I knew we shouldn't have bought that. I had a feeling you were wrong. What's the matter with you?"

No, you are the covering. You are the head, and you are to accept responsibility for the mistake and learn from it, not cast blame and try to make your wife the scapegoat.

And Speaking of Money...

Another aspect of the covering that a husband provides for his wife and family has to do with providing for them materially and financially. Some husbands allow their wife to bear the responsibility of the finances in the home. They kick back without a care in the world while the wife takes care of balancing the checkbook and paying the bills. She is the one responsible for determining whether there will be enough money to pay bills.

From an emotional standpoint, women weren't designed for that responsibility as long as there's a husband in the house. The husband was destined by God to be the responsible party in the area of finances. Remember, he's the protector and provider. He's the one who should make certain there's enough money to pay the bills. He needs to be the one who ultimately decides what the family should and shouldn't spend — not so he can be a control freak but so he can provide his wife with emotional and financial security. She should know that everything's going to be all right and that the future is bright. (We'll talk more about the subject of "men and money" in another chapter.)

Number Three: A Man Is Responsible To Lay Down His Life

Jesus made the first move toward the Church — "the joy set before Him" (Hebrews 12:2) — in His ultimate act of sacrifice on the Cross. He loved the Church, His Bride — the Body of Christ — not for what the Church could do for Him but for what He could do for the Church.

Christ was a Servant-Leader. He spoke truth in love always. He knew God in Glory and, in fact, had been seated with Him. Yet He left all of that for us; He gave it all up. He lived a sinless life as a mortal human and yet very much God. In taking our place, He took responsibility for that which He was not responsible — the sin of mankind.

How do we apply that to a man's responsibility in the home? For one, he must "crucify" his own flesh and his own desires for the good of his family. For instance, after a long day at work, he may want to come home and be left alone to sit in front of the TV. His flesh is crying out for food, sex, and sleep! But his wife wants to talk!

So what does this husband who's laying down his life do? He denies his own flesh and gives himself up for her. He dies to what his flesh wants in order to spend some quality time with his wife and children. No matter how difficult work was or how bad the traffic was on the way home, he must do what's best for everyone, not what he thinks is best for him.

In an environment like that, a man's family feels loved, protected, and safe. They feel secure, knowing that the head of that home will do everything necessary to provide for their needs financially, emotionally, and so forth.

I have a saying that when you're single, you have your whole self (submitted to the Lord, of course). Then when you get married, you lose half of your self. And when you have kids, you lose the other half. Later, when your kids are grown, you get half back!

Yet the fact remains that when you're married, you are not your own; you do not belong to yourself but to your spouse.

Don't Be a Backslidden Romantic

If you're a married man, think back to your dating relationship with your wife. In that phase of the relationship, you were actually engaging in the process of giving up your life. You were experiencing those over-whelming feelings of love, and you felt in your heart, *I'm going to do this the rest of my life!*

Then you got married, and the demands of work and family relation-ships hit you hard. You became busy, and you began reacting to life instead of taking life by the horns. After a time, you wondered where that loving feeling had gone.

When you were dating your wife, you used to spend hours on end talking about everything. In fact, did you ever call your wife and say, "What are you doing?" and she answered, "Thinking about you"? Have you ever talked on the phone for hours while watching TV together — you at your house and her at hers?

What were you doing? Laying down your life. You probably weren't making nearly the amount of money you're earning now, yet you found the money to take her out as often as you could. And you planned ahead; taking her out wasn't an afterthought but a carefully planned outing or event.

All of that took time, effort, and some creativity. But you gave yourself to it. You were walking out biblical principles whether you realized it or not! Then in marriage, after you won her, perhaps you started to backslide, and you let those principles slip. You started thinking more about your needs and what you could get out of the relationship. You began doing more taking than giving. Then you wondered where the romance went. If you will go back to doing those "first works" (see Revelation 2:5), you will find that the romance between you and your wife is right where you left it — at the exact place in the road where you ditched those acts of love.

Number Four: A Man Is Responsible To Value His Wife

Many young men pride themselves in working hard to make the best life possible for their family. They're ambitious, and they go in to work early and stay late. They're trying to provide the dream for their wife and family.

Given your responsibility as provider and protector, can you relate to that as a husband? But have you ever felt conflicted because your wife wants you to leave work at the earliest possible moment so you can spend every possible moment at home with her? That can create some tension. Your wife wants you to be great, but she also wants to know that you'd give it all up for her.

Most women are romantics at heart, and they have a deep need to know that their husband is willing to sacrifice for her and that she is the most important thing in his life next to the Lord. She may like nice things, but, ultimately — if she had to choose — the kind of house or the neighborhood she lives in, the kind of car she drives, and her dreams for material blessings don't matter more to her than her relationship with her husband. What matters most in comparison to those things is her marriage, because if everything you have was gone tomorrow — but you still had a loving relationship that had been nurtured and cared for — you could still be happy because you have each other. You'd still have what you valued the most.

I believe God put it in a woman to highly value relationships. A wife needs to know that you value what she values and that you would sacrifice everything for her. Once you prove that you would, she'll be content and at rest in the relationship.

Oftentimes there is tension when a husband has a sports night or a poker night once a week with the guys. His wife constantly nags him to stay at home to be with her instead. He's at home six nights a week, so he's wondering why there's a struggle. The real issue is that she wants him to prove to her that she means more to him than his friends and that he would give up his night out for her.

If this is your situation, instead of struggling with your wife, let her know that if you didn't have a single friend in the world but her and God, you'd still be happy. She really needs to know that you're willing to lay down your life because you value her. Once she is convinced of her value in your eyes, she'll likely be very gracious about your having time with your buddies. You will have placed her in the position of honor, esteem, and value where she rightfully belongs.

There can also be tension in a marriage with in-laws, especially if your wife doesn't feel more valuable or important to you than your parents. (Do I need to say here that it's never a good idea to side against her in favor of your parents?)

> *...a man shall leave his father and mother and be joined to his wife, and they shall become one flesh.* (Genesis 2:24)

> *...a man shall leave his father and mother and be joined to his wife, and the two shall become one flesh.* (Ephesians 5:31)

Cleaving is all about becoming one flesh. When you look at the original Hebrew translation of Genesis 2:24, it means that both the wife and the husband are to "leave and cleave." We can see the wisdom and logic in obeying that by not living with your parents as a young married couple! But what about cleaving to your spouse in other ways? Did you know that you can drag your parents into your marriage without living in the same house with them?

If you talk to your parents about every problem that comes up between you and your spouse, you are not "leaving and cleaving." Instead, you're creating discord between your spouse and your parents; you're going against God's design and order. Your spouse now has in-law troubles — and you caused it!

Also, it's not wise to discuss with your spouse any issues you have with your own parents — not if you want your spouse to love and honor your parents as he or she should. Whatever you share with your spouse may cause him or her to become offended at your parents. Then you will have created a situation in which your spouse is having problems letting go of that offense. You may get over your issue with your parents, but your spouse may never get over it.

And never, ever get angry with your in-laws to your spouse. After all, your spouse is a direct "product" of his or her parents, just as you are of yours. So if you dislike or disapprove of your spouse's parents — even if they're wrong about a particular thing — your spouse is subconsciously hearing that you dislike him or her.

You Can 'Leave' and Love

You can "leave and cleave" — leave your parents and cleave to your spouse — and still love your parents and your spouse's parents. In fact, one of the greatest things you can do for your marriage is to love your spouse's parents unconditionally and to show acts of love toward them every chance you get. For example, take your mother-in-law out for Mother's Day. For Father's Day, take your father-in-law on a short outing. Go "overboard" for your in-laws. Doing so will pay great dividends in your family relationships.

I'm not saying that loving your parents means you have to allow them to interfere in the affairs of your life or manipulate the decisions you and your spouse make for your own family. But you must show the God-kind of love toward them.

As a man, you have the responsibility of showing value and honor to your wife, of guiding the affairs of your home and protecting it from outside interference, and of keeping peace within the borders of your home and family. That doesn't have to be a balancing act if you understand your responsibilities and priorities and put first things first.

A part of your job of keeping peace is to protect your home from strife, including where parents and in-laws are concerned. If your wife becomes upset with her parents about something, you need to point her back to them, not side against them. It may be okay for your wife to spout off something about her parents in frustration, but it's not okay for you to say it! If you say it, you're creating separation, not making peace.

No matter how legitimate your wife's complaint may be, you should continually point her to the good things about her parents and yours, encouraging her to think on things that are "lovely" (see Philippians 4:8). Even bad parents do a lot of good things, and focusing only on the bad plants a seed that will eventually produce a harvest. That harvest is intended to spring up and trouble you and your house (Hebrews 12:15). It could spring up and be in full blossom when you least expect it, such as at a holiday party or other family gathering.

You must not allow this, but you must encourage peace. And you must do it in love instead of criticizing and condemning your wife for her negative feelings. Remember, she must know that you value your relationship with her the most.

There's No Room for God's Best on the Path of Selfishness

A married man must lay down his life for his wife. He can either take the attitude, This is not what I bought into when I committed to marriage, or he can dig in by the grace of God and commit himself to make the best life possible for his family. Then as he lays down his life — his will and desires — for the good of those he is now responsible for, he will reap so much more joy than if he had followed a selfish path.

Think about it. Jesus laid everything down to come to earth as a man. Then He laid it all down again when He gave up His life — spirit, soul, and body — for His Bride, the Church. But look at what He reaped! God raised Him up in glory, and Christ is still reaping a harvest each time a person gets saved.

Remember, we identified the woman as a "wombed man," who will incubate, nurture, and produce based on what her husband sows into her life. If he lays down his life for her, she will give life back to him. In fact, the only way for a husband to be truly happy and fulfilled in life and in marriage is if he gives his life wholly to his wife. He will reap infinitely more than he could ever receive by holding back and hanging on to his life.

Jesus said, "He who finds his life will lose it, and he who loses his life for My sake will find it" (Matthew 10:39). Jesus was saying that the one who gives up his life gains life, but the one who holds on to his life loses out. In other words, if you give up your low life, you will gain the high life. But if you hold on to your low life, you'll lose the high life. If you hold on to your poker parties and your buddies, you will do so at the expense of your marriage. You will cheat the marriage and yourself and lose out on building the Kingdom, Heaven-on-earth marriage that God wants you to enjoy.

Number Five: A Man Is Responsible To Have a Vision for the Future

Many men lose out with their wife because they're shortsighted. They don't see "the joy set before them" in marriage. Instead of thinking ahead about what they want to ultimately reap in life, they think only about what they want and need at the moment.

Years from now, what kind of memories do you want to have as a husband and father? Sometimes the future is difficult for us to wrap our minds around. But can you think about next month? For example, if you spend hours at a time in the front of the TV this next month, watching sports and channel-surfing instead of spending time with your wife, what do you hope to gain at the end of the month? Will you remember any of the scores of the games you watched? You may remember some things, but years from now, the things you saw on TV that month will be a vague memory at best.

I don't ask this to condemn you but to make a point. One evening alone with just you and your wife can create memories that will last a lifetime. One evening giving your children your undivided attention can produce priceless memories that will shape their lives for years to come. You must decide what is most valuable to you in the long run and sow your time wisely into those things — into things that last.

Fulfill Your Dying Wish Today

Perspective plays a part of being a great husband and father and taking responsibility for leadership in the home. At the end of your life, the memories that you have with your wife and your children and family will be your most important possessions. The life you built with your wife will have laid the foundation for your children to build their own families on the solid foundation of God's Word.

The happiness you all share as a family — not just your own happiness — will be your crowning reward and delight in life. Yet how many men lack this perspective when they're young? Then when they're old, their lives are so empty and filled with regret.

The saying is true that no one says on his deathbed, "Oh, how I wish I'd watched more TV or gotten drunk more often with my friends." No, unfortunately, the last thoughts of many men turn to the shortsightedness of their youth and to the deep regret they feel for not investing more in the things of priceless value: their own family.

Get on the Same Page With God

Anytime you undervalue something that God deems as valuable, you're going to end up with regrets if you don't make the change to love what He loves and hate what He hates. He created marriage and the family. He values that, and He loves it. And He desires that you show the same care for it, nurturing these valuable relationships in your life instead of neglecting them.

Yes, man has a certain authority in his home. It was given to Him by God to bless his family, not hurt or destroy them. And before authority, a man must take responsibility. That is no small undertaking!

Putting the cart before the horse and emphasizing a man's authority without teaching him his responsibility is a recipe for disorder and chaos in the home of the worst kind. But as a man faithfully fulfills his duties as a husband and father — and does it as unto the Lord — his rewards will be great. The blessing he sets in motion for his family will last and be perpetuated for generations to come.

True Romance: A Marriage Beyond the Dream

6

'Where Art Thou,' O Man — And Why Aren't You Taking Out the Trash!

Dr. Tom Anderson

And the Lord God called unto Adam, and said unto him, Where art thou? (Genesis 3:9 KJV)

The Bible is clear that although the husband is the head of his wife in marriage (Ephesians 5:23), that position of leadership is one of responsibility as much as it is one of authority. It was designed as a part of God's divine order for the home in order to bring blessing to the man and his family.

However, far too often in marriage, the husband has abandoned this position of responsibility and is "missing in action" where real leadership in the home is concerned. But God is calling Christian husbands to fulfill, not neglect, their God-given roles of leadership in marriage.

'Husband, Come Forth!'

This sort of reminds me of the situation in the Garden of Eden after Adam and Eve had sinned and had hidden from the Lord. God called to Adam, "...Where art thou?" (Genesis 3:9 KJV). Of course, God knew Adam's precise whereabouts, so He wasn't trying to locate Adam. Instead, God was calling on Adam to come out and to be accountable.

The same is true today. God is calling husbands everywhere to lay aside the things that have held them and their families back from experiencing His highest and best. It's time to remove those hindrances — to take out the trash — and take your place "front and center" as the head of your home.

Hang Up on Your Hang-Ups

Ephesians 5:25 makes it very clear that the husband has a responsibility to give up his flesh — his selfish desires — for his wife and family. There's only one small problem with that: The flesh does not like giving itself up! The flesh has a lot of "hang-ups"; it wants to do what it wants to do when it wants to do it. That means that when the Bible says a husband should act like Christ and wash his wife with "the water of the Word" (Ephesians 5:26), the flesh will not enjoy obeying that! The flesh doesn't want to sow into anyone but itself. But sowing to the flesh will only reap corruption, not life (Galatians 6:8).

> *Husbands, love your wives, just as Christ also loved the church and gave Himself for her, that He might sanctify and cleanse her with the washing of water by the word.* (Ephesians 5:25-26)

Responsibility has been given to the man to sow good words into his wife — not just in public but in private as well. It's one thing to be a man of principles at church or in public, but we need to be men of integrity and love "behind closed doors" when we're at home with our family. No one knows what goes on in the privacy of a man's home except his family. As husbands and fathers, we need to regularly ask ourselves, What does my family see in me?

For example, does your family see you gossiping about and slandering your boss or co-workers? You may drive home from church bashing your pastor's sermon and think nothing of it — but what is your family taking away from that experience? In talking against your pastor, you're teaching your children by your actions that you don't live under authority and that it's okay for them not to live under authority, either.

As I've said before, establishing yourself as a godly leader in your home is really about establishing relationships of trust in your family. Our family won't be able to trust that we can lead them successfully if they don't believe we know where we're going ourselves.

Your loved ones need to see your love for God and your dependence on the Word of God demonstrated consistently on a daily basis. There are many ways you can show them your love and deep reverence for God and His Word. Spending just a couple of minutes with your children over breakfast, sharing the Word of God with them, sends the message that God's Word is a priority in your life and that you're not just a Sunday morning Christian. Also, when you share testimonies of answered prayer, your family is encouraged, and they feel safe and secure knowing that you're trusting God and that your faith is bearing fruit.

Your wife and children must trust you, no matter what, at all costs. You need to keep your word with them before you keep it with anyone else. But even if you do that —yet they see you lying to others — it's going to affect their trust in you.

Do your children hear you make up excuses to others when you don't want to accept an invitation? If they perceive you as dishonest, when you tell them you want to spend time with them, hear what they have to say, or even that you love them, they may question your sincerity.

And what about your wife? If you stretch the truth with others, and then you get home late from work and tell her that traffic on the expressway was horrific — that may well be the truth, but she's thinking, Well, he lies to everyone else; maybe he's lying to me too.

Make It Count

It is absolutely amazing the power of the man's responsibility in the home. The example you set before your family, especially your children, is so critical to their emotional well-being as well as their own character. Kids follow exactly what they see Dad doing, more so than they follow what Mom does. Everything a father does and says is constantly on display. Little eyes are watching, and little hearts are forming belief systems based on what those eyes behold. So much is happening just by the husband and father's presence in the home. It is his God-ordained assignment that he make his presence count!

What kids witness in the home will directly affect their own behavior in marriage one day.

As a man, your responsibility is the dying to your flesh and to what your flesh wants to do. You won't always be able to say everything you're thinking. You won't always be able to do everything you'd like to do, because it could prove harmful to your children and their well-being.

For example, you may want to enjoy an occasional beer — but if drinking beer is going to harm your family, you need to give it up. Your drinking a beer or glass of wine — or smoking a cigarette or puffing on a cigar — might lead your children to do the same one day, and that could prove harmful to them.

Do you see the gravity of your responsibility as the head of your house? This responsibility calls for the dying of your flesh to those desires that are not profitable and that may be harmful to yourself and those you love.

Setting the right example is not always the easiest task, but it is a powerful one. And it's critical that you as a man accept that responsibility. In fact, if you're single, and you don't want that responsibility, I have to recommend that you not get married. Men who get married and refuse to give up their "me-centered" lifestyle hurt others as well as themselves in the long run.

A Man's Greatest Gift to His Children

It's been said that the greatest thing a man can do for his children is to love their mother. How true that is! The biggest thing you can do for your children is show them a picture of Christ and the Church in your marriage. Not only will your happy marriage produce within them feelings of security and well-being, it will also contribute to their building a happy home life of their own one day.

Children live what they see. So if you treat your wife right, your sons will likely treat their wives right when they grow up and get married. And your daughters will quickly perceive the difference between a man "who talks a good game" and one who demonstrates godly character consistently, over the long haul.

And since children live what they see, if you maintain a devoted relationship with God, they'll also grow up having a relationship with Him for themselves. When what you have with God is real, you will show your children the Heavenly Father. You will demonstrate His Word in your everyday life. And your children will want to cultivate that kind of relationship with the Lord for themselves.

Demonstrating Honor

As I said, a man is responsible to his wife to "wash" her with the water of the Word (Ephesians 5:26). He must invest his faith, love, time, and prayers in her. He should build her up consistently and value her uniqueness and her calling. He must esteem her as the queen of his house — and then ensure that the children in his house properly esteem her as Mom. He must teach them to show honor to their mother, but he does this primarily by demonstrating honor toward her himself.

When our children were growing up, I took responsibility for teaching them to honor Maureen. They always remembered her in a special way on her birthday, on Mother's Day, and on holidays. And I never allowed them to speak disrespectfully to their mother. That kind of behavior was simply not tolerated, and I took responsibility for enforcing that. (It was a well-understood rule in our house!)

It's important that a husband honor his wife, but he must also instill honor for her in the lives of their children. By his actions, he needs to show them — not just tell them — that she is queen of the castle! She is the most important woman in his kids' lives, and it's important that Dad treat her in a loving, respectful manner at all times and that he teach his children to do the same.

Very often we see fathers allowing their kids to speak any way they want toward the mother. He knows what's going on, but he just kicks back in front of the TV like nothing's happening. But God forbid that the child who's sassing his mother messes with Dad's remote control! As soon as he finds his remote missing, he'll jump up to deal with that posthaste!

If kids are not honoring Mom in the house, it's because Dad hasn't trained them to do it. In teaching them to show the proper honor and respect in the home, a father is setting his children up for success in their own families one day, and he is positioning them to receive a blessing promised to them by God.

> *Children, obey your parents in the Lord, for this is right.*
> *"Honour your father and mother" — which is the first*
> *commandment with a promise — "that it may go well with you*
> *and that you may enjoy long life on the earth."*
> (Ephesians 6:1-3 NIV)

Children will grow up doing what we do, not what we say. A man's children are watching the way he treats their mother — as well as the way she shows respect toward their father. And they take to heart how both Dad and Mom respond to and interact with them. Children are extremely sensitive to their parents' feelings and emotions. What kids witness in the home will directly affect their own behavior in marriage one day.

You Will Gravitate in the Direction
of Your Choices

Perhaps you grew up in a very godly, Christian home — and taking your place as a great husband and father is natural to you. Or maybe you grew up in a dysfunctional home, and you realize as an adult that you don't have a clue about what it means to be a great husband and father.

Have you ever found yourself doing or saying something unseemly and you thought, Oh, no! I'm just like my father? Actually, you probably have traits — both positive and negative — that you saw in your dad when you were a child, and now those traits are being demonstrated in your own house. But if you're a Christian, you can lay an axe to the root of every negative, harmful, dysfunctional trait, and you can refuse to pass that on to another generation.

No matter what your upbringing, being a great husband and father is not a choice that you make just once — and sometimes it's not even a choice you make every day. Sometimes it's a choice that you make many times in one day! There is a natural struggle that takes place with dying to self. I believe that most men desire to be good husbands and fathers — but their flesh just keeps winning over them.

The key is this: If you choose as though you were what you want to be, you will become what you want to be. After a period of making the right choices, you will form the habits necessary to be a good husband and father. In other words, you will gravitate in the direction of your choices, whether good or bad.

An Exercise to Help You

Allow me help you start this process in a positive direction if you haven't done so already. The next time you're driving home from work, begin to work through this out loud:

If I were a great husband, what would I choose to do when I get home? Would I turn on the TV right away, or would I sit down and talk to my wife about her day? After that, if I were a great father, I would help my children with their homework or class project and spend time talking to them about their day.

You don't have to wait until you're driving home from work to begin practicing this. If you feel as if you're not where you want to be in terms of being a good husband and father, you can practice these "if" scenarios anytime.

If I were a good husband, I would take my wife out tonight. She's been working hard lately without a break. I don't want her to have to cook tonight. If I were a good father, I wouldn't yell at my family. I would be patient with my children and teach them how to do what I want them to do. I would discipline them in love and not in anger so that they're always secure in my love for them.

As you practice doing this, after awhile, you won't have to ask or think about it anymore. You will have formed the habits that make you a great husband and father. It may not happen overnight, but stay with it. With God's help, you will change for the better, your wife will change for the better, and your family life will never be the same again!

When our children were growing up, I decided that when I got home from work each evening, the very first part of my time at home would go to Maureen. I made certain to show my kids how much I valued her. Then I made sure that I chose them over television time. I made the choice to spend some quality time with my children every single night, even if I was exhausted and just wanted to go to another room and shut myself off from everyone.

Early on, I had to consciously think about that — and those decisions were not always easy to make. My flesh fought me hard. But I made no excuses and no provision for my flesh because I had a committed, made-up mind that I was going to be a great husband and father and have the happiest, healthiest family life possible — for my sake, for my wife's sake, and for the sake of my children and their own families one day.

Excuses, Excuses — How To Stop Growth and Progress in Its Tracks

The lazy man says, "There is a lion in the road! A fierce lion is in the streets!" (Proverbs 26:13)

A person doesn't become great at some sport, profession, or trade by making excuses and refusing to work at and invest time in getting better. Yet how often in marriage do we see people making excuses for why their home life is in shambles and why it doesn't model anything remotely close to the relationship of Christ to His Church?

I have actually heard men say, "I am who I am. My wife's just going to have to deal with it." A man who says that stops growing right there at the point of his statement. And oftentimes, he makes those kinds of statements as an excuse for not changing. In other words, he has no intention of changing for anyone.

Many people take a very hardened approach to marriage and to life. They act like the clay pot that has already been fired and is now eternally unchangeable! But God wants us to be pliable and yielded. He wants to mold us into Christ's image (see Romans 8:29).

Well, for clay to be molded, it must be kept wet. We are kept wet by "the washing of water by the word" (Ephesians 5:26). When we continually read, study, pray, and meditate on the Word of God, we keep ourselves from becoming selfish and hardened.

Crucify Your Flesh, Fulfill Your Purpose

Have you ever read some of the things Jesus said in the Gospels and thought, That's just too hard? For instance, some people read in Matthew and the other Gospels, "…'If anyone desires to come after Me, let him deny himself, and take up his cross, and follow Me" (Matthew 16:24), and they say, "That's asking too much." But that verse doesn't mean we're to take up a physical cross and be crucified. It simply means that we are to crucify our flesh and deny it its desires in order to "take up" and fulfill our God-ordained purpose.

Our cross symbolizes our purpose. And when we got married, part of our purpose as men became to be great husbands. Well, how are you going to fulfill that? How are you going to become great at being a husband? The same way you became great at softball, golf, accounting, plumbing, or whatever it is you're good at: You simply have to apply yourself to your purpose as "husband." And that means you're going to have to change.

Suppose you played softball, and your softball coach told you that you really needed to practice batting. Then what if you said to him, "Hey, this is just the way I am. You knew how I batted when you put me on the team. Sorry, I'm just not the best batter. That's all there is to it."

Sound ridiculous? Of course it does! You would never say that. Instead, you would probably go to the batting cages and work on improving your skills. You would put in the time and apply yourself to becoming a better batter.

Similarly, we must apply ourselves to marriage. Perhaps you've said in the past, "I'm just not a good communicator." Instead of saying that, you need to make the effort to become a better communicator!

You can learn how to communicate. I did. It was tough, because for most of my life, I hardly ever communicated. I just didn't talk much. My wife finally said to me, "Why don't you just say what you're thinking?"

I said, "Really?" Now she's trying to figure out how to shut me up, because I'm thinking all the time about a lot of things.

Love Brings Out the Best

That He might present her to Himself a glorious church, not having spot or wrinkle or any such thing, but that she should be holy and without blemish. (Ephesians 5:27)

Let's look at that phrase "holy and without blemish." This means, in effect, prepared for the plans and purposes of God. Now let's apply that to the husband loving his wife "as Christ loved the Church" (v. 25). The Word of God has been symbolized as both the seed and water. Just as Christ sowed the Word into the Church and watered it, causing His Body to bear fruit, we as husbands are to plant the Word of God into the life of our wife. Then we're to water that Word with more Word. And she, like the Church, grows stronger and becomes more and more fruitful as a result.

As Christ sows His Word into the Church, the responsible husband also sows into his wife. But if a husband is always complaining about his wife and saying things, such as, "My wife is such a nag," he's probably not sowing the seed of the Word into her life as he should.

All things being equal, a woman is good soil — and whatever her husband plants in her is going to produce a harvest. In other words, if you sow love, you'll get love. If you sow romance, you'll get romance. If you sow laziness, you'll reap laziness. And if you sow one seed, you'll get a hundred back! So if you sow a little anger, for example, you'll get a whole lot more anger in return.

It's been said many times before, but it bears repeating: If you don't like the harvest you've been getting in life, change the seed you've been sowing! So if you don't like your marriage, begin to plant some different seeds.

When you take a genuine interest in your wife and in her becoming the best she can be, you will reap the reward of that. However, too often a man isn't interested in sowing into his wife's life. He is too interested in his own needs and what pleases him to be able to invest in her.

Can you imagine Jesus taking that attitude toward the Church? Can you imagine Him saying, "You don't ever let me do what I want to do. What about My needs? What about Me? You're not doing enough for Me, and you want what?" No, you never heard the Lord say that, and you never will. He knows that His joy is in His sowing and that His reward will surely be reaped as He fulfills His place and performs His part as the Head of His Body.

Why clamor for your own needs when you've been given the position as head of your house? Why not focus on sowing the right seeds and reaping the fruit of that? Certainly, you can sow the seed of the Word, and you should do that. But there are countless different kinds of seeds you can sow into your wife.

What if on your way home from work, you spent 15 dollars on some flowers and a card for your wife? Then when you got home, you spent 20 minutes or so just talking to her? You will have invested less than 20 dollars and about a half hour of your time — just a small seed — but your harvest would be incredible.

It's interesting that many husbands don't want to sow anything into their wife or their marriage, yet they want to reap something. It can't be done. You simply cannot reap where you have not sown!

The Bible was given to us to change our thinking to come in line with God's way of thinking. We need God's Word to change our mentality about so many things. For instance, many men have had the mentality that they can just take love without giving any love. No one wins in a relationship like that.

But if a man will give love, he will get love too. In fact, if we want to be truly happy, we must figure out what we want most in life and then give that! The Bible is clear: Whatever you sow, you will reap (Galatians 6:7).

Love Her First

As we've already seen, husbands are a picture of Christ and wives are a picture of the Church. By nature, men are initiators; women are responders. A wife will usually respond to what her husband initiates. That's the way God ordered it. Just as we love God because He first loved us (He initiated a relationship with us), a wife loves her husband because he first loved her.

Loving your wife first is the sowing process. We reap the harvest because we participated in the process. So if you want a harvest in your marriage, you can't just sit around making excuses. You must be willing to do something toward bringing that harvest about. It takes time and effort.

If a farmer plants corn one morning, he doesn't go out the next morning looking for his ears of corn! No, it takes time for the corn to grow. He must plant, but then he must water and nurture what he has planted.

Here's what often happens in marriage. For some reason — through ignorance, stubbornness, or laziness — a husband plants a lot of weeds into his marriage. And those weeds spring up and start taking over the relationship. Then he receives some light and revelation in his heart about marriage, so he decides to plant some good seed into his wife. But he can't weed out in one day a garden of marriage that's been overrun with weeds for months and even years. He's going to have to stay with planting the right seeds for a while before he sees the harvest of a happy, healthy marriage.

So if you've been sowing "weeds" into your marriage — but then you begin bringing home cards and flowers — you might not get an immediate harvest. In fact, your wife may even question your motives. Because of the bad seeds you've planted, distrust has sprung up in the marriage, and she may wonder whether or not you're sincere.

Many men are resistant to this idea of being the initiator and of taking responsibility to sow into the marriage. They have the attitude, As soon as she becomes a great wife, then I'll begin to love her.

A man with this kind of attitude doesn't see that when he begins to love his wife, then she'll become a great wife. He must begin the action; then she becomes what he desires. As he treats her as an amazing wife, she will become that in his life.

Sow Love Into Your Wife and
Reap Favor With God

If you're not loving your wife purely for what it will do for her, think about what it will do for you!

Husbands, likewise, dwell with them with understanding, giving honor to the wife, as to the weaker vessel, and as being heirs together of the grace of life, that your prayers may not be hindered. (1 Peter 3:7)

When you don't treat your wife according to biblical knowledge, your prayers are hindered. That's how serious this issue is to God. I wonder how many men flounder and fail in life because they're treating their wife poorly. They might be praying and believing, but their praying and believing are rendered ineffective because they're mistreating or neglecting their wife.

The Bible has a lot to say about sowing and reaping in the area of finances. But Malachi 2:13 talks about sowing and reaping in the area of relationships, in particular, the marriage relationship.

> ...*You cover the altar of the Lord with tears, with weeping and crying; So He does not regard the offering anymore, nor receive it with goodwill from your hands. Yet you say, "For what reason?" Because the Lord has been witness between you and the wife of your youth, with whom you have dealt treacherously; Yet she is your companion and your wife by covenant. But did He not make them one, having a remnant of the Spirit? And why one? He seeks godly offspring. Therefore take heed to your spirit, And let none deal treacherously with the wife of his youth.*
> (Malachi 2:13-15)

I tell the men in my church that when they're giving offerings, yet they're seeing no harvest, they need to look at how they're treating their wife. In fact, if my prayers seemed to be hindered, my relationships would be the first place I'd look. I would check my heart to make sure I'm walking in love and not holding a grudge against anyone. And I would certainly look at the way I've been loving my wife.

Study the Love of God and
Learn To Love Yourself

Loving someone else begins with loving God first and then loving yourself. When you realize the great love God has for you, you will begin to value yourself the way He values you. A revelation of the love God has for you equips you to love others.

Some people are very selfish in relationships, because they don't understand the love of God, and they very often don't love themselves. They may act as if they love themselves, but it's not real love. They're looking out for "number one" —they're only out to get what they want regardless of what others want or need.

But real love is not selfish (see First Corinthians 13:5). When you really love God and understand His great love for you, you're in a position to really give yourself to someone else and be truly happy in a marriage.

Depression and the 'Me' Syndrome —
How To Break Free By Breaking All the Rules

Some people become so steeped in self-thought that they become depressed. In fact, most depression stems from selfishness and self-centeredness. Secular psychology tells you that to deal with depression, you need to make it more about you. But doing that usually only leads to more depression.

This is exactly opposite of God's way. God's way is to sow what you want in life. If you want joy and to be free from depression, you're going to have start breaking some of the "rules" you've learned from the world. You're going to have to sow joy into someone's life who needs it. In other words, get your mind on God and His Word instead of on yourself. God will meet your needs and the needs of those you're sowing into!

Problems occur in marriage when the husband doesn't love himself; therefore, he cannot truly love his wife as God intends. The husband who doesn't love himself can't treat his wife right because he has so much junk in him — in his soul and his thinking — such as rejection, low self-worth, and low self-image. I'm not making excuses for a husband who finds himself in this position; I'm simply explaining why he behaves the way he does toward his wife. He needs to identify the problem and deal with it head-on instead of burying it and continually struggling in his marriage.

Time To Take Out the Trash

If you're in your 30s, 40s, or 50s, and you know you don't love yourself the way you're supposed to and that you don't treat your wife right, I have a question for you. How long have you been aware that you have issues? No matter what hurtful experiences you've suffered or how badly you've missed it with your own family, it's time to face those issues head-on. It's time to train yourself to think, act, and live in line with God and His Word.

For example, find scriptures that tell you who you are in Christ and who you are to the Father. Ask the Lord to show you which books to read or which audio or video teachings on the subject you need. Just as you'd go to the batting cages to practice batting to improve your skills, you must "practice" understanding the love of God. You must put forth the effort to learn of His love for you and to love your wife as you love yourself.

Unfortunately, our society teaches us to put so much value in our looks, or our appearance, that many people live very shallow lives on the inside. But the Bible teaches us to place value on Christ within us. Being beautiful on the outside does not promise beauty on the inside. A person who is ugly on the inside will eventually show ugly on the outside. So spend time working on the inside, on your own self-worth. Learn about who you are in Christ and how valuable you are to the Father.

What Are You Feeding Your Marriage?

Ephesians 5:28-29 says, "…he who loves his wife loves himself. For no one ever hated his own flesh, but nourishes and cherishes it…." Well, if you're hungry, you feed yourself, right? Similarly, you need to regularly "feed" your marriage relationship.

Men sometimes have the attitude that they fed the marriage last Friday, so why should they have to feed it again today! But you need to nourish and cherish your marriage daily. Just as you don't go prolonged periods of time without eating, you shouldn't starve the physical and emotional needs of your wife.

I'm so glad that Maureen prayed for me in the early days of our lives together and that I had a teachable and determined heart to win at this thing called marriage! I'm also glad that we received the revelation early on that biblical submission in marriage meant that I was the head of our marriage with Christ as my model. Both Maureen and I would have suffered for it if she had just submitted to my every whim and had been complacent about the junk I had in my life because of my upbringing. Had she just accepted that as the standard in our lives, I would have become a spiritually indifferent and undisciplined man on the road to nowhere. But she expected the best from me, and I knew God was calling me higher in my walk with Him, in my personal life, and in my marriage. I knew it was time to "take out the trash" and take my place as a godly, loving leader in my home.

What about you? Is God looking at your home and finding that the leadership position has been neglected or abandoned? When He calls, "Where art thou?" how will you answer? So much is riding — even future generations — on what you'll say to the Lord in response to His call on your life as husband, father, and leader in your home.

7

'You Want Me To Do What?'
The Wisdom of Biblical Submission

Drs. Tom and Maureen Anderson

To understand the roles and responsibilities of the husband and wife in marriage, we must look to God, who created the institution of marriage and joined the first man and the first woman in this holy relationship. Understanding their beginnings at Creation helps us see God's purpose for the unique design of the man and the woman.

> *Then God said, "Let Us make man in Our image, according to Our likeness; let them have dominion over the fish of the sea, over the birds of the air, and over the cattle, over all the earth and over every creeping thing that creeps on the earth." So God created man in His own image; in the image of God He created him; male and female He created them.* (Genesis 1:26-27)

The word "man" here is masculine-feminine. In fact, the word "Adam" in the Bible means mankind or humanity. So when God created man, or Adam, He created mankind, and He created mankind in His own image.

Notice this verse also says that when God created Adam, He created them, plural. So first — before God ever brought Eve forth in the Creation — God created the human being, Adam, as male and female "in His own image," or with the same attributes that existed in Him (v. 27).

Tom:

God Created 'Woman' as Equal and Indispensable

Then the rib which the Lord God had taken from man He made into a woman, and He brought her to the man. (Genesis 2:22)

The word "rib" in this verse doesn't mean rib as you and I understand anatomy today. Think about it. If God simply took woman from a rib, that act wouldn't have placed a lot of value on her. After all, a man can get by without a rib — but he can't get by in life without his wife.

The Hebrew translation of "rib" in creation portrays half a temple. In other words, God took this masculine-feminine being, Adam, and separated "half a temple" to make two distinct beings, one man and one woman.

And Adam said: "This is now bone of my bones and flesh of my flesh; She shall be called Woman, Because she was taken out of Man." (Genesis 2:23)

The word "bone" means substance or self-same substance. So Adam was in effect saying, "As I am strong and powerful, so is she strong and powerful."

Not only is a husband responsible to protect his wife, as we've seen, but the wife is also responsible to protect her husband — to surround him with faith and love, to help him, and to be a lover, friend, associate, and companion. Woman is the "completion" of man, equal and indispensable.

Let's back up to a time before God brought forth woman from Adam.

So Adam gave names to all cattle, to the birds of the air, and to every beast of the field. But for Adam there was not found a helper comparable to him. (Genesis 2:20)

The word "helper" in this verse means aid, assist, or protect; the completion of man. Adam was able to say, "She is bone of my bone and flesh of my flesh; she's similar and powerful. She completes me."

Putting the Puzzle Pieces Together
Woman was created to complete man in life, to assist him as a magnificently created companion, not as a servant or slave. And we've seen that God created man with an innate calling to lead and to take responsibility. Yes, he stands as the ultimate authority figure in the family — under the authority of God Almighty. But God conferred more than authority on Adam; He charged him with certain responsibilities where the marriage was concerned. And one of Adam's primary responsibilities was to protect and provide (see Genesis 2:15).

Often in marriages today, we find the role of protector and provider being filled by the wife instead of by the husband. The position is vacated because, for some reason, the husband isn't fulfilling his responsibility; he's taking a passive role in the marriage. But no matter how he arrived at that place of passivity, it's still in his God-given nature to lead and to be responsible for the well-being of his family.

Out of Position, Out of Order
Some wives are viewed as overbearing or domineering. They're seen as women who want to take the lead in the marriage or "wear the pants" in the family. But I believe that because of her own purpose and design, a woman actually wants her husband to take his place as a responsible leader. Yet in some cases, a woman feels she has to step in and accept the leadership role because no one else is doing it. Once this shifting of roles takes place, the marriage becomes lopsided and out of order. The only way for the situation to be righted is for the wife to vacate the role and responsibility of leader, because the position must be open in order for the husband to fill it.

A husband is called to be at his wife's side in the role of leader, protector, provider, and lover. And one of his biggest responsibilities in this role is over the family's finances. I'm not saying that a husband must handle every aspect of the finances, especially if the wife has better bookkeeping skills. But he still must take the lead in the marriage and be responsible to know the state of his family's financial affairs. (In another chapter, we'll look at the subject of how to handle money wisely.)

I've seen so many women stepping in to fill this role of "financial manager" because the husband failed to do it. But a wife must be very careful not to carry this responsibility emotionally, because in her attempt to create order, it will instead create disorder and disharmony in the marriage. She must allow her husband to fulfill his God-given responsibility to manage his household before God.

A wife who's trying to fill her husband's role in the marriage is like a missing piece of a puzzle. Until she fills her own role in the marriage and allows her husband to fill his role, God's picture of an ideal marriage will remain incomplete in their lives. As a husband fulfills his role as leader, protector, provider, and lover, his wife can then "complete" him. She is the completion of man, not the man.

Leading With Love as Your Motivation

As we've seen, a husband's position as leader is one of responsibility as much it is as one of authority. And as a leader, he must examine his motives as he makes decisions concerning his family. In other words, he must ask himself, Am I acting in the best interest of my wife and children, or am I being selfish, doing only what's best for me? When a husband proves over time that he makes decisions prayerfully and lovingly — putting his family's interests above his own — his wife and children will feel secure and loved, and they will trust him to lead and guide the family. They will willingly submit to that kind of leadership because it reflects leadership as Jesus would do it.

Often we hear about husbands attempting to force their wife submit to them. But that's not how submission works. Submission is a voluntary act on the part of the one doing the submitting. Remember, Christ and His Church — His Bride — is the model, and the Bible says that Christ gave Himself for the Church. A woman submits to her husband because he genuinely cares for her and "gives himself" for her, not because he's a dominating ruler.

> *First John 4:19 says, "We love Him because He first loved us." Since Jesus and His relationship with the Church is the picture of the husband and wife in marriage, we can see that the husband should be the initiator in the marriage. In other words, he is the teacher and the example in the marriage. His wife loves him because he loves her first! And from the love he gives to her, she loves him back! If he fails to love her, she will struggle in her effort to complete him (see Ephesians 5:28-29).*

MAUREEN:

The Interdependent Marriage

We know that marriage is a picture of the beautiful relationship between Christ and the Church, and God does not want that picture broken. Ephesians 5:21-33 provides wonderful instruction for the way a marriage should operate based on the model of the Christian's relationship with Jesus. However, there has been so much error and extremism concerning this subject of submission that it has caused havoc in marriages.

Let's go to the Word and see what God has to say about the interdependent relationship that should exist between a husband and wife.

> *Submitting to one another in the fear of God. Wives, submit to your own husbands, as to the Lord. For the husband is head of the wife, as also Christ is head of the church; and He is the Savior of the body. Therefore, just as the church is subject to Christ, so let the wives be to their own husbands in everything. Husbands, love your wives, just as Christ also loved the church and gave Himself for her, that He might sanctify and cleanse her with the washing of water by the word, that He might present her to Himself a glorious church, not having spot or wrinkle or any such thing, but that she should be holy and without blemish. So husbands ought to love their own wives as their own bodies; he who loves his wife loves himself. For no one ever hated his own flesh, but nourishes and cherishes it, just as the Lord does the church. For we are members of His body, of His flesh and of His bones. "For this reason a man shall leave his father and mother and be joined to his wife, and the two shall become one flesh." This is a great mystery, but I speak concerning Christ and the church. Nevertheless let each one of you in particular so love his own wife as himself, and let the wife see that she respects her husband.* (Ephesians 5:21-33)

The first two verses of this passage lay a foundation or springboard for the "rules" and roles of marriage. Verse 21 says, "Submitting to one another in the fear of God." You've no doubt heard the saying, "There's no 'I' in 'TEAM.'" This verse simply means that a husband and wife should combine each other's strengths and use them to build a life together as one.

In other words, they're a team. They're "two" functioning together as "one." Each one must assume certain responsibilities and carry part of the load. Many couples understand this principle — but some of them need help putting it into practice so they can join forces without killing each other!

Verse 22 says, "Wives, submit to your own husbands, as to the Lord." One definition of the word "submit" in this verse is to adapt or yield. So a wife is to adapt and yield herself to her husband's leadership, but she is not be trampled on by a laundry list of unreasonable demands!

Teammate or Slave?
'Who's Rowing the Boat in This Marriage?'

When I became born again, Tom and I were already married. We were members of a very traditional church that taught that the husband was "lord" over the wife and bore absolute power and rule over her like a dictator. The strong implication was that the wife was nothing; she simply obeyed without question whatever her husband told her to do.

Well, Tom wasn't a dictator by any means, but I went along with that teaching because I loved God and I wanted to please Him. However, after about three or four years in that particular church, I felt completely worthless as a wife and as an individual. It was like I was being drained of life itself! I had no joy, no peace — I was miserable! And I couldn't shake the continual feelings of worthlessness that plagued me.

I knew something was wrong with this church's teaching, but on the other hand, I didn't exactly know the right teaching, either. I simply knew that the fruit wasn't good. Tom recognized what this teaching was doing to me as a person. He wasn't happy, either. So we began to seek the Lord.

We learned that when Scripture says wives are to submit to their husband, it simply means that a wife is to bond to, participate with, and stand shoulder-to-shoulder with her husband. It means she's to be "in the same boat" with him. It means that she's to be a team player!

Have you ever heard the saying, "We're all on the same page"? That means that everyone involved is together in his or her thinking, aim, and mission. They're like a team in that they're putting their heads together and pooling their talents and resources to pursue a common goal. In a manner of speaking, they're one — one unit consisting of two or more individuals.

Certainly, a wife is to respect the husband's ultimate responsibility to make certain decisions that guide or provide direction for the whole family. That's his God-given assignment. But she has a part, too, and a wise husband will listen to his wife's input. He may or may not agree, but he should respect her wisdom and insight. Then, ultimately, He must prayerfully do what he feels the Lord is telling him to do or what he thinks is best.

In the Garden of Eden, God created Eve as a "helpmate" for Adam (Genesis 2:18, 20). And God intended that the two complement each other and function together. Eve was created to stand side by side with Adam — not under his feet as a servant or slave.

Contention or Celebration?

Many a marriage has fallen short of what God intended simply because of ignorance concerning the different roles of a husband and wife — and because couples failed to recognize each other's gifts and strengths in the marriage. Because one spouse didn't understand the other as a valuable and unique individual, the couple's differences became points of contention instead of celebration.

Instead of fighting about our different gifts and strengths, Tom and I have always endeavored to celebrate our differences. We have worked wonderfully together as a team all these years. Tom is a visionary. God gives him dreams and plans for our life and ministry. I'm an administrator. In matters pertaining to ministry, almost as soon as Tom shares the plan or vision, I'm "on it" to help bring it to fruition! In fact, as soon as he communicates what he sees in his heart, I usually have staff and volunteers praying and interceding over that vision! I'm not trying to take over. That's simply my strength; I'm simply taking my place with Tom to assist him in the work God has called us to do.

Tom and I are a team. He needs me, and I need him. I'm not a visionary; I'm a builder. I need vision in order to know what to build. Tom is the head of this team, but he's not a builder. He values my strengths to bring forth what he sees as the visionary — and he allows me to operate in those strengths because that's where I function best and am the most effective.

As a pastor, Tom spends long hours praying and seeking God. He studies the Word of God and writes sermons. He has the pulse of the congregation because it's his job to know what the needs and concerns are of the members of our church. He doesn't have time to organize departments and oversee volunteers. That's an administrator's job. If we both did my job, who would take care of the spiritual oversight of the church? On the other hand, if we both did Tom's job, who would facilitate the vision and the day-to-day operation of the ministry?

My strengths are not Tom's strengths. And his strengths are not my strengths. But together, we complement and strengthen each other and our marriage. We don't feel threatened by each other's gifts; we esteem and appreciate those gifts, and that's why we're able to benefit collectively from them. By recognizing the gifts in each other and combining our strengths, we've been able to build a successful family and a ministry together.

Progress on the Sea of Life

A wife needs to get on board or "get in the boat" with her husband. She can't have her own separate boat and expect to be truly happy and fulfilled in marriage. A husband and wife must be in the same boat together and combine their strengths so that they can make steady progress and fulfill destiny on the sea of life.

A healthy marriage in which there is unity and solidarity can accomplish great things in the Kingdom of God. The enemy has tried to undermine marriages by pitting one spouse against the other. He knows that marriages are strengthened when we complement each other with our differences — but that a marriage is weakened when we use our differences to attack, ridicule, and reject one another. If we would give place to the love of God in our hearts and accept one another's gifts and strengths, the enemy would be defeated in his attempts to hinder our progress or even to destroy our marriage.

Sometimes a husband is intimidated by his wife's gift, so he doesn't draw from it properly. In fact, he might try to smother her gift and not permit it to develop and flourish. Similarly, a wife can ill-esteem and demean the gift of God in her husband. She may lack the desire to see that gift grow, and in a case like that, very often the gift never comes to fruition. Everyone loses in those kinds of situations — the couple, their family, and the calling that's on their lives as husband and wife.

Tom:

'My Husband Made Me Do It'

For the husband is head of the wife, as also Christ is head of the church; and He is the Savior of the body. Therefore, just as the church is subject to Christ, so let the wives be to their own husbands in everything. (Ephesians 5:23-24)

These verses concerning the roles of the husband and wife are often taken out of the context and misunderstood. The context is the analogy of Christ and the Church. So the teaching that a wife must submit to her husband "no matter what" is erroneous. I have actually heard ministers teach that a wife must do whatever her husband says to do, regardless of whether it's legal, moral, or ethical or right in the eyes of God!

In other words, this teaching purports that if the husband wants to go to a bar and wants his wife to accompany him, she must do it even if going to the bar violates her convictions. If he wants to commit some sin and invites her to participate in that sin, she must do it even if that sin goes cross-grain to her own desires or to the voice of her conscience. If he wants her to commit a crime, she must do it despite the consequences she may face with the law!

To say that a wife must do whatever her husband commands regardless of the consequences is a perverted teaching. We are each individually responsible to God for our walk with Him and for whether we obey Him. The excuse "My husband made me do it" won't hold water with God. Colossians 3:18 says, "Wives, submit to your own husbands, as is fitting in the Lord." So a wife is to submit to love, because God is love. But she isn't to submit to abuse or to things that go against her heart or her conscience.

Now, I'm not saying a wife should refuse to submit to some decision her husband has made just because she doesn't agree with it. Certainly, he should hear her out and consider her thoughts about the matter, but, ultimately, it's his responsibility to do what he believes the Lord is leading him to do.

I'm aware that there are situations in marriage in which a husband doesn't care about his wife's feelings or value her input in family matters. And some husbands aren't walking in godly reverence and submission to the Lord. It's also true that some women don't care as much about what the Lord — or their husband — wants as much as they care about what they want! But when two people in a marriage sincerely desire to do what's right according to God's Word — and not fight for their own rights or selfish desires — they are "submitting to one another in the fear of God" (Ephesians 5:21), and God will bless that kind of attitude and devotion.

To Love as Christ Loves

Husbands, love your wives, just as Christ also loved the church and gave Himself for her, that He might sanctify and cleanse her with the washing of water by the word, that He might present her to Himself a glorious church, not having spot or wrinkle or any such thing, but that she should be holy and without blemish. So husbands ought to love their own wives as their own bodies; he who loves his wife loves himself. For no one ever hated his own flesh, but nourishes and cherishes it, just as the Lord does the church. (Ephesians 5:25-29)

Again, this passage is talking about husbands and wives and about Christ and the Church. Remember, the relationship between Christ and His Church is a picture of the relationship between a husband and wife. So when Paul writes, "Husbands, love your wives, just as Christ also loved the church and gave...," he's showing a husband how to love his wife: by giving himself to her.

After Paul tells us that husbands are to love their wives in the same manner that Christ loves the church, verse 26 says, "That He might sanctify and cleanse her with the washing of water by the word." A husband loves his wife when he gives himself for her and when he lays down his life by praying for her and speaking the Word of God over her — spirit, soul, and body.

I've seen miracles happen in relationships in which husbands fulfilled their responsibility to speak the Word over their wives. In many cases, situations of childhood abuse or other negative experiences were hindering the wife from becoming what God had designed her to be. But the Word of God spoken over her by her husband "washed and cleansed" her, and those deep-seated issues fell by the wayside! She was released from issues of the past, and her gifts began to flow in the marriage, which added another dimension to her husband's gifts as she "completed" him.

When a husband speaks the Word of God over his wife, that Word washes and cleanses her from garbage in the world that tries to bombard her mind. Negative thoughts of the enemy can be washed away by the power of the Living Word spoken in faith from the lips of her husband.

MAUREEN:

The Temptation To Quit
Just Short of the Prize

The husband has a big responsibility in the marriage relationship. He lays down his life for his wife, and that is not always easy, convenient, or comfortable.

As a husband, you may feel as if you're sweating "great drops of blood" as you die to self and to your own desires. But just as Jesus said to the Father in the Garden of Gethsemane, "Not My will but Thine be done" (Luke 22:42) — you're going to have to voluntarily give up some of your rights for the sake of your wife. You may have to pray to God yourself, saying, "Not my will but Yours be done." And you may have to do that more than once!

The other side of this truth is that the potential exists for a husband to produce in his wife a selfish, self-centered, spoiled brat! In other words, he becomes the giver, and she becomes the taker without ever giving back, showing gratitude, or caring for his happiness. We must never forget that we're called to submit ourselves to one another in the fear of God (Ephesians 5:21) and to serve one another in love (Galatians 5:13). Our attitude should be, What will make my spouse happy? Lord, help me meet his [or her] need. When we're loving, giving, and serving each other in marriage, we'll reap the rewards of a marriage that's Heaven-blessed!

TOM:

The Real Purpose for Authority in Marriage

At least four times in the New Testament, God says to the husband, "Love your wife" (Ephesians 5:25,28,33; Colossians 3:19). Remember we said that love is not a feeling but a choice. In other words, a man chooses every day to show love to his wife.

> *Husbands, love your wives and do not be harsh with them.*
> (Colossians 3:19 NIV)

Women are emotional creatures who don't respond well to yelling and harsh tones. So when a husband is harsh toward his wife, that doesn't set very well with her. His attitude may be, Hey, I was just trying to make a point. But his point was not received because it wasn't delivered with tenderness and gentleness. So God is not being mean or unreasonable when He says to men, "Don't do that." He's simply trying to impart wisdom to a man's heart and blessing to his marriage.

> *Husbands, likewise, dwell with them with understanding, giving honor to the wife, as to the weaker vessel, and as being heirs together of the grace of life, that your prayers may not be hindered.* (1 Peter 3:7)

Look at the phrase, "…as being heirs together of the grace of life…." A husband must see his wife as a co-heir. He must be a team player, and he must see her as a member of his team and then dwell with her accordingly. Without this understanding, he risks having his prayers hindered.

One of the husband's responsibilities in the marriage is to pray for his wife. Most people have the idea that women are supposed to be the intercessors and that it's a wife's job to pray for her family. Certainly, both the husband and wife are responsible for their individual prayer life and their own fellowship and relationship with God. But as a figure of authority in the marriage, the husband has a certain responsibility to "watch and pray" where his wife and children are concerned. He must be spiritually alert and sensitive to God's guidance for that family — as well as to any spiritual attack that may be stirring against them.

Christ is the Intercessor over the Church. Hebrews 7:25 bears this out: "Therefore He is also able to save to the uttermost those who come to God through Him, since He always lives to make intercession for them." And God has called husbands to be the intercessor over their home and family. It is the husband's privilege and responsibility to pray for his wife. And he has the spiritual authority to do it! God will honor and answer the prayers a man prays on behalf of his family.

Maureen grew up dealing with oppression at various times in her life. Her father dealt with mental illness, and I believe this affected Maureen's emotions as a child. As a grown woman, she continued to struggle from time to time with oppression. Three different times after we were married, she experienced oppression so dark that it seemed to swallow her and render her helpless and paralyzed. She was so overwhelmed with life, she couldn't even pray for herself.

We didn't know the exact source of this oppression — we just knew it didn't come from God! One night, I stayed up all night praying in the

Spirit for Maureen. And by morning, that darkness lifted from her, and she never had a problem with oppression from that day on.

I'm not sharing this to brag. I simply took my place of authority in my home and refused to allow the enemy to have a place in my wife. I still don't know what it was exactly that was oppressing Maureen, but I knew it had probably gained some kind of hold in her life when she was very young. And I knew I had authority over it and that it had no place in my home.

I am in no way giving the wife a free pass so that she can just have her husband do all of her praying for her. As a Christian, she's an intercessor too. But the husband is called to watch over the affairs of his house and to guard and guide his household. He is the protector naturally, but he is the protector spiritually too. And he must die to self and take his place of authority and responsibility over those in his own house whom God has entrusted to his care.

MAUREEN:

Just for Women

We've established the fact that the relationship between Christ and the Church is the picture of the relationship between a husband and wife. So when we read about Christ and His Church, we can see the role a husband is to have in his marriage.

Similarly, in reading about Christ and His Church — His Bride — a wife can also understand her role in marriage.

> *...let the wife see that she respects and reverences her husband [that she notices him, venerates, and esteems him; and that she defers to him, praises him, and loves and admires him exceedingly].* (Ephesians 5:33 Amplified)

Think about those words — respect, reverence, esteem, love, and admire. One of our biggest roles as wives is to set our husband up for success. We send him out to "conquer the world," because we believe in him, and we believe that he can do it!

He Can 'Hear' You

As a wife, what you think about your husband affects him. Even when the two of you are apart, your thoughts, words, and emotions affect your husband positively or negatively. You are "one flesh" with him (Genesis 2:24), so your attitude toward him is vitally important.

A husband can sense whether his wife is standing with him in life. Remember, his successes are your successes, too, so I encourage you to stand by your husband, even in your attitudes, and help him believe that he is a success.

'On the Same Page'

To submit to our husband means we're to "be on the same page" with him. We are to pull together with him and add our strength to his. When a husband and wife join forces to accomplish a common goal, they can do great things in life. But if a wife is constantly pulling against what her husband desires to accomplish, she hurts him, but she hurts herself too.

A wife is a helper to her husband, "equal and indispensable." However, that doesn't mean she shouldn't submit to her husband's godly counsel and authority. There have been many times when Tom has discerned that some direction I was about to take wasn't quite right, and I have always respected that. I've backed off those situations to give myself more time to pray about them.

There are also times when the wife will sense direction from the Lord in some area of their lives, and, certainly, her husband should listen to her. Wisdom can be found in her mouth (Proverbs 31:26) if she's been meditating on the Word of God. Because of what's she been meditating on regularly — the Word of God — the wisdom of God that's needed for a particular situation may come through her.

Recognizing Faith and Fear

However, it's important to note that just because we as women are "incubators," that doesn't mean we're always going to come up with the answers to the dilemmas of life. In other words, just because we're meditators by nature doesn't mean we're always meditating on the right thing! Sometimes the "wisdom" on our tongue that we're speaking forth is nothing more than fear!

I remember when we first started our church more than twenty year ago. We'd had a word from God, but at the time we stepped out to obey Him, I still had a lot of fear in me about it. From fear comes the need to control, which can in turn produce fear in others. I wanted to have a lot of control in the church, and I went to Tom day after day about what I thought we needed to do. My ideas mainly consisted of rules everyone needed to follow.

After a period of "reasoning" with Tom and presenting my arguments, very gently but firmly, he finally said to me, "We're not going to do that." Then he explained why, saying, "It's not of God, because it's based on fear."

I had to take a step back and evaluate my motive for wanting my own way. Tom was right, and I needed to respect his decision. I needed to get free of fear and the need to control situations as a way of managing fear. Neither Tom nor I wanted a church just based on rules. We wanted people to come to church because they loved God and wanted more of Him, not because they were afraid the pastor (or the pastor's wife) was going to be angry if they didn't attend.

Respect the Lord and the Beautiful Order
He Created for Marriage

Some women get upset if their husband overrides their wishes. But we shouldn't want our husband to be passive and just cater to our every whim. A man needs to be able to hear from God and obey Him to the best of his ability without having to struggle with his wife to do it. And he needs to gently but firmly "stand up to her," so to speak, when she's operating in fear and not in faith.

Remember, in the beginning, it was Eve who took Adam down a wrong road. Yet Adam allowed it. A man's passivity or failure to act when something defies his deepest convictions can spell disaster for his family.

> *Marriage was created to reflect God's love — and for the New Testament saint, it should portray the beautiful relationship between Christ and the Church.*

As pastors, Tom and I see that in many marriages today. The husband bows to the wishes of his wife even though he knows they should go a different direction. He wants peace at any cost, but his compliance ends up being far more costly than "rocking the boat" and standing up to his wife as he should.

In review, Ephesians 5:21-33 tells us how we should treat our spouse. That means there is a certain way, as defined by God, that husbands should think, speak, and act toward their wife — and that wives should think, speak, and act toward their husband.

So when it says, "… let the wife see that she respects her husband" (v. 33), it's telling us as wives how we should be thinking, speaking, and acting toward our husband. And The Amplified Bible beautifully expounds on that, saying, "…let the wife see that she respects and reverences her husband [that she notices him, regards him, honors him, prefers him, venerates, and esteems him; and that she defers to him, praises him, and loves and admires him exceedingly.]"

Keep Those Big Dreams Alive

Those are amazing words for guiding our thoughts, words, and actions where our husband is concerned. In other words, we should be focusing on his positive traits as we "notice" him. We should study him, and know his likes and dislikes, his strengths and weaknesses. We should esteem him in our mind as well as in our words and deeds. We should believe the best about him and expect the best. We should expect him to fulfill the dreams God has put in his heart.

As a wife, you need to have big dreams for your husband, because God has big dreams for him. I encourage you to send your husband off to work each day a winner. Help him see himself as successful.

Also, don't just think about your husband's good traits. Praise him for what you admire about him. In other words, point those things out. This must be your commitment to God and to your husband as a godly wife.

You might be thinking, *I don't feel any of those things for my husband. You don't know the man I'm living with!* If that describes you, I understand your feelings. But I ask you to obey this verse — Ephesians 5:33 — by faith, because you love God and desire to be obedient, not because your husband is doing everything perfectly or just right.

If you as a wife will respect your husband as unto the Lord, because you reverence and respect God, your feelings will eventually change. And who knows what God will do in your husband! I urge you to say out loud, even if it's by faith: "I admire my husband. God gave him to me. He's a man of God. I respect him. I honor and esteem him. I love my husband!"

Say this every chance you get — as you're getting dressed each day, as you're driving your car, and every time a negative thought about your husband comes to your mind. Let your words develop positive thoughts and images in your mind and your spirit, and your thoughts will eventually change your emotions.

Friend, no one gets handed a perfect marriage in life. Great marriages are built over time. Sometimes one or both people in the marriage don't even know how to build a happy life together. Many would work at building a better marriage if they understood how or if they had the right tools. But ignorance has robbed them. Their ignorance of God's Word has stolen from them the very thing that God intended to be a blessing in their lives: their marriage.

I'm not saying that the responsibility for the success or failure of a marriage belongs to the wife. But since I'm addressing the wife here, I think it's important to emphasize the power of a wife's thoughts, words, and emotions to set the tone in her home and to either build up her marriage or help tear it down (see Proverbs 14:1).

Here is another practice that will help you develop the right thoughts and attitudes about your husband. Every little thing that he does right or that he does to help you, say, "Thanks! I appreciate you." In other words, prize your husband; value him even if he's not everything you'd like him to be. This is not just forcing your emotions to go in a certain direction; rather, it's a powerful tool to bring about real change in your home life and to take your marriage to the next level.

Tom talked about a husband's responsibility to pray for his wife. But as a wife, you can pray for your husband, too! In fact, your prayers can make the way easier for God to communicate truth to your husband. You must not neglect this important ministry, because through your faith, love, and prayers, God can move mightily in the life of your husband to establish godly order and to bless the entire family.

Marriage was created to reflect God's love — and for the New Testament saint, it should portray the beautiful relationship between Christ and the Church. God has given us His wisdom and instruction for marriage, so let's sift through those erroneous teachings that bring bondage and steal our joy. Instead, let's submit to God and His Word — and then to each other in reverential honor of the Lord. We'll be pleasing to God and blessed in our deeds if we do.

8

If It Takes Two To Tango, Whose Turn Is It To Lead?

Dr. Tom Anderson

This Book of the Law shall not depart from your mouth, but you shall meditate in it day and night, THAT YOU MAY OBSERVE TO DO according to all that is written in it. For then you will make your way prosperous, and then you will have good success.
— Joshua 1:8

In preparing for a marriage seminar that Maureen and I recently taught, I wrote down seven attitudes or mindsets that a husband must have if he ever hopes to experience "Heaven on earth" in his marriage. These seven things have become so important in my own marriage that I feel I must share them with you if you're a husband or if you hope to become a husband one day.

Each of these seven attitudes is based firmly in Scripture, and if you'll meditate on these truths, you'll become capable of doing them — or practicing them — as the Bible says, and you will see scriptural results and the blessings of Heaven in your marriage. It won't take long before you and your wife will enter the next level in a "Kingdom" marriage — a marriage relationship as God intends.

These seven attitudes are not difficult or complicated; however, they can be very humbling. But I believe they're positive because they help us as men deal with some of the "macho" mentality many of us have been raised to have. We as men will never become just like women — and we don't want to! But we do need to grow in areas that have traditionally been associated with the feminine gender, such as gentleness and kindness. Some men don't consider those characteristics as masculine. Yet they are listed among the fruit of the Spirit in Galatians 5:22. They are characteristics of God, so we should exemplify those same traits too.

Are you ready to transform your thoughts and attitudes about marriage and take a step up to enjoy the kind of relationship that God desires you to have?

Let's begin.

Mindset Number 1:
'There Isn't Anything I Wouldn't Do for My Wife'

The first attitude I pondered in preparation for our marriage seminar is this: There isn't anything I wouldn't do for Maureen.

The Bible teaches us very clearly that in the marriage relationship, the woman is looked at as the Church, and the husband is looked at as Christ Jesus. Is there anything that Jesus wouldn't have done for His Bride (see Romans 8:32)? No, and there's nothing He wouldn't do for His Bride today. Remember, Jesus said, "I didn't come to be served but, rather, to serve" (see Matthew 20:28; Mark 10:45). So Jesus becomes our Example in service. We as husbands have a responsibility to serve our wife.

Just think about how far societies — including the Church — have gotten away from this in the last 2,000 years. Marriage overall is often looked at as the wife primarily serving the husband. This "switch" in mindset is interesting, but it isn't biblical, and it isn't workable.

Let me say it very plainly. What we largely see in marriages is husbands expecting the wife to serve them. Many husbands believe that if they simply make money and bring it home, that is enough to maintain a marriage. But that is not the truth; that is not the way it's supposed to work!

Man Is the Primary Sower of Seed
Woman was designed a specific way by God to help motivate her husband to "conquer the world"! And man was designed by God to lay down his life for his wife. Isn't that contrary to much of what you've seen and heard taught? Is that contrary to the way you've been living?

The good news about serving is that when you as a husband serve your wife, it is a sowing process, and you do reap a harvest! In other words, service comes back to you. Yet "service" needs to be put in the right order, because as a man, you — not your wife — are the seed-sower. She is the receiver, incubator, and bearer of the seed you sow. This fact alone should cause you to pause and consider what you're sowing into your marriage. It's so important what you sow, because what you sow is what you're going to reap.

As I said, there isn't anything I wouldn't do for Maureen. Whatever she asks me to do — short of divorcing her — I will do!

You might be thinking, That seems like such a tall order! That's why I said you need to meditate on these things in light of the Word of God. Let this attitude grow within you. Then you'll be enabled to do it and do it with the right motivation — love for God, love for your wife, and a desire to experience marriage at the level of blessing and fulfillment that God intends.

Meditation, Not Manipulation

Meditating on God's Word will help you get the truth into your heart and then act on that truth from a heart of love. But what happens when a husband and wife do the right things, but they do them for the wrong reasons or with wrong motives? Manipulation is the result. Manipulation is of the flesh, and it will suck the life right out of your marriage. But God's Word will give life to the relationship you have with your spouse.

Maureen and I did not get to where we are in our marriage today by simply reading a few books or attending a seminar or two. In other words, it didn't happen overnight. (But over the years, we have read books, listened to audio teachings, and attended meetings on marriage. Those things are important.) We got to this place of fulfillment in our marriage by continually meditating

When Maureen and I got married, we made a decision together — an absolute, solid, resolute commitment — that neither one of us would ever cheat.

on and practicing the Word concerning the marriage relationship. We finally got to a place where we could "observe to do it" (Joshua 1:8). After a time, we could put it into practice successfully and experience the rewards of being "doers of the Word" (see James 1:22).

Now it's nothing for me to get up and make breakfast and do whatever I can to serve my wife. I don't make our breakfast every day, but I am willing to do it as often as possible. I want to do whatever I can to serve Maureen and to be a blessing.

Certainly, I'm not saying that this attitude of service shouldn't work both ways in a marriage. Maureen serves and blesses me too. However, I discovered years ago that I am the primary sower of seed and that I was to take the lead if we were ever going to have the kind of marriage and live the kind of life God desired for us.

Mindset Number 2: 'I Will Never Cheat on My Wife'

When Maureen and I got married, we made a decision together — an absolute, solid, resolute commitment — that neither one of us would ever cheat. Making that kind of quality commitment takes so much out of the equation where marital problems are concerned. Every marriage faces problems in life that must be resolved and overcome. Why add to those problems fear, worry, or concern about issues of marital faithfulness and trust?

So much is encompassed in that one commitment, or pact, of absolute fidelity in a marriage. My faithfulness to Maureen will never be a concern to her. And her faithfulness to me will never be a concern to me. Unfaithfulness is not on the table, so to speak. It's not a possibility in either one of our lives.

The commitment to marital fidelity is so powerful. Amid all the twists and turns of life, that solid, unwavering, unswerving commitment brings a tremendous level of security to both people in the marriage. And security and trust are the foundation of a marriage; they are vital to the success of that union as husband and wife.

So many people get married with the attitude, We'll try it to see if it works. Usually, those marriages don't work. When we got married, Maureen and I made a commitment to each other for eternity. We vowed that there was no turning back, no giving up, no possibility of not making it. Our attitude was this: We're going to do this thing, and this is how it's going to be. That has been our hearts' determination from the beginning. Divorce was never an option.

I took the initiative in making that firm determination. I didn't leave Maureen to carry the weight of trying to ensure an insulated marriage, safe and free from the outside forces that invariably attempt to work their way into a marriage to destroy it. Adultery is an insidious thing that tries to come into a marriage relationship. And once it is allowed access, it's either impossible or, at best, very difficult to get past. The Bible teaches that adultery is a valid cause for divorcing. Can you see why making a commitment to forbid adultery in your marriage can have such positive, long-lasting effects on the quality of a marriage?

No matter what your past, if you haven't done so already, now is the time to make this firm commitment to be faithful in your marriage. And you need to make this commitment face to face with your wife.

Mindset Number 3: 'My Wife Is a Gift From God to Me'

The third attitude I've cultivated over the years is that my wife is a gift from God to me. With that mindset uppermost in my thinking, I make Maureen first place in my life next to the Lord. No sport or other activity — including my ministry or job or time with my children or grandchildren — is going to take the place of time with her. She is a gift from God to me. I will not allow anything to occupy a place in my life that would take me from her.

The Bible says, "He who finds a wife finds a good thing, and obtains favor from the Lord" (Proverbs 18:22). Your wife is a gift to you from God, and when you meditate on and grasp this truth in your heart, it will change the way you prioritize your time. And when you let your wife know that she is number one — that she's second to nothing on earth — it further builds trust and security, and it strengthens your marriage relationship.

Mindset Number 4: 'I Will Give My Wife Everything I Possibly Can'

I have also made the heartfelt commitment over the years that I will give Maureen everything in life that I possibly can. Today we are doing well financially, but that wasn't always the case. However, my commitment has always been to work hard and do everything I possibly could to provide the best life possible for her.

Some husbands seem to have that truth turned completely around! But it's not the wife's job to provide for her husband; it's his job to provide for her. I'm not saying it's wrong for both husband and wife to earn income. But he is primarily the responsible party for what they have, where they go, and the kind of lifestyle they live.

In our marriage, I accept responsibility for that. There simply isn't anything that I wouldn't provide for Maureen that was in the power of my hands to give her, and I have always felt that way — whether it meant working one job, two jobs, or even three jobs (and I have done all of those!).

Don't misunderstand me. In the early days of our marriage, we weren't well off. And there were times Maureen went without some of the things she wanted. But that didn't stop me from working as hard as I could to get her as much as I could.

I'm not talking about a certain, set standard of living that a husband must attain to. I'm talking about his doing the very best he can with the attitude that there's nothing he would ever withhold from his wife that he could possibly provide for her.

Some husbands hoard their money or keep a separate account so they can buy their own "toys" and things. But he should always put his wife first. This may seem like a hard pill to swallow. But if you will embrace this truth, it will change your life and your marriage.

Now, a husband's eager desire to provide the best for his wife doesn't negate her commitment to him if he falls on hard times or is struggling financially. Maureen is committed to me, and I'm committed to her. If I lost everything tomorrow, we would still have each other, and with God's help, we would rebuild our lives financially. We don't fear abandonment by the other if times get tough. We are secure in our relationship, and we don't fear risk and loss. We have the courage to take a shot at the "next level" because we know that we know that even if all else fails, we will always have each other.

When you make God and your marriage foundational to your life, it also keeps you from becoming attached to things. I like material things as much as the next person. But I refuse to allow my life to become so attached to those things that they become more important than my relationship with God and my relationship with my wife. I'm attached to God, and I'm attached to my wife. As a result, things have no hold on me. I am free from the unnatural attachments of the world because of the priority I've placed on God's Word and on my marriage.

Mindset Number 5: 'Everything I Invest in My Wife Must Have Life or Give Life'

Everything that I invest in Maureen must meet the criteria of having life or giving life. In other words, I won't steal from her. I won't sow anything destructive into her life. I will support her dreams and goals — and what is important to her will always be important to me. I esteem the dreams God has placed in my wife's heart. I make it my aim to do everything I can to help her go wherever she believes God wants her to go. I will never belittle her vision or her significance in the Body of Christ or the plan of God.

When I invest words into Maureen, I make certain those words are filled with life, not death. If I want to walk in life and not destruction, I have figured out over the years that I must take the initiative to sow life. Therefore, I determine that my words will be filled with love, not with criticism, anger, or harshness.

Have you ever heard the saying, "Happy wife, happy life"? It's so true! Usually, when you hear that saying, you hear it in the context of a wife acting contentious when things don't go her way. That's not what I'm talking about. I'm talking about a harvest of the happy life a husband will reap when he purposes to sow into his spouse only those things that have or give life.

Mindset Number 6: 'I Will Infuse My Wife With Seeds of Praise, Appreciation, and Honor

The sixth attitude I have cultivated in my marriage is that I will always attempt to infuse Maureen with seeds of praise, appreciation, and honor. I highly value my wife, and I purpose that every word I speak reflects this attitude. I believe with all my heart that a husband's thoughts, words, and actions planted in his wife's life will yield fruit and cause her to be what he has planted!

Seeds of Thoughts, Words, and Deeds

Seeds of praise, appreciation, and honor are very powerful things that will produce powerful results. Even the thoughts you think are seeds, so don't ever allow negative thoughts about your wife to get into your head, because it will eventually produce a "harvest" of a bad word or action. So don't even go there. Take your thoughts captive (see Second Corinthians 10:5). Think positive thoughts about your wife and discover the power of your thoughts when you begin to see your marriage in a positive light.

Why would Paul exhort us to take our wrong thoughts captive if thoughts weren't powerful or capable of working great damage? You might think, *It's just one small thought.* But think of the power of a small twenty- or forty-watt light bulb in your refrigerator! When you open the door to your fridge in the middle of the night, it could be pitch black in your house, but that very small light will illuminate the inside of the refrigerator so brightly and even "spill over" into the kitchen were you're standing. One small light? Yes. But it produces a big result!

I'm not talking about a negative thought that passes through your mind that you refuse to think on or allow to remain. I'm talking about little things that are negative (not having or giving life), yet they seem harmless. And you dwell on those. You concentrate on the faults and failures of your wife. In doing that, your "secret" thoughts are creating a power that's going to vividly manifest in your marriage sooner or later. The lights are going to come on, so to speak, and the effect will be damaging.

That's how much power and energy your concentrated thoughts have on your home environment, including on your wife and children. Your thoughts can affect your wife's emotions and demeanor, especially if she's nearby — in the same vicinity or area of the home.

Your Words and Beyond

Face it. The words we speak are either going to build up or tear down. Words are seeds that will produce a harvest, whether a good harvest or a bad harvest. So you need to ask yourself, Do I want to build my marriage up, or do I want to tear it down? If you want to build up your marriage, then begin by using the appropriate words.

What about your actions or your body language? What about your tone of voice when you speak to your wife? Do those things count? They count, and they are critical!

The Bible says, "Do not be harsh with your wife" (Colossians 3:19). Where does harshness come from? Most of the time, it doesn't come from actual words. Harshness is manifested in one's tone of voice. It can also be manifested in one's body language. For example, if your wife is talking to you, and you're watching TV or reading the newspaper, that comes across as harsh indifference to her. You're minimizing her importance and significance, and, remember, she is a gift from God to you.

So what should you do? When your wife talks to you, put down the newspaper and focus your attention on her. What you're reading is not more important than her. And what you're watching on TV isn't more important, either.

If you want to go to the next level in your relationship with your wife and experience a marriage that's like Heaven on earth, make certain that everything you think, say, and do is a seed of praise, appreciation, and honor — a seed of everlasting value to God and to your wife.

Mindset Number 7:
'I Give to My Wife in Spirit, in Soul, and in Body'

The seventh attitude I've cultivated that has taken Maureen and me to the next level in our marriage is that I give to her in spirit, in soul, and in body.

How do you give to your wife "in spirit"? Well, how often do you pray for your wife in a heartfelt way? In spirit, I give Maureen prayer. In fact, the first thing I do every morning is to pray over her. I don't pray a long prayer — maybe two to four minutes — but I lay my hand on her and pray the blood of Jesus over her. I "cover" her for the day. As her husband, I have that authority and responsibility.

Husbands are a spiritual covering for their wife (Ephesians 5:23). They have a right to pray for their wife, and they have a responsibility to do so. And as Maureen's covering, I pray for her divine destiny and the things she's believing for. I pray that no outside influence will ill-affect her emotions. Because she asks me to, I even pray about her ability to maintain her weight. I pray for the things that are important to her life.

Praying for your wife is so important because, first, if it's a believing prayer, you are releasing your faith for God to work in her life. Second, you are accepting spiritual responsibility in your home and establishing God's will and order in your house. God can bless a home and a marriage in which the husband is taking his God-ordained place.

What about giving yourself to your wife "in soul"? You must practice the last attitude we looked at, sowing only seeds of praise, appreciation, and honor in your thoughts, your words, and your actions.

The way I give to Maureen in soul is, I make sure that I keep my thoughts in alignment with what is positive and encouraging. To the best of my ability, I let no words come out of my mouth that don't build her up. I'm not perfect at doing this, but because I've practiced it for so many years, I keep getting better, and I'm actually pretty good at it now!

In the realm of the soul, I desire to minister to my wife. For example, I am completely committed to Maureen. Commitment comes from the will. My commitment produces calmness and confidence in her. She is never stressful or anxious about whether or not I'll be faithful to her or about whether or not we'll always be together. In the area of the mind and emotions, I simply attempt to be sensitive to her at all times.

I'll only touch briefly on the area of giving to your wife "in body," because we're going to talk in greater detail about sex later in the book. In effect, I give to Maureen in body by giving her the best sex I know how to give her. I make it a point to do that by reading and studying wholesome materials that deal with this very subject. And I take care of my health so that I'm at my best during our times of physical intimacy.

These seven attitudes or principles from Scripture will ensure the best, happiest, and most fulfilling relationship with your wife that you can imagine. But you must practice them as a lifestyle, and doing that takes renewing your mind to these principles. Romans 12:2 says, "And do not be conformed to this world, but be transformed by the renewing of your mind, that you may prove what is that good and acceptable and perfect will of God."

Certainly, it takes two people, both the husband and the wife, to enjoy a happy, successful marriage — just as, very often, it takes two people to fail in a marriage. We've heard the phrase, "It takes two to tango" referring to the fact that it's usually never just one person's fault when something goes wrong in a particular situation or circumstance. But if marriage were to be compared to dancing the tango, someone does have to take the lead. And scripturally, the responsibility for leadership in the marriage points squarely in one direction: to the husband.

If you haven't already done so, as a husband and man of God, it's your turn to take the lead in your marriage. So I ask you, will you take hold of these truths and meditate on them until you're able to lay down your life for your wife in much the same way Christ laid down His life for the Church? Will you make the sacrifice necessary to always choose the right thoughts, words, and actions despite your feelings that may lean to the contrary? Yes, there will be a time of sacrificial sowing into your marriage, but those acts of sowing can also become your highest joy. And the harvest you'll reap will be beyond anything you could imagine.

Perhaps you need an overhaul in your thinking concerning how you're to treat your wife. Or maybe you simply need to make a few adjustments as you step up to the next level in your marriage relationship. But one thing is certain: As you meditate on these things and allow them to sink into your heart, you'll be empowered to do them. And as you do them continually, as a lifestyle, you will never look at marriage the same way again. And life will be gloriously different and infinitely better than you ever thought possible!

9

How To Avoid a Train Wreck in Your Marriage

Dr. Maureen Anderson

Love is the foundation of every great marriage. So a vital part of having a great marriage is understanding this love — what it is and what it isn't. Many of us understand that love is not a feeling; it's a choice and a commitment that stands the test of circumstances and time. We've learned to draw on the love of God that has been poured out in our heart by the Holy Spirit. And we've learned that this kind of love is also based on giving. The saying is true that love isn't love until it's given away.

Yet feelings can be involved in love. And in their place, those feelings can be good and beneficial. But they can also be very destructive. In fact, the "feelings" part of love and marriage can either keep a relationship on track over the long haul — or derail it when a couple least expects it.

In this chapter, we're going to study the emotions that often accompany love.

The 'Infatuation' Phase of a Relationship

So many couples date and get married without ever understanding the difference between love and infatuation. In short, true love is about the other person; infatuation is about you.

In the following chapters, we're going to look at the subject of love in marriage, but in this chapter, we're going to take a hard look at infatuation — the "feelings" of love that are often present in the early stages of courtship and marriage. Infatuation can actually help build a relationship — but the other side of the coin is that it can also destroy a relationship. Like a locomotive at full-throttle, infatuation can act as a means of getting you from one place to the next in your relationship. But if it's misused, it can cause a serious "train wreck" in your marriage and bring much pain and sadness to you and to those you love.

So we need to understand infatuation. First, we need to know that although feelings of infatuation motivate and compel us to do things that are loving and kind, those feelings are not the same as love, as we will see.

Infatuation — Physiological in Origin

As I said, infatuation isn't negative or wrong in itself. Infatuation is chemical in nature and physiological in origin. In other words, infatuation has its basis in emotions that are the product of certain chemicals released in the body.

God created each of us spirit, soul, and body (see First Thessalonians 5:23) — and we know that what God creates is good (Genesis 1:31). Every cell of our physical body is controlled by our brain. And our brain is controlled largely by our thoughts. This truth is illustrated in Proverbs 23:7, where it says about man, "For as he thinks in his heart, so is he...."

It is perfectly normal that our thoughts produce stimuli in the brain — and that in response to our thoughts, our brain releases chemicals that can in turn stimulate strong emotions. For example, if you've ever experienced a close call with an oncoming vehicle while driving your car, you've probably felt that involuntary wave of fear sweep over you as adrenaline coursed through your body in those brief seconds. Of course, those feelings subsided almost as quickly as they came. But the medical community has proven that our emotions over a prolonged period of time can have drastic effects on our body — our physical health — and our relationships, whether positively or negatively.

At the Wheel and in Control

Although it's true that feelings and emotions are powerful forces, they do not have to control our lives as believers! Remember, we are a spirit, we have a soul, and we live in a body (1 Thessalonians 5:23). As spirit beings, we can be in complete control of our thoughts and emotions instead of our thoughts and emotions controlling us.

Have you ever heard someone talk about falling in love as if he or she just couldn't help it? Or have you ever heard someone say, "It was love at first sight"? What that person was referring to probably wasn't love at all. It was simply physical attraction or infatuation. We have control over those feelings of "love," as we will see in the following pages.

Medical research has discovered that when we allow ourselves to be attracted to the opposite sex, our brain releases a chemical called phenylethylamine (abbreviated PEA), which is also found in certain foods, such as chocolate. And that chemical produces positive feelings of happiness, goodwill, and a desire to serve and bless that other person — the object of his or her attraction.

When PEA is operating within the confines of God's will and order, it can be a very good thing, because infatuation serves the purpose of laying the foundation for a relationship that lasts — for a permanent marriage relationship. In other words, the purpose of infatuation and the releasing of PEA by your body is to mentor you, to train and develop you, to build a healthy relationship with another person in the context of marriage. (We'll talk more about that later in this chapter.)

PEA stimulates in the brain feelings of optimism and euphoria. It inclines a person to think positively — on things that are "…true…noble…just…pure…lovely…of good report…" (see Philippians 4:8). In other words, when we're infatuated, all we see is the good, the beautiful, and the praiseworthy things about the other person. Yet

> *Infatuation is a stepping stone to love, but it's not love. Love steps in when infatuation has run its course, and love continues the momentum of loving, giving, and serving.*

it's an unrealistic observation of the situation. We're seeing that person through the rose-colored glasses of infatuation.

Don't misunderstand me. I'm not saying that's necessarily wrong. I'm simply saying that we need to understand infatuation — that it's chemically based and not real love at all. Very simply, real love is a commitment and a choice that's based on giving. If we fail to grasp the difference between love and infatuation, we'll misunderstand our emotions or find ourselves floundering when those emotions finally subside.

When Infatuation Leads to Sex Before Marriage

Because many people don't understand the purpose of infatuation, they often enter into a sexual relationship with their partner prior to marriage. But since God intended infatuation as a precursor to marriage — and sex to be enjoyed in the confines of marriage — that is a misuse of infatuation that always results in some type of destruction or harm.

But when we use infatuation for the purpose it was intended, we will focus on blessing that other person, not gratifying ourselves. We will be interested in building a long-term relationship with that person, and we'll be consumed with his or her happiness to the point that we constantly think about how we can bless and help that person and meet his or her needs.

Well, that's what love does, doesn't it? Love gives; it isn't selfish or self-seeking. And infatuation is a precursor and a stepping stone to love.

Feelings of Love Will Prompt Acts of Love

Have you ever noticed that when two people begin to be attracted to each other —and the brain chemical, PEA, begins to flow — they have excessive energy? They don't seem to need much sleep. They think about each other constantly, and all they want to do is bless each other. They want to write notes and give gifts to each other. They want to continually affirm each other. They want to do acts of service for each other. They want to spend as much quality time together as possible, and they definitely want to show affection! They want to do all the "love languages"!

What motivates a person to do these things? Infatuation and PEA, or the chemical associated with thoughts of attraction. The infatuation phase of the relationship is teaching the person the right way to act in marriage.

For example, even if you're not a communicator by nature, when you're infatuated with someone, that PEA is in a sense teaching you to communicate and spend quality time with the other person. You may have grown up never having been taught generosity toward others, but now, suddenly, you desire to continually give to that person who has become the object of your infatuation. And you want to serve that person by making dinner, baking something, cleaning his or her car, and so forth.

Studies indicate that the strong emotions which initially motivated you during the infatuation phase of your relationship will begin to dissipate within six months and will totally subside within approximately two years. But what those strong feelings teach you to do should remain so that you continue those actions long afterward, motivated by a commitment and a choice to love with God's love and to bless, serve, and meet the needs of your spouse.

Infatuation — Then What?

When the levels of PEA produced in the brain begin to wane, does that mean the relationship is over? No! It means that what you learned about blessing your partner during that time must now be sustained by love that lasts. But if you don't allow infatuation to do what it's supposed to do during that period of time, you will revert to the person you were before, and that "training period" won't benefit you, your partner, or your marriage.

Infatuation is a steppingstone to love, but it's not love. Love steps in when infatuation has run its course, and love continues the momentum of loving, giving, and serving. Then it becomes your choice to continue to love, give, and serve in the way that the chemical PEA has motivated and mentored you to do. That's God's plan for building a Kingdom marriage, or a marriage that's like Heaven on earth.

But because so many people don't understand infatuation, when those feelings of infatuation subside, they are either ready to give up on the relationship altogether, or they find themselves unhappy and ill-equipped to sustain a happy, healthy marriage. When the chemical is gone that motivated them, they fail to understand that they're now on their own to continue building a marriage that's Heaven on earth by yielding to the love of God that is always motivated to give and to serve.

The Power of No!

Problems also arise in a marriage when people allow themselves to be attracted to someone else other than their spouse. But as I said, they have the power to resist those thoughts and even the strong feelings and emotions they've already given place to. Yet very often they don't resist, because they don't understand the power of no!

You see, your body is not you. Your spirit is the real you. You are a spirit — made in the image and likeness of God (Genesis 1:26). You have a soul, and you live in a physical body. And within your spirit and soul is the ability to exercise freewill and to choose rightly or wrongly. That's where love comes in. God is love (1 John 4:8), so when you're walking in love, you're walking in God — in the light of His Word. And you will be motivated to choose rightly — to do the right things for the right reasons.

So what happens if you feel an attraction for someone other than your spouse? You exercise your power of choice, because you have to power to say, "No, I'm not going there. I plead the blood of Jesus over my life, and I refuse to allow my mind to think about that other person." Merely stopping your thoughts in their tracks can prevent the release of phenylethylamine in your brain before it's ever triggered.

But even if you miss it and let your thoughts go in the wrong direction, as you repent and continue exercising your will to do the right thing, your brain will eventually stop producing that chemical, and the feelings you have for that other person will subside.

Keep [or guard] your heart with all diligence, For out of it spring the issues of life. (Proverbs 4:23)

We have the power to guard our own heart and mind against thoughts, feelings, and emotions that go against God's will and plan. But if we fail to keep our heart concerning relationships, we become dysfunctional; we won't function in relationships as God intends.

Relationships are a blessing from the Lord, especially the marriage relationship. Marriage is a gift from God to believers to be a picture of the relationship between Christ and the Church.

But having a relationship is similar to eating — we can do it correctly or incorrectly. In other words, eating is healthy and, certainly, it's God's will that we eat. But on the other hand, being a glutton is wrong! And eating the wrong kinds of food over a prolonged period of time will have negative consequences on our body.

Sleeping is another good thing when used properly or as God intends. God planned that we require sleep to stay healthy — and He desires that we get the appropriate amount of sleep every day. But if we're lazy, that's wrong. The Bible calls laziness sin.

Similarly, sex is a good thing. God created it to be enjoyed between a husband and wife. But outside of marriage, it's sin and it becomes harmful and destructive.

Just as people get into trouble when they misuse food or other necessities of life, they can also get into trouble because of wrong relationships. And many who become involved in these illicit relationships will claim they "just couldn't help themselves." That kind of reasoning is not biblical — therefore, it is simply not true.

How Reverence for God
Can Keep Your Marriage Safe

How can a married couple keep their marriage safe from the dangers of sin and infidelity? By walking closely with the Lord in holy reverence and fear.

When I talk about fearing the Lord, I'm not talking about being afraid of Him like you'd be afraid of a dangerous wild animal. I'm talking about having an attitude of reverence toward the Lord. Proverbs 8:13 says, "The fear of the Lord is to hate evil…." When you fear, or reverence, the Lord, you love what He loves and you hate what He hates. When you hate what He hates, you won't get involved with it, including relationships that are wrong.

The Bible has much to say about the protective power of fearing God! For example, the Bible says, "The fear of the Lord is the beginning of wisdom, and the knowledge of the Holy One is understanding" (Proverbs 9:10). So a person who fears the Lord and has a heart to walk in the light of His Word will be a person of understanding. He will be in a position to be kept from the evil he hates.

A part of having understanding is understanding how things operate and function, even in the natural realm. So when it comes to having a great marriage, you have to understand the Word of God concerning marriage, but you also have to understand the various components of marriage that make it great. A lack of understanding in this area can completely destroy a marriage relationship.

The Word of God says that people are destroyed because of a lack of knowledge (see Hosea 4:6). That verse is talking about the knowledge of God and His Word and an understanding of His creation. How many times have you seen someone's life practically ruined because he or she lacked understanding in some area, whether it was health, finances, relationships, and so forth?

As pastors, Tom and I have seen marriages destroyed because one spouse in the marriage didn't understand the very thing I'm talking about in this chapter. The husband or wife became attracted to someone else, and instead of willfully shutting down those thoughts immediately, he or she allowed those chemicals to flow, and the feelings and emotions associated with infatuation ensued.

Instead of resisting, the person continued allowing those feelings to dominate his or her thoughts and actions. Soon that person was in a very bad situation with many people getting hurt as a result. The person never intended to destroy the marriage or family. But his or her lack of knowledge and understanding caused a disaster to take place that never should have happened.

For wisdom will enter your heart, and knowledge will be pleasant to your soul. Discretion will protect you, and understanding will guard you. Wisdom will save you from the ways of wicked men, from men whose words are perverse, who leave the straight paths to walk in dark ways, who delight in doing wrong and rejoice in the perverseness of evil, whose paths are crooked and who are devious in their ways. It will save you also from the adulteress, from the wayward wife with her seductive words. (Proverbs 2:10-16 NIV)

Say to wisdom, "You are my sister," and call understanding your kinsman; they will keep you from the adulteress, from the wayward wife with her seductive words. (Proverbs 7:4-5 NIV)

Notice the words "protect," "guard," "save," and "keep: in these verses. Walking in the fear of the Lord brings wisdom, knowledge, and understanding to your life that will protect, keep, preserve, guard, deliver, and save you and your marriage!

'Truth or Consequences?' —
One King's Nightmare

When a married couple chooses to walk in the truth and in the light of God's Word, they will avoid the devastating consequences of sin.

Do not lust in your heart after her beauty or let her captivate you with her eyes, for the prostitute reduces you to a loaf of bread, and the adulteress preys upon your very life. Can a man scoop fire into his lap without his clothes being burned? Can a man walk on hot coals without his feet being scorched? So is he who sleeps with another man's wife; no one who touches her will go unpunished. (Proverbs 6:25-29 NIV)

Verse 29 says, "So is he who sleeps with another man's wife; no one who touches her will go unpunished." The same is true for a man or woman who sleeps with someone other than his or her spouse. The Bible is clear that adulterers will not go unpunished. In other words, they will face consequences for their actions.

You probably know the story of David and Bathsheba, who was the wife of Uriah the Hittite. You can read this account in Second Samuel 11 and 12. David was the king of Israel, anointed of God. He had sent his army off to battle while he remained at home. One night, he went to the roof of his palace and saw a neighbor, Bathsheba, taking a bath on the roof of her home.

Immediately, a thought hit David's mind! David was attracted to the lovely undressed woman in the rooftop bathtub. But instead of saying no to his thoughts, he allowed the chemical, PEA, to flow. He permitted the attraction to persist, and a flood of emotions began to influence him. Still, he didn't resist. He continued yielding to those feelings and emotions until he became consumed with them, and they began to dominate his every thought and action.

Perhaps David thought, Well, I'm the king. I could just sleep with her, and then it will all be over. What his exact thoughts were, we don't know. But we do know that he sent men to inquire about Bathsheba. In other words, David knew she was married before he ever had relations with her!

So David has Bathsheba brought to the palace. Her husband Uriah is one of David's soldiers on the battlefield, laying down his life for his country. But David, still refusing to resist the strong temptation to commit adultery, acts beyond reason and beyond what is right. David sleeps with another man's wife, and soon it is discovered that she's pregnant with his baby!

David tries to maneuver the situation by bringing Uriah off the field so that he'll have relations with his wife and then believe that the child she's carrying is his. But Uriah is too loyal to his fellow soldiers still on the field. He refuses to indulge himself in the pleasure of sex with his wife and chooses instead to sleep outside the doors of David's palace until he receives new marching orders.

Now David is in a real predicament! So he concocts a plan to get rid of Uriah permanently so that he can take Bathsheba as his wife. He orders Uriah to be sent to the frontline in battle completely unprotected, and Uriah is eventually killed.

David is now an adulterer and a murderer! God sends the prophet Nathan to David, and Nathan finally gets through to him that God has seen David's selfish, arrogant actions and has revealed it to His prophet. Then Nathan delivers the really bad news that David is going to suffer the consequences of his actions.

Now therefore, the sword shall never depart from your house, because you have despised Me, and have taken the wife of Uriah the Hittite to be your wife. Thus says the Lord: 'Behold, I will raise up adversity against you from your own house; and I will take your wives before your eyes and give them to your neighbor, and he shall lie with your wives in the sight of this sun. 'For you did it secretly, but I will do this thing before all Israel, before the sun.' (2 Samuel 12:10-12)

It's just as Proverbs 25:27-28 says — when you allow yourself into a situation like that, you're playing with fire, and you will be burned. In other words, you're going to be hurt. And not just you, but you're your family will suffer the consequences of your sinful actions.

There is no such thing as "private" sin. The sin you engage in will eventually directly or indirectly affect others around you. In the case of adultery, not only is a spouse betrayed and emotionally devastated, but children, friends, and extended family members are often hurt as well.

After David's affair with Bathsheba, he never had complete peace in his circumstances again. Consider the following consequences of David's actions:

- His firstborn child with Bathsheba died (2 Samuel 12:18).
- His daughter was raped by his son (2 Samuel 13:11-14).
- His son mocked him by sleeping with his concubines in the presence of all Israel (2 Samuel 16:21-22).
- His own son tried to overthrow his kingdom and kill him (2 Samuel 17:14-26).
- His son was killed (2 Samuel 18:14-15).

That was a huge price to pay for one moment of attraction that David yielded and gave himself over to! Influenced by thoughts and overcome by emotions induced by brain chemicals, he brought much destruction and ruin into his life.

But each one is tempted when he is drawn away by his own desires and enticed. Then, when desire has conceived, it gives birth to sin; and sin, when it is full-grown, brings forth death. (James 1:14-15)

Death and destruction are what King David experienced in his life because he "despised" God and His commandments (2 Samuel 12:10). In other words, David failed to walk in the light of God's Word. But before we judge David, when a person commits adultery today, he, too, is despising the commandments of God.

Remember we said that God is love (1 John 4:8). So if we're walking with Him, we're walking in love — in the very love of God. And that love will not intentionally violate His Word. The love of God within us will compel us not to do anything to hurt our spouse or family.

The Power of a Thought

We talked about the fact that thoughts affect the brain, which physiologically can affect the emotions — which in turn can even affect the body. So how do we keep ourselves from giving undue place to infatuation — infatuation outside the context of marriage? It begins with the fear of the Lord — with our relationship and our walk with God — and with our thoughts!

> *...I [Jesus] tell you that anyone who looks at a woman lustfully has already committed adultery with her in his heart.*
> (Matthew 5:28 NIV)

It's amazing how many people entertain sexual thoughts about someone other than their spouse and somehow think that because they haven't "acted" on those thoughts, it's okay. But when thoughts come, and they entertain those thoughts, lust is being conceived in their heart.

It's not just young people who fall prey to giving wrong thoughts, feelings, and emotions a place in their lives. Even older people are ignorant of how phenylethylamine, or PEA, can work against them through the power of just a thought. Although it has been discovered that it can occur in middle-aged women as well, men are especially vulnerable to what has been termed the midlife crisis. Both genders go through a sort of "change of life" in which chemical changes occur in the body that can seriously affect behavior in the unlearned and naïve.

Have you ever seen a man who approached mid-life, and, suddenly, he leaves his wife, buys a sports car, and marries a significantly younger woman? He leaves "the wife of his youth" (Proverbs 5:18; Isaiah 54:6; Malachi 2:14-15). He devastates his family, including his own children,

129

affecting generations to come. But this misguided man is flying high with feelings of euphoria at being "in love" with someone else.

Then after a couple of years when the chemical PEA begins to wash through the man's body and subside, he often realizes that the new life he created for himself is not that great. But it's too late. Lives have been hurt, and lifestyles have been forever altered. In cases like this, God can restore individual lives, but the families will likely remain broken. And to think it all began with one thought that went unguarded and unchecked.

Take Action Now

The life we live here on earth is just a vapor, but eternity goes on and on without end. So why live foolishly and with regret? Whatever you may be experiencing in your mind at this stage of your life, there is help in God, and the time to take action is now.

The Spirit of God will lead you into all truth in every situation and circumstance (John 16:13). You may need to see a good doctor who can test you for hormonal imbalances. You may need to talk to your pastor. Whatever you do, don't allow your marriage to be destroyed. In the face of temptation, invite God into your situation and pray earnestly about it. He can do more than you can ask or think — "exceedingly abundantly" above and beyond your own wisdom, power, or feelings (Ephesians 3:20)!

How Looking Ahead Can Keep
Your Marriage From Being Derailed

Most marriages that fail don't just collapse overnight. In most failed marriages, there were certain conditions the couple allowed to persist that made their relationship vulnerable to destructive forces. Had those couples exercised a little more diligence and foresight in their marriage, they could have seen the dangers that loomed ahead, and their relationship could have been salvaged and healed.

Some people are emotionally numb and "distant" in their attitude toward their spouse, and that condition in the marriage is a setup for failure. Perhaps the husband has devoted so much of his life to making money that he has become indifferent to having an intimate relationship with his wife. Or maybe the wife has been so consumed with her children or other interests and activities that she no longer desires her husband.

Priorities can change and cause real damage to the relationships in our lives that God considers the most important. Next to your relationship with Him, your marriage is the most vital relationship you have. So why not invest the time, effort, and energy necessary to keep your priorities in check and your marriage closer to the top of the list where it belongs?

There are times in life when we need to reflect on what we truly value — what really matters to us. When you value something, you're more inclined to protect and preserve it. You'll spend time and money to keep what you value in tip-top shape.

Tom and I have a great marriage. We are so happy, and we are very close as a couple. We're truly best friends. We enjoy being with each other, and we hate being apart. But it hasn't always been that way. Our marriage is blessed, but it took a lot of work — a lot of time and effort — to get to where we are today.

Tom and I weren't saved when we got married, and when we did get saved, we were first-generation Christians. There was a lot of divorce on my side of the family, and Tom's parents were also divorced. We both brought a lot of baggage into our relationship. But we were determined to get it right! We valued the institution of marriage and our commitment to each other. And we knew we could have God's highest and best if we worked at it. We also knew that if we didn't work at it, our relationship would ultimately be derailed, and we would become just another statistic in the record books of marriage and divorce.

People can get their priorities out of order, and over time, marriage can seem to lose its value. Many couples don't value the relationship they have with each other. They value jobs and other activities more than the marriage.

Or maybe only one person in the marriage values the relationship. One party works on the marriage while the other party sort of floats along, indifferent in his or her attitude. That hurts a marriage, because it takes the effort of both the husband and the wife to nurture and grow a marriage into something beautiful and fruitful.

When marriage doesn't hold the place of honor and importance that it should, that's when a husband or wife becomes more susceptible to outside interferences to the marriage. For example, you may be a wife whose husband is negligent toward your relationship. But at work, a handsome man pays a lot of attention to you, and you sense an attraction between the two of you.

If you don't shut those thoughts down, before long, you're going to begin thinking, *I've fallen out of love with my husband, anyway. He isn't* doing right by me or the marriage. Now you're "in love" with Mr. Right at work. But it's not even the real thing. You have feelings of love, but it's infatuation — the result of the chemical PEA — and feelings that are also very real, yet deceiving.

Or if you're a husband, your wife could be so wrapped up in your children and their activities that she has neglected herself and has really let herself go in terms of her appearance. Maybe she's overworked and just doesn't care anymore. You go to work, and there's a secretary there who's always well dressed, and she tells you that you're the smartest man in the world. She always looks nice, smells nice, and acts nice. Before long, you're thinking, I deserve better than what I'm getting at home. My wife is always telling me what's wrong. I want to hear something good for a change.

Both of those arguments may sound reasonable and convincing, but they're not biblical or justifiable. However, if you allow yourself to be consumed with thoughts of being with someone other than your spouse, your senses will eventually override the voice of your conscience, and you will begin traveling a path of deception and destruction in your marriage.

What so many people are calling true love is nothing more than infatuation, and medical science bears that out. Why, then, are so many otherwise intelligent people deceived by these feelings? Oftentimes it's because they've traded the value of their marriage for the value of having their own needs met, despite what the consequences will mean to their spouse or their marriage. Human love is selfish, but the God-kind of love puts others first. And it's that kind of love that ultimately never fails! (See First Corinthians 13:8.)

How To Restore 'Lost' Love

A person's relationship with the Lord is closely connected with his or her relationship with others. In fact, the closer you walk with the Lord, the better you'll treat others and the better you'll do at marriage, successfully navigating the storms and the twists and turns of life that come against every married couple. When you walk closely with the Lord, you make a much better marriage partner than someone who doesn't walk closely with God.

But what happens if your walk with the Lord needs to be restored as badly as your marriage needs to be restored? Of course, you know you can ask the Lord to forgive you, and you can be restored in your relationship with Him. Well, it's possible to restore your relationship with your spouse as much as it's possible to restore your relationship with God. Perhaps you've thought that the love between you and your spouse can never be regained. But with God, it's possible to discover and renew that love again.

I think back to when I was first saved. I was so in love with Jesus that all I wanted to do was talk to Him and spend time in His Presence. It wasn't physical attraction, but I was so consumed with His love for me that I gave myself totally to the Lord in my thoughts, words, and actions. And guess what? My brain released that PEA. I was on a "high," so to speak. Now, I realize that everyone doesn't react or respond this way when he or she gets saved. But that was my experience. I wanted to pray and read the Bible day and night. Thoughts of the Lord consumed me continually.

This is the experience of many Christians. But just as the infatuation stage of a relationship between a man and woman is designed to teach them how to act, this early stage of a believer's walk with the Lord is supposed to teach him how to act to retain his joy over the long haul, not just for a brief period of time.

So often a believer who began his relationship with the Lord in a euphoric state of mind doesn't continue those "first works" after those strong feelings for the Lord subside. And this is not a unique scenario. In Jesus' seven messages to the seven churches in the Book of Revelation, He said the following to the entire Church at Ephesus:

> *Yet I hold this against you: You have forsaken your first love. Remember the height from which you have fallen! Repent and do the things you did at first....* (Revelation 2:4-5 NIV)

Jesus had commended this church for their good works in certain areas, but then He delivered to them the hard truth that they had forsaken their first love, or the first love they had for Him. Then He told them to repent, or change their minds completely, and to do the things they did at first — when they first got saved and had a revelation of God's love for them (a love which hasn't changed, by the way). He told them, "Remember the height from which you have fallen! Repent and do the things you did at first…" (v. 5 NIV).

How does this apply to the "fallen" relationships in marriages that we see today? Since our walk with the Lord affects our relationship with others, especially our spouse, it is very much connected. If your relationship with your spouse has reached this "fallen" state, I'd say you've forsaken your "first love" for your spouse, and I encourage you to remember the height from which you have fallen in your relationship with him or her. Then repent, turn around, and do those things you did at first!

In other words, in the same way that we need to remember the works we did when we first got saved, we need to remember the "first works" we did when we initially became attracted to our spouse.

I encourage you to think back and recall the "consuming" feelings of euphoria you felt in the beginning of your relationship with your spouse. Remember the fun times you enjoyed together and the thoughtful things you did for him or her when you began dating. Were you more attentive to your spouse then than you are now? Were you more supportive? Protective? Kind, gentle, and thoughtful? These are great questions to ask yourself. You can relive your fond memories again and again until you bring those loving feelings back into your marriage.

In Psalm 51:12, David wrote, "Restore to me the joy of Your salvation, and uphold me by Your generous Spirit." With God, restoration is possible no matter how far you've fallen — in your relationship with Him and with your mate. So I encourage you to meditate on these truths and apply them to your heart and to your marriage. In so doing, you will begin to understand the difference between mere emotions born of the senses and love, which is real and lasting. This understanding will not only preserve you spiritually and morally and prevent a potential "train wreck" in your marriage, but it will also restore joy to the relationship you have with your husband or wife.

'But I Married the Wrong Person'

As I said before, when the strong feelings of infatuation subside in their marriage, some people think that the person they're with is not the right person for them. That couldn't be further from the truth! Also, did you know that when you get married, that person becomes the will of God for you, because marriage is sacred in the eyes of God. It's not a game. When you entered the covenant of marriage, you made a vow to God and that other person, and your marriage then became the will of God.

So don't ever let the enemy tell you that you married the wrong person. You need to "stand down" every thought that comes to your mind to that effect, and you need to say, "No, my spouse is the right person for me."

Certainly, I'm not talking about situations in which one partner is being physically abused by the other. Some marriages end, not because God necessarily willed the marriage to end but because one person made ungodly choices that endangered his or her spouse, and that person refused to seek help to make the necessary change.

There are extenuating circumstances that sometimes make it impossible for a marriage to continue. But those cases are few and far between. What we see happening with divorce in the world today — and even in the Church — is more or less the result of a lack of understanding about God's Word and a lack of understanding about relationships and, in particular, our physical makeup. In other words, an alarmingly large number of people don't understand the difference between infatuation and love.

But if you have Jesus in your heart, and your spouse has Jesus — then no matter where you're at in your marriage — God is in your marriage, and He's for it, not against it. The Holy Ghost lives in you both, and He is working in both of you the desire to do God's will and to be changed by Him from faith to faith by the power of His Word (Romans 1:17). He can do great things with even the most hopeless situations. So I encourage you — don't break up before you get your breakthrough!

A Word to Singles

Understanding the difference between love and infatuation is so crucial for someone who's single. Infatuation is fleeting because it's based largely on the senses, and it can change with the seasons of life. But love that is grounded in God and His Word is stable and committed through every season.

If you're single and you're in a dating relationship with the wrong person, you can turn those feelings off gradually or suddenly, but you have to begin somewhere. First, you need to say no and keep saying no until your thoughts that you're not going to allow that relationship to continue begin to affect your brain, which in turn will affect your feelings and emotions.

We know that the Bible says, "Do not be unequally yoked together with unbelievers. For what fellowship has righteousness with lawlessness? And what communion has light with darkness?" (2 Corinthians 6:14). Now apply what you know about infatuation, and you can see that even though a sinner says and does the most loving, romantic things for the one he "loves," once that infatuation phase is over and the phenylethylamine, or PEA, begins to wane, that unsaved person is still who he or she was before.

Unless the person has gotten saved, he or she is in the exact same lost condition as before when the couple became physically attracted to one another. Phenylethylamine can be released by a person's brain whether or not he's saved! This chemical that causes such feelings of euphoria is physiological in nature, not spiritual.

Infatuation in Its Place

Infatuation has its specific place in a relationship. If you're single, its purpose is to bless you and the person you're going to marry. If you're married, its purpose is to bless you and your spouse. Outside of that, infatuation has no place in your life!

Although it's certainly important to be physically attracted to your spouse, physical attraction and infatuation cannot sustain a permanent marriage relationship. Those things can help lay a proper foundation for marriage, but they can't act as the foundation itself, causing that relationship to last as a healthy, happy marriage.

So infatuation in itself isn't wrong, but we must know its purpose and its place. When infatuation is laying the foundation for a permanent relationship that's blessed by God, it can be a blessing. The Holy Spirit can work with infatuation if you're teachable, and He can use it to develop you further in your love walk than you ever thought possible. Even after you're married and you're long past being infatuated with your spouse, you can be anointed to be the husband or wife that God intended you to be and enjoy a marriage that's Heaven on earth. I know it's true because Tom and I are living our "dream marriage" today.

Of course, I know of people who have gotten married and never seemed to go through the infatuation stage in their relationship. I'm not saying that infatuation is necessary to have a good marriage. I'm simply saying that when present, those strong feelings and emotions have a purpose — to mentor and train you to be the lifelong partner that God intended.

10

What To Do When You're 'Just Not Feeling It'

Drs. Tom and Maureen Anderson

Over the years, we've witnessed many marriages that seemed shattered and broken beyond repair but that were restored by God's bountiful grace. However, His grace was only effective as these couples embraced the help that God offered them — and offers every couple today — through the pages of His Word.

Because of the finished work of Christ, there is victory available to us in every circumstance of life, but we must eagerly avail ourselves of that victory through our willing obedience to the Word and the will of God in every area of our lives, including our marriage.

If there's one thing we've learned in our own lives and in ministering to others, it's this: Great marriages are made of great people, and when two people in a marriage strive to build up the other person, the marriage, as a matter of course, will always blossom and thrive.

But what happens when a couple loses all hope concerning their marriage? They're "just not feeling it," and the future looks anything but bright. There is hope in God! God extends hope to every person willing to believe beyond his or her feelings and beyond the challenges of the moment.

Tom:

From 'Caterpillar' to 'Butterfly' in Your Marriage

And do not be conformed to this world, but be transformed by the renewing of your mind, that you may prove what is that good and acceptable and perfect will of God. (Romans 12:2)

We know that our emotions stem from our thoughts. And our thoughts come largely from the words we hear, including the words we speak! By purposely changing our words, we can eventually change our thoughts. And changing our thoughts will change our beliefs and our actions. It will transform us and our circumstances, unlocking our potential in much the same way the metamorphosis of a caterpillar takes place, and it is transformed, or changed, into a beautiful butterfly.

Thoughts are so powerful, and we see this in the study of human behavior. For example, scientists have studied the brains of people who seem to bounce from relationship to relationship. In one study, it was discovered that these types of people have unusual neurological patterns associated with thinking negative thoughts over a prolonged period. These subjects developed certain "ruts" and "grooves" in their patterns of thinking. In other words, after thinking along the same negative lines over time, something happened in the brain that caused them to behave erratically, especially in their relationships.

Volunteers in this study were then given an assignment: to think and speak only positive thoughts for the span of two months. In a nutshell, after just two months of successfully completing the assignment, brain scans revealed those "grooved" patterns had been reversed!

Isn't it amazing that just the act of thinking and speaking positively can break cycles of destructive behavior in a person's life?

We Build — or Destroy — With Our Words

Proverbs 18:21 says, "Death and life are in the power of the tongue, and those who love it will eat its fruit." In the same way that our words can tear down and destroy, they can also build up and give life. When you sow life with your tongue — with the words of your mouth — you'll reap the fruit of life. So as a husband, when you bless your wife with words of praise, you're sowing life into her spirit and into your marriage as well.

We know that man is the provider of seed. We also know that the Word of God is referred to as seed (Mark 4:14; Luke 8:11). So as a husband, when you speak the Word over your wife, you're planting seeds into her heart and mind. She can incubate those seeds and cause them to germinate and grow, and when they do, they will return to you — the sower — the harvest of a wonderful marriage.

You Can Create the Marriage of Your Dreams

By faith we understand that the worlds were framed by the word of God, so that the things which are seen were not made of things which are visible. (Hebrews 11:3)

Your vision for your marriage will come to fruition based on what you're speaking or confessing. And I'm not just talking about the words you quote by faith to God and to your own heart; I'm talking about the words you speak to each other.

You can "fashion" your marriage, put it in order, and equip it for its intended purpose by the words of your own mouth! For example, simple words — such as, "I admire you"; "I appreciate you"; "I'm so in love with you"; "you're the love of my life"; "I'm blessed to have you"; "you're so good-looking"; and so forth — are words that build and heal your spouse instead of tearing him or her down and inflicting injury and pain.

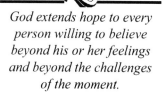

God extends hope to every person willing to believe beyond his or her feelings and beyond the challenges of the moment.

Think about how loved you'd feel to hear your spouse say these things to you! Words are powerful — they are carriers of energy. Loving words carry and convey love. No matter how far from grace you think you've fallen in your marriage, positive, love-filled words — spoken consistently — have the power to save that relationship and cause it to flourish. Remember, love never fails (1 Corinthians 13:8).

Stop It Before It Starts — How To Stop Wrong Words in Their Tracks

We've already seen that women are great meditators, or incubators, of words — good words and bad words. For example, when a woman "broods" over the Word of God in the midst of a challenge, wisdom and blessing come forth. She meditates and meditates until wisdom is produced. But I can't talk about this facet in a woman's design without addressing the potential problems that can occur when she meditates on the wrong things. When she over-thinks the wrong things, it can produce an emotional reaction that can be harmful.

We're all accountable to God for the thoughts we meditate on. In other words, we can control our thoughts; we can choose what we will and will not think on.

Through the years, I haven't always been the example of a model husband toward Maureen. I'm not perfect, but I'm growing. I'm further along now than I was years ago, and I'll learn and grow even more as long as I'm alive on this earth! But during those years when I was developing myself to be a good husband, there were times when I said things to my wife that weren't appropriate.

But that's not the end of our story. Maureen had the ability not to receive those words — and she did refuse to receive them. When I said things that were wrong, she decided to let those words go rather than allow them into her heart to incubate as seeds and produce something harmful to her emotions and, ultimately, to our marriage.

A woman who knows God and knows the Word has the ability to refute thoughts that come to her as a result of wrong words that are spoken into her life. She can say, "No, that isn't worth building a situation out of."

Of course, Maureen has the freedom to address me when I miss it and say to me, "That was inappropriate." And because I choose to walk reverently before God and tenderly toward my wife, I am man enough to respond to her, "You're right, and I'm sorry. Can we put those words to death and move on?"

I'm not perfect, and I don't always say everything just right. And there are also times when I say one thing, but she hears another. But rather than try to argue the point, we've found ways to work through those situations, and we do it through communication and trust. In other words, Maureen isn't easily offended, and she is patient and calm enough to ask, "Here's what I just heard you say. Is that what you meant?" And if she has misunderstood me, I'll explain what I intended to communicate.

This is where integrity and trust come into play. I have to be honest with Maureen. For example, if I said something in a sarcastic tone, I know it, so I have to own up to that. I can't lie to her and say, "I did not say it like that. What's your problem, anyway?"

And because Maureen knows my character, she trusts that I would never lie to her or purposely hurt her. So through honest communication, we've been able to work through situations in which one or both of us has miscommunicated something or misunderstood something the other one was saying.

It's very difficult for a wife to trust her husband if he has earned a reputation with her over the years of being very volatile and unsteady in his treatment of her. When he continually hurts her week after week, month after month, and year after year, she has a problem trusting that he won't do it again.

You've seen people who are what you might call moody or "up one day and down the next." It's not easy to trust a person like that. In fact, he or she hasn't earned any trust, because trust is earned over time. When you display certain godly characteristics over a period of time, you build trust with those around you. Then when something happens to cause someone to momentarily doubt you, you can easily work through it. Because of your overall good character, one misunderstanding or even a lapse in judgment won't be enough to destroy the trust that you've built over time.

Although she is a meditator and incubator of words, a woman has the ability to stop wrong words from being sown as seeds into her heart. She can uproot them and keep them from growing. In fact, she must uproot them, because the principle of seedtime and harvest works, no matter what it is that we're "seeding" or sowing. Whether grains of corn or hateful words, every seed that's planted has the potential to produce after its own kind!

But we don't have to allow the sowing or planting process to take place. We don't have to nurture and grow everything that's been planted into our lives. In fact, we need to destroy those things that we don't want to reap a harvest from!

> *Let no corrupt word proceed out of your mouth, but what is good for necessary edification, that it may impart grace to the hearers.* (Ephesians 4:29)

I don't understand husbands who know this principle of sowing and reaping, yet they continue to sow grief and pain into their marriage. A man who does this will never enjoy the great marriage God intended for him, because he refuses to sow the right kinds of seeds. He shoots himself in the foot, so to speak. The power to have a great marriage is in his grasp, but whether through ignorance or stubbornness, he refuses to do the right thing. Because of the wrong words he speaks, his wife constantly struggles to keep herself spiritually healthy and emotionally stable — while her trust in him has fallen by the wayside.

As a husband, you can't expect your wife to have the wherewithal to bless and minister life to you if you're filling her with death and destruction. To expect blessing when you're sowing cursing defies the law of sowing and reaping, and it will not work. Woman is truly the "wombed man." So why not sow romance and tenderness into her life? Instead of reaping "corruption" because you're mistreating her, you can choose to enjoy a harvest of blessing.

The Word of God in Your Marriage

All Scripture is given by inspiration of God, and is profitable for doctrine, for reproof, for correction, for instruction in righteousness, that the man of God may be complete, thoroughly equipped for every good work. (2 Timothy 3:16-17)

God desires that our marriage be strong — complete and "thoroughly equipped." But we're going to have to follow the instruction and correction of the Word of God in order to have the blessing of God in our marriage.

Romans 1:16 says, "For I am not ashamed of the gospel of Christ, for it is the power of God to salvation for everyone who believes, for the Jew first and also for the Greek." God's Word is His very power to do in your life whatever needs to be done. In other words, there's enough power in God's Word to change you and your circumstances, including your marriage. But you have to be open to God's Word. You have to eagerly accept and embrace the truth when you hear it. If you'll do that, the Word of God will change your life for the better.

Romans 12:2 says, "And do not be conformed to this world, but be transformed by the renewing of your mind, that you may prove what is that good and acceptable and perfect will of God." This verse was written to believers, not to unbelievers, or to those who are unsaved. As believers, we are a new creation in Christ. Second Corinthians 5:17 says concerning the New Birth experience, "Therefore, if anyone is in Christ, he is a new creation; old things have passed away; behold, all things have become new."

This verse is talking about your spirit, or your heart. Your spirit was reborn — made completely new — in the New Birth. But what about your soul? Just as you still had the same body after you got born again, you still had the same soul. Your body and soul did not become "new" in the New Birth. So you still had many of the same attitudes and beliefs that had been formed over the course of your life, largely due to your circumstances and environment. Many of those beliefs were wrong; they didn't line up with the Bible. That's why Romans 12:2 says you must renew your mind with the Word of God. You must allow your mind to be transformed — changed — by the power that's in God's Word.

> *Submit to God and be at peace with him; in this way prosperity will come to you.* (Job 22:21 NIV)

> *Agree with God, and be at peace; in this way good will come to you.* (Job 22:21 NRSV)

When we are truly submitted to God, we will agree with and yield to His Word and His will for our lives — including our marriages. And great good will come to us as a result. His blessing will be upon us and our household. We have His Word for it!

MAUREEN:

A Focused Mind and a Guarded Heart

> *Keep your heart with all diligence, for out of it spring the issues of life.* (Proverbs 4:23)

Although a husband is responsible to guard his words and "let no corrupt word proceed from his mouth" (Ephesians 4:29), a wife has some responsibility in building and strengthening her marriage too. She must "keep her heart with all diligence" (Proverbs 4:23). In other words, she must guard her heart concerning her marriage, because from her heart will flow an attitude of life or death regarding her relationship with her spouse.

I'm talking about focus. As a wife, you can choose to focus on your husband's faults, or you can focus on his strengths. If you focus on his faults, those faults will become magnified, and they will eventually cause a wedge of separation or division between you.

The Birth of an Emotion

Every emotion is born from a thought. Women must understand that they are incubators; therefore, we need to think on and nurture the right kind of thoughts. If we fail to think correctly, we will develop the wrong kind of emotions — strong negative emotions that will affect our marriage.

The right thoughts equal the right emotions.

When a woman comes to me and says, "I just don't love my husband anymore," by talking with her, I can usually take her back to the place where she began to incubate negative thoughts about her husband. In some cases, the wrong thoughts a woman nurtures over time produces such strong emotions that she's ready to act on those feelings in divorce court. A woman in this position usually doesn't need to change her marital status — she needs to change her thoughts and emotions.

Some women become so ingrained with wrong emotions that they are completely captive to their feelings. Their emotions are more real to them than the truth of God's Word. But thoughts and feelings can change. You can change your feelings the same way you got those feelings in the first place: by changing what you've been thinking about.

It's sad when marriages fail because a wife doesn't grasp this important truth. She buys into the lie that her husband will never change and that "the grass is greener on the other side."

The Wisdom of Guarding Your Thoughts

The wise woman builds her house, but with her own hands the foolish one tears hers down. (Proverbs 14:1 NIV)

This verse in Proverbs can apply to men too. By our thoughts, words, and deeds, we are creating the marriage that we'll either be privileged to enjoy or be forced to endure. If we want the right kind of marriage — marriage as God intends it — we'll think on His Word, speak His Word, and act on His Word concerning marriage.

When you feel unhappy with your spouse, the first step to overcoming that is to recognize it as just a feeling. Then you need to resist that feeling so you can work constructively, not destructively, on the problem. If you act on what you believe according to God's Word instead of on your negative feelings, positive feelings will eventually follow. But so many people don't want to take that first step because it involves "casting down" the wrong thoughts and replacing them with the right thoughts, and that takes work!

Casting down imaginations, and every high thing that exalteth itself against the knowledge of God, and bringing into captivity every thought to the obedience of Christ.
(2 Corinthians 10:5 KJV)

144

We know that thoughts produce feelings, whether good or bad. Good thoughts produce good feelings; bad thoughts produce bad feelings. In order to cast down bad thoughts, we must replace them with good thoughts. And we do that by speaking good words, especially God's words.

That sounds simple enough, but it seems that women especially struggle with this. Many don't understand that feelings are just that — feelings — and that they can control those feelings and emotions by controlling their thoughts.

Change Your Thoughts and Change Your Life!

How do you turn negative thoughts about your marriage into positive ones — and feelings of frustration and unhappiness into feelings of joy, peace, and contentment? One way is by remembering the good times, by remembering what caused you to fall in love with your husband in the first place.

You know you can do this, because how many times have you done it in reverse? In other words, how many times have you relived an argument with your husband or some painful moment in your marriage? Just as you can relive a bad moment, you can relive a season in your life when you had intense feelings of love for your husband. You can think about the things that made you laugh together. If you can't remember those times, ask the Holy Spirit to help you remember. Then as He brings those things back to your remembrance, write them down. Rehearse them in your thinking over and over again.

What are you doing when you actively replace negative thoughts with positive ones? You're doing battle in your mind! It won't always be easy, but if you'll fight for your marriage, you can win these battles of the mind and enjoy the reward and the victory that will ultimately come.

Doing spiritual battle means you're not always going to go with your feelings. When your feelings contradict the Word of God, you're going to go with what the Word says instead. You're going to be a doer of the Word (James 1:23) instead of just responding to your feelings and fleshly impulses.

Casting down arguments and every high thing that exalts itself against the knowledge of God, bringing every thought into captivity to the obedience of Christ. (2 Corinthians 10:5)

You can stop the cycle of negative thought patterns by guarding your heart and by taking every negative thought captive to God's Word. And when your thoughts are "talking loud," clamoring for your attention, you can talk even louder! You can boldly and confidently say, "I don't feel it right now, but I appreciate my husband. I admire and esteem him. I choose to respect him."

> *...and let the wife see that she respects and reverences her husband that she notices him, regards him, honors him, prefers him, venerates, and esteems him; and that she defers to him, praises him, and loves and admires him exceedingly].*
> (Ephesians 5:33 Amplified)

I've heard many women use the excuse that because their husband had done so much that was wrong, they could no longer respect him. Instead of using their thoughts to think on their husband's positive traits, they were using their thoughts to meditate on his faults, failures, and shortcomings. And those wrong thoughts produced the wrong kind of emotions.

When you think on your husband's strengths and take notice of his accomplishments, you feel better about him and your marriage. He may not be where you want him to be, but one thing is certain: He's never going to get there while you're being negative!

If you look for your husband's weaknesses, you will find them. But if you look for his strengths, you will find those too. Most people are very trained and adept at looking for weaknesses, so it may take some time to train yourself to meditate on your husband's strengths. But once you begin thinking more and more about your husband's good points, you'll start talking about them more.

I realize that many women struggle with this verse in Ephesians; they struggle to respect their husband. But I'm telling you that it's possible to obey this verse, and it starts with a willing heart. Then you must practice thinking the right thoughts. You may have to pray about it and ask the Lord, "Show me his strengths." But God will answer you, and He will bless your acts of obedience every step of the way.

Dreams Don't Just 'Come True' —
Sometimes You Have To Call for Them

…(as it is written, "I have made you a father of many nations") in the presence of Him whom he believed — God, who gives life to the dead and calls those things which do not exist as though they did. (Romans 4:17)

(As it is written, I have made thee a father of many nations,) before him whom he believed, even God, who quickeneth the dead, and calleth those things which be not as though they were. (Romans 4:17 KJV)

Abraham "called those things which be not as though they were." He walked by faith in what God had said despite what he could see with his natural sight. We can take a lesson from Abraham. We can talk about what we want our husband to become instead of what he appears to be right now. We can call "those things which be not as though they were." When we do that, our thoughts will produce the right emotions. We will be building a positive environment of faith in which God can work in us, in our husband, and in our marriage.

By faith we understand that the worlds were framed by the word of God, so that the things which are seen were not made of things which are visible. (Hebrews 11:3)

With our words, we create our own world. And with God's words in our mouth, we create the kind of life that He desires for us. He wants us to prosper in our health, in our finances, and in our relationships — especially in our marriage.

But marriages don't come prebuilt. We have to put forth the effort to build a life together with our spouse. Often people will look at a couple that has a great marriage and say, "I wish I had a marriage like theirs." Those people don't realize the work that went into building that great marriage.

Romans 1:16 says, "For I am not ashamed of the gospel of Christ, for it is the power of God to salvation for everyone who believes…." God's Word is His power! In other words, His Word is self-fulfilling. The opposite is true too. You can speak negative things over and over, and those negative things you speak will come to pass too! They will produce negative

147

emotions and negative consequences in your life. So why not speak the Word of God's power over your marriage?

Years ago, I ministered to a woman who overcame her negative feelings toward her husband and helped restore her marriage by doing what I'm sharing with you. In fact, this woman's feelings went beyond having feelings of disrespect: She literally despised her husband.

This woman needed help. She didn't want to feel that way about her husband, but she felt trapped by her thoughts, emotions, and beliefs concerning the man she'd married. She opened her heart to the Lord and to His Word, and she began "arresting" every negative thought that came to her mind about her husband. Instead of thinking on a negative thought, she began quoting scriptures that deal with marriage, especially those that talk about a godly husband, or a man who fears the Lord.

When she first began doing this, she'd get angry, because emotions flooded her mind and thoughts assailed her: You're lying! Your husband is NONE of these things! In fact, every time she tried to speak out the Word of God over her husband and her situation, she was attacked by negative thoughts and emotions that had become strongholds in her mind. She had allowed those thoughts to work in her, so she had to own up to that and deal with it before she could move on.

But this woman kept at it. And over time, it became easier and easier to nip wrong thoughts in the bud about her husband and her marriage. The Word of God in her heart spoken out by faith began to change her, and, gradually, her husband began to change. Instead of allowing her emotions to control her, she took control of her emotions. And today this woman and her husband have a beautiful, loving marriage!

A Wife's Responsibility

A woman can build her home and her marriage instead of tearing it down by thinking and speaking negatively (see Proverbs 14:1). It's true that women are incubators of words, but we are also responsible for what we incubate and grow. We must focus on thinking positive thoughts and speaking words that are based on the Word of God.

> *When they observe the pure and modest way in which you conduct yourselves, together with your reverence [for your husband; you are to feel for him all that reverence includes: to respect, defer to, revere him — to honor, esteem, appreciate,*

prize, and, in the human sense, to adore him, that is, to admire,
praise, be devoted to, deeply love, and enjoy your husband].
(1 Peter 3:2 Amplified)

As a wife, you might be thinking, Help me — I just don't feel that
way about my husband anymore! But you can develop those feelings and
emotions once again. God wants you to have feelings for your husband,
and He's showing you how to get those feelings back. You don't have to
have them all back by midnight tonight! But you do need to begin now
restoring your emotions by the power of God's Word.

It's not only possible — God is calling you to do it! You're going to
have to pay the price to lay down your old thoughts and to pick up new
ones. Your emotions will change when your thoughts change. You may
flip-flop in your emotions when you first start out. But in time — as you
consistently think on the right things — your emotions will change. The
atmosphere in your home will change and so will your marriage. Your
husband will be free to be everything God has called him to be.

Many women don't want to take that kind of responsibility. They don't
want to hear that they're the ones who could be making or breaking their
marriage. The saying, "Behind every great man is a great woman" is true.
What is a great woman? One who has faith in her man — not someone
else's man, but her man! She looks at him as a man of greatness, no matter
where he is in his walk right now. Why? Because God says he's great!

Every man is born with a purpose; God has a plan for every person.
But a man has to realize this fact, understand God's plan, and have the
support of his wife and family if he's ever going to carry out his God-
ordained purpose.

I've known wives who were married to their husbands for years, and
those men just seemed to be going nowhere in life and taking their families
with them! These wives had just about "had it" and were ready to throw
in the towel concerning their marriage. I counseled some of these women
to do the things I'm sharing with you, and within months, their marriages
and their lives began to turn around!

Where did my marriage go wrong? Many women wonder. Somewhere
along the way, there were disappointments and hurts in the marriage, and,
although the wife made the decision to forgive and be at peace with her
husband, her emotions didn't recover and "catch up" with her decision to
forgive. Now she must aggressively change her thinking process and retrain
herself to think positively so she can produce positive emotions.

Emotion-Driven or Spirit-Led?

Emotions are a powerful, driving force in our relationships. They can be used for good, but they can also be very destructive to the wife, her husband, and their relationship.

Although we as women are emotional by nature, we must guard against being led by our emotions. We must be Spirit-led, not emotionally driven. If we "incubate" the Word of God and let the Word develop in us, that Word will take us where our heart wants to go.

No woman wants to feel cold toward her husband. No woman wants to disrespect the man in her life. Most women desire a passionate relationship with their husband that just keeps getting better and better over time.

Years ago, the Lord spoke to me and said, "Every day, I want you to look for something good in the man I've given you. Then I want to tell him the good that you see." So I would look for something in Tom every single day. And every day, God would show me something. I'd find a way to tell Tom, "I'm so proud that you're a great leader," "You're so wise," "You take such good care of me and the kids," "You're so handsome," and so forth.

Those words blessed Tom and made him happy. Who wouldn't be happy to hear words of affirmation every day from someone you loved?

The Male Ego: Handle With Care

God created man with an ego, and that ego can be easily crushed. A man should be able to trust his wife not to bruise his ego, yet a wife can bruise or even crush her husband's ego like nobody else.

A man is at his best and functions at this highest potential when his wife believes in him. He doesn't function well when his wife is upset with him. So as a wife, you have a tremendous amount of influence in your husband's life. It's a great responsibility, and you must fulfill it with love and great care.

Psalm 100:4 says about our worship of God, "Enter into His gates with thanksgiving, and into His courts with praise. Be thankful to Him, and bless His name." Your thanksgiving and praise to God gives you entrance and access into His gates and courts. Similarly, your praise of your husband's good qualities opens his heart so that emotional connection is possible. Your words of praise and affirmation also build trust, and they build him as a person.

Remember, great marriages are made of great people. In the process of building up your spouse, you're building your marriage, too, and causing it to become a relationship that honors God and brings blessing to your own life. In thought, word, and deed, your marriage is happy and blessed!

11

True Love: The 'Constant' Through Life's Changing Seasons

Dr. Maureen Anderson

Years ago, a secular song hit the top of the charts that asked the question: What's love got to do with it?1 Since there seem to be so many different kinds of love, a better question might be: What is true love?

People often talk about love in various contexts, such as their love for a certain kind of car, food, clothing, jewelry — or even a favorite song. Of course, people also talk about love as it relates to those they hold dear, such as spouses, children, parents, siblings, and friends. And what about the deep fondness some feel for their pets? Love can have various meanings and applications to many. But what does God say about the subject of love?

We know that God is love (1 John 4:8). And we know that He gave us — mankind — His very best in the Gift of His Son Jesus Christ (John 3:16). So right away, we know that true love originates from God and that giving is a characteristic of someone who loves. And since marriage is the picture of "Christ and the Church" (Ephesians 5:25), we know that love is unconditional. Christ loved the Church and gave Himself for it — not because we did anything to deserve or merit His sacrifice, but because He loved us unconditionally, with an everlasting love.

Simply put, true love in marriage is about your spouse, not about yourself. And to love your spouse effectively — in the way that he or she best receives love — is not a lofty goal that we can never attain. Romans 5:5 says, "…the love of God has been poured out in our hearts by the Holy Spirit who was given to us." So if we're saved, we can love!

We know that love is not a feeling. It will become a feeling when we choose to love as an act of our will. In other words, love is about giving

— but it's about a choice to give, serve, and bless our spouse. So we must will, or choose, to give the love that's already in our heart as a believer.

Because marriage is a picture of Christ and the Church, one purpose for the love of God in our hearts is marriage! A Christian marriage is designed to show how much Christ loves the Church, His Bride — and how much the Church loves Christ. It's how we give place to God's love in us that determines the level of fulfillment we'll experience in marriage. If we allow love to flow out of us freely, we'll reap the benefits that go along with sowing love into the life of our spouse.

Seasons in Marriage

There are seasons in every marriage — high seasons and low seasons. Low seasons come when a need is not being met over a period of time. It's in those low seasons when many couples begin to focus on the negative qualities in the relationship and in the other person. They begin to focus and meditate on the faults and failures of their spouse. In other words, they forget about love! This is very dangerous to the marriage because negative thoughts often have a way of coming to fruition and bearing very bad fruit.

We must guard against thinking on the negative thoughts that come to our mind, especially during the low seasons. When our needs go unmet over a period of time, certain chemicals are released in the body that can cause us to begin to think negatively. As our emotions become affected, our thoughts and feelings can spiral further downward into discouragement, depression, and, eventually, complete hopelessness.

But hope is not lost in the low seasons. We must fight against negative thoughts that are induced by those brain chemicals or neurotransmitters — and we do that by thinking positive thoughts. As we work harder to love our spouse by choice, we become more rooted and grounded in the Word of God and the love of God, which helps us grow to the next level in our marriage.

Finally, brethren, whatever things are true, whatever things are noble, whatever things are just, whatever things are pure, whatever things are lovely, whatever things are of good report, if there is any virtue and if there is anything praiseworthy — meditate on these things. (Philippians 4:8)

What you think about will eventually produce strong feelings because emotions are always borne out of thoughts. Once negative emotions start flowing from the negative thoughts that you've allowed to persist, those thoughts become even more powerful because emotions are even more difficult to control.

Many married people find themselves in this very situation. They've meditated so long on the negative things in the marriage that they become discouraged and confused. They simply don't know what to do. They don't have a vision of victory on the inside of them, and, unfortunately, that's when many opt to end their marriage instead of fighting for it.

Recognize Your Season and Formulate Your Plan

It's important in marriage to recognize the low seasons when they come so that you can grow through them and come out on the other side stronger and more deeply rooted in love. This begins with a determination that you're going to have a Kingdom marriage no matter what. You'll have to invest your time to study the Word of God and materials on enjoying a successful marriage. You'll need to fellowship with your spouse — and you'll certainly need to know how to fast and pray! But you must be willing to walk by faith concerning your marriage and to pay the price to succeed, remembering that faith works by love (see Galatians 5:6).

When you recognize that your marriage is in a low season, that is the time to guard against every negative thought that comes to your mind about your marriage and your spouse. Did you know that you can plan your thoughts! You can plan to think only on positive things where your marriage and your spouse are concerned. You can plan to think only on things that are loving, kind, and praiseworthy.

You might need pen and paper to formulate your "thought plan" by writing down your mate's strengths and the things you love about him or her. Then you can record memories of when you first met and of your dating experience. You can recall and relive the days when you sort of "glowed" when he or she walked into a room.

Here is a simple exercise that will help you to keep the right attitude during a low season so that you can grow and go to the next level of love in your marriage stronger and better than you were before.

Concerning your spouse, simply ask yourself, What are the positives about this person? So often, we focus on the negatives, but what are your spouse's positive traits? I encourage you to write down five good things about your spouse at the beginning of each day — five things that you are grateful for. Do it first thing in the morning. Don't wait until you've had time to become frustrated again. Then tell your spouse that you appreciate those things about him (or her). Rehearse these characteristics to yourself. Talk about them constantly so that you can form new, positive thoughts to replace the negative ones.

Do this every day. Begin with a new list each day. Think about traits you admire in your spouse. Think about and relive fun times you've enjoyed together. Think about things that remind you of your love and dedication to each other.

For example, if you're a wife, does your husband have a job? Does he go to that job every day to earn a living? Write these things down and focus and meditate on these things instead of on the negative thoughts that come to your mind. It may help you to talk about what you've written — to rehearse out loud the positive things about your spouse that you've written. Also, if you've recorded a fun activity that you remember, perhaps you can make plans to do that activity again.

People do this simple exercise "in reverse" all the time. They may not keep a real, written list of things they don't like about their spouse, but in the low seasons, they will focus and meditate on those things until those thoughts form negative emotions and strongholds, or belief patterns, that become difficult to change. Then they'll starting talking negatively about their spouse — because emotions demand expression. Out of the abundance of the heart, the mouth speaks (see Luke 6:45)!

After they've meditated on and spoken those negative things continually over a period of time, unfortunately, the next step is to act on that, or do it, and many divorces occur out of the low seasons in a marriage as a result.

The following is provided as a guideline to record the thoughts you plan to think about and meditate on when negative, accusing thoughts assail your mind.

My spouse's greatest characteristics:
1.
2.
3.
4.
5.

My favorite memories together:
1. I met my spouse at _____
2. He [or she] looked _____
3. I knew I was in love when _____
4. We went _____
    on our first date.
5. My favorite memory is the time when _____

Someone might argue, "I remember all the good times, but things just aren't that way anymore." Although that may be true, continuing to think that way will not change anything for the better. Very simply, if you want to re-create those feelings from your days of dating and courtship, it begins with your thoughts and emotions — with reliving those moments when your thoughts were positive and your emotions high. If you truly want to see a change for the better in your marriage, you must get rid of your old way of thinking and begin to think positive, faith-filled thoughts.

Remember, love is not a feeling. But your thoughts of love can produce feelings of love. And when you sow thoughts and words of love that are in line with God's Word, the feelings you re-create won't be fleeting like the thoughts that come and go. Instead, your thoughts and feelings will become habit. In time, they will develop within you feelings of love that will last a lifetime.

Think about it!

How To Turn a Mountain Back Into a Molehill

You've no doubt heard the saying, "You're making a mountain out of a molehill." That's actually what happens when you continually think and meditate on your spouse's faults and shortcomings. Negative emotions always follow, and you create a destructive mountain on the inside. The more you think on those negative things, the larger that person's faults loom high above any possibility of marital happiness!

But you can reverse that process. The same way you created your mountain, you can also diminish it. You can turn your mountain back into a molehill!

Here is another simple exercise you can do during a low season in your marriage when you're feeling frustrated with your spouse. Write down three characteristics of your mate that you would like him or her to change. In other words, list the things that seem to come up over and over again when you're in a low season. Then ask the Holy Spirit, "How do these characteristics show up in me."

Usually, what we don't like in someone else are traits that exist in us. We might become bothered from time to time about these things in our own life, yet they seem to be magnified or intensified in the lives of those closest to us.

> *"And why do you look at the speck in your brother's eye, but do not consider the plank in your own eye? Or how can you say to your brother, 'Let me remove the speck from your eye'; and look, a plank is in your own eye? Hypocrite! First remove the plank from your own eye, and then you will see clearly to remove the speck from your brother's eye."* (Matthew 7:3-5)

> *The thing that really bugs you about your spouse is a "speck" in him or her, but it could be a "plank" in you! So before you try to change your spouse, you need to ask the Holy Spirit, "Is this a problem in my own life? If so, how can I get free from this myself? How can I get victory in this area?" But if you criticize and become hyper-sensitive about what the other person is doing, the Bible says that while you're judging that person, you're condemning yourself* (see Romans 2:1).

Low Seasons Do Not Have To Be Long Seasons

In the low seasons of marriage, remembering and meditating on the good times will positively affect your emotions and help usher in the high seasons again. Your low seasons don't have to be long seasons! By thinking right, speaking right, and purposely reminiscing and reliving the high, positive seasons, you can quickly reverse the low seasons of your marriage.

Let's look at a Spirit-inspired prayer the Apostle Paul prayed for the Church concerning the love of Christ — a prayer we must continue to pray today.

> *...that Christ may dwell in your hearts through faith. And I pray that you, being rooted and established in love, may have power, together with all the saints, to grasp how wide and long and high and deep is the love of Christ, and to know this love that surpasses knowledge — that you may be filled to the measure of all the fulness of God.* (Ephesians 3:17-19 NIV)

What does love have to do with the seasons of life? Thoughts, words, and acts of love can act as a "constant" in the changing seasons we all experience. They will produce within us positive emotions even when dark clouds of negativity assail. Expressions of love can sustain a relationship, strengthen it, and help propel it to a higher level of love in the next season.

Another facet of love in the changing seasons is dealing properly with conflict and differences. In the low seasons, conflicts often escalate and can bring destruction to a marriage if those conflicts aren't resolved.

When Hope Seems Lost —
What To Do When You Don't Know What To Do

As we've seen, when a person's needs go unmet for a period of time, the body releases a chemical that begins to influence emotions. But that doesn't mean you have to go the way of your emotions. You can resist that process by guarding your thoughts and by going to God in prayer. He is the great need-meeter. He is our first Husband, and He ever lives to meet our needs.

Instead of praying and resisting negative thoughts, many people just allow their emotions to bring them down. They forget that Jesus is their High Priest, who ever lives to meet our needs (Hebrews 7:26 NIV). We can always go the Lord with whatever is bothering us, and He will be a present help in time of trouble.

God is our refuge and strength, a very present help in trouble. (Psalm 46:1)

Let us therefore come boldly to the throne of grace, that we may obtain mercy and find grace to help in time of need. (Hebrews 4:16)

In our own experience, prayer and fasting has made all the difference in how Tom and I relate to each other today. Although we both came from broken, dysfunctional homes, our families were opposites and so were we. In fact, our dysfunction was just about the only thing we had in common! Not only did Tom and I have adjustments to make and hurdles to overcome, we faced obstacles in our marriage that seemed like impossible mountains! In the early days of our marriage, we had small struggles, and we had huge, enormous struggles! Of course, God gets all the glory that we came through those early years with a love story greater than we ever thought possible. We have a marriage that's Heaven on earth — a Kingdom marriage. We're so in love, and Tom and I are very best friends because we learned the secret of true love in marriage. But God could not have taught us if we'd not been determined that we were going to overcome no matter what the price or cost.

Remember, the goal of marriage is to create intimacy between the husband and wife. But emotional baggage often interferes with the intimacy we should be experiencing in marriage. To say that Tom and I entered marriage with a lot of baggage is an understatement. We had freight trucks and moving vans full of baggage that we each brought to the table in our relationship. My father was abusive, and my parents divorced when I was eight years old. I never really had a dad in my life. Tom's mother left him and his family when he was four years old. So what we had in common were abandonment issues, rejection issues, and issues of worthlessness and low self-esteem.

These are the kinds of things that had been planted into our minds and subconscious from a very early age, so every response and reaction as adults was based on those negative thoughts and emotions. Naturally speaking, we were a divorce waiting to happen. But to God, we were a challenge, and He was more than up for it!

How To Share Your Relationship Baggage

Before God could help us, He first had to work within both of us a willingness and eagerness to have His best and to honor Him with our obedience and our marriage. So every time an issue would arise, we had a prearranged way of settling them. Instead of screaming and yelling for days or giving each other the silent treatment, we would pray together and ask God to show us what to do.

When Tom and I had a problem, we would sometimes go on a three-day fast together, and we'd spend as much time as possible over those three days earnestly praying and seeking the Lord. We would allow Him to speak, and He would speak! We would allow the gifts of the Holy Spirit to manifest on our behalf (1 Corinthians 12:8-10). And the Lord came through with the wisdom and the answer we needed every time! He would reveal the root of the problem, so we always knew exactly whose issue was causing the problem — mine or Tom's. But it didn't matter whose issue it was. We were in it together — Tom's victories were my victories, and my victories were Tom's victories. So together we would rid our marriage of that particular piece of baggage for good.

In a low season in marriage, that is not the time to drift apart but to draw even closer together. Even if only one spouse is going through a difficult time, you are a couple — a team. You need to pray and seek God together. As Christians, you both are indwelt by the Holy Spirit, who will lead you into all truth (John 16:13).

Oftentimes when one spouse is dealing with intense emotional issues, the other spouse sort of "abandons" him or her to deal with it alone. But you're not supposed to abandon each other in marriage. You're supposed to stand and fight together, united as one in purpose, shouldering each other's issues. That's love in action, and doing that brings the favor, power, and provision of God into whatever it is you're dealing with.

Now, when I say that Tom and I stood together in our marriage, I'm not saying we never were angry with each other or that we never spoke a harsh word. But we had to get over our offenses quickly and learn to walk in love and forgiveness. Otherwise, we would have become isolated from one another — and it's in those places of isolation where people become vulnerable and fall prey to discouragement and hopelessness.

Communication Do's and Dont's in Marriage

Fasting and prayer is a big key to resolving conflict and getting rid of the emotional baggage that can destroy a marriage. Communicating is another big key to resolving conflict. Even if you have to talk and talk about the same issue over a period of time, if you're communicating truthfully and peaceably — in a godly manner — you can eventually work the issue out with God's help. But when you stop talking, it's almost guaranteed your problem will not be solved.

I know of husbands and wives who sleep in separate rooms at night because they stay constantly offended at each other. Early in our marriage, there have been times I've been tempted to close myself off from Tom when we were dealing with something. But he wouldn't allow it. He'd follow me into the other room! And he would pray in the Holy Ghost all night at times. Tom has never been passive about our relationship. But how many men just let things drag on for weeks and months at a time — and sometimes let the relationship deteriorate until it is completely destroyed?

You can walk into some people's homes and just sense strife and offense in the atmosphere. Why? Because conflict was left unresolved and unchecked, and it continued building and gaining momentum until everyone became affected — the husband, the wife, and the children in the home.

You don't have to allow those attitudes to dwell in your home. You have the power — especially if you're the husband, the head of the home — to "take the bull by the horns" and determine that you're not going to give up on God or your marriage until you've reached the other side, and you're both enjoying Heaven on earth in your marriage.

Wrong Ways To Handle Conflict
That Yield Very Wrong Results

People react differently to difficulty and hardship — to the "low seasons" of life — so don't expect your spouse to react the same way you do in every situation and circumstance. Instead, accept each other's differences and stay positive and supportive. Give one another the benefit of the doubt. In other words, walk in love!

So often during hard times, we become impatient and intolerant of others — especially our spouse — and that only makes matters worse. In many cases, if couples simply knew what not to do during the storms of life, they'd be a lot further along in their marriages than they are now. That's why I want to share with you four negative responses to difficulties — criticism, withdrawal, defensiveness, and contempt — that we must recognize and overcome if we're to endure the low seasons so we can enjoy the high seasons of marriage and of life.

Negative Response Number One: Criticism

The first negative habit some people fall into when they feel disappointed is criticism. When they're dissatisfied — especially if they're dissatisfied with the marriage — they often use words that tear their spouse down instead of build him or her up. Obviously, that's not the wisdom of God, because the Bible says that a wise woman builds her house, but a foolish one tears hers down (Proverbs 14:1).

Of course, this can apply to men too. When a husband is frustrated over some behavior of his wife, he can begin pointing out all her faults and failures. His needs aren't being met, so he uses criticism as a mechanism to deal with it.

Using criticism to try to get your needs met doesn't work. When a husband and wife pick each other apart with their words, they tear the marriage down. Marriage is an institution involving two people — and when those people are torn down, the marriage goes down with them.

I urge you to avoid being critical at all cost. Criticism doesn't produce anything godly in a marriage. There's no building involved in criticism, only destroying or tearing down. In fact, nothing constructive at all comes from criticizing your mate in a critical, mean-spirited, or demeaning way.

The root of criticism is impatience. In other words, if you're critical, you want to see a change now, even if it's a forced changed. You want to have your say now, even if feelings get hurt in the process. A critical person is emotionally driven, and when you're emotionally driven and not Spirit-let, your conversation can be very destructive. Criticism doesn't build intimacy in relationships; instead it tears down any intimacy that was present to begin with.

People who struggle in this area also deal with feelings of pessimism and extreme negativity. They're the ones who see the glass half empty. They're blinded to what they have in life because all they can see is what they don't have.

If this negative habit describes you, make a commitment before God today that you're going to search for, acknowledge, and be thankful for what you have and praise Him for it. Even if you have to get a journal and write down the good things you have — including the good qualities in your mate — I encourage you to do it. Write down the things you're thankful for and meditate on those things. Begin each day reviewing what you've written.

Thankfulness and praise open our hearts and allow connection to happen.

> *In everything give thanks; for this is the will of God in Christ Jesus for you.* (1 Thessalonians 5:18)

> *Give thanks in all circumstances, for this is God's will for you in Christ Jesus.* (1 Thessalonians 5:18 (NIV))

This verse doesn't mean that God brings every circumstance into our lives, whether negative or positive. And it doesn't mean we're supposed to be thankful for everything. It means we're supposed to be thankful in everything.

Here are a few more verses about being thankful.

And let the peace of God rule in your hearts, to which also you were called in one body; and be thankful. (Colossians 3:15)

Enter into His gates with thanksgiving, And into His courts with praise. Be thankful to Him, and bless His name. (Psalm 100:4)

Thankfulness and praise open our hearts and allow connection to happen. When you and your spouse show gratitude to each other, you are building trust. Even emotional gates that have been closed in the past can be opened again where love and appreciation are being shown.

The opposite is true in atmosphere of un-thankfulness, negativity, and pessimism. Darkness prevails in this kind of environment. Romans 1:21 says, "…although they knew God, they did not glorify Him as God, nor were thankful, but became futile in their thoughts, and their foolish hearts were darkened."

An unthankful heart becomes darkened. And a darkened heart can bring a marriage down lower and lower unless the person makes a decision to change. Showing gratitude is a choice just as showing love is a choice. And since God has told us to be thankful, that means we can do it!

The person who's critical must be willing to change. Instead of criticizing, he or she must learn to pray. Then that person must be willing to have an honest, healthy conversation with his or her spouse — one that builds intimacy instead of destroying it. (In the next chapter, we'll look at how to peacefully and effectively communicate with your spouse.)

Negative Response Number Two: Withdrawal

The second negative response to frustration and discontentment is withdrawal. The person who employs this mechanism doesn't use words at all. He or she simply withdraws. That person is there, but not really. Instead, he or she becomes emotionally distant. When the other person asks, "Is everything okay?" the withdrawn party will usually respond, "Yes, everything is fine."

But everything is not fine. That person is dissatisfied, and instead of dealing with the issue biblically, he or she pulls away from the other party.

This behavior is so destructive. You can't bury needs, pretending they don't exist, and expect to be happy. It's emotional dishonesty, and it breeds confusion in the marriage because of the person's unwillingness or inability to be open and upfront.

When you bury your emotions instead of dealing with them, those emotions don't just die. Although they're buried, they remain alive, and whether you're consciously dwelling on them or not, they grow and produce destructive fruit in your heart and in your marriage — hatred, bitterness, wrath, resentment, and so forth. Withdrawing as a means of "dealing" with negative emotions doesn't work!

People who use withdrawal are usually very sensitive to criticism. They don't like to be told what to do, and criticism makes them feel inadequate. So when you criticize this kind of person, he or she will quickly withdraw. They seem isolated, but they inwardly long for connection, not isolation. Yet what they long for, they will never do.

If you have a spouse that withdraws, you need to hug that person! That's what he or she really wants. You need to tell your mate, "You're not going to withdraw. We're going to talk about this and work it out."

As I said, the person who withdraws often does so because he or she has some deep need that's not being met. For example, the person may have a passion about something and wants his or her spouse to share that passion. Perhaps that person loves the outdoors and desires to spend quality time with his or her spouse doing an outdoor hobby or activity. But if the spouse doesn't share that passion — and has no desire to learn to like it — withdrawal can be the result.

We've all been guilty at times of neglecting the dreams and passions of those we love. We don't hear the excitement in our loved one's voice when something greatly interests him or her. We're not as interested as we should be in that person's heart and in what God is doing in his or her life. Often, that person senses the lack of interest and, over time, begins to "check out" emotionally.

Since people who withdraw have difficulty expressing themselves, communication can present a special challenge. They often don't know how to express their issue, whether it's some kind of emotional injury or a fear that mentally tortures them. If you're a "withdrawer," for the sake of your own emotional health and the health of your marriage, you must simply make the decision that you will communicate! And you must do it in a healthy manner, not when adrenaline is flowing at a "high."

Perhaps you can begin with an email or voicemail message or a letter. Just purpose in your heart to start somewhere until you can sit down with your spouse and engage in a healthy conversation.

This will be especially challenging, because a person who withdraws is not the kind of person who usually seeks out connection — yet that's the thing he or she needs the most. I'm not making excuses for the one who withdraws, because it's a trait that needs to be overcome. I'm simply saying that being sensitive to people like this — and loving them in spite of the walls of isolation that they throw up — is a big key to drawing them out and helping them make the change to communicate more effectively and to take personal responsibility in their relationships.

Those who withdraw need to determine why they're withdrawing and what their real needs are. Then they need to practice communicating those needs in a loving manner. Only then can "withdrawers" begin to break this destructive habit in marriage.

Negative Response Number Three: Defensiveness

The third negative behavior many resort to in low seasons is defensiveness. Defensiveness is born out of hopelessness and then turns to defiance. Someone who's hopeless might say things, such as, "I can never please her [or him]." Being defensive is the attitude that causes anger to erupt, so strife and fighting usually ensue when a person gives place to defensiveness.

When one person in a marriage becomes consistently defensive, there's usually an underlying problem that's manifesting in that negative behavior. Defensiveness includes denying personal problems and failing to be responsible. And the root of defensiveness is usually a feeling of hopelessness that you'll never be able to please your spouse. You have nurtured the belief that you'll never be able to make that person happy. A voice inside you declares, "You're not good enough." And nothing you do seems to change that belief. You respond to every word and action defensively because you find it difficult to separate your behavior from you. You identify so closely with your behavior, which provokes more of the same defensive behavior (see Romans 7:19).

You need to realize that your behaviors and attitudes are not you; they simply live in you, in your soul. Understanding that you are a new creature in Christ (2 Corinthians 5:17) will help you drive those attitudes far from you. It may not happen overnight, but as you meditate on the truth of God's Word that you're a beautiful new creation in Christ —made in His likeness and image — those attitudes from the past will fall by the wayside.

If "defensiveness" describes you, you need to realize that you're responding from a place of hopelessness, and that's not of God. God is the God of hope! You're going to have to pray and perhaps do some fasting. Ask the Lord to show you how to deal with the doubt and the judgmental attitude — toward yourself and your spouse — that has taken hold in your life.

Defensiveness leads to arguments and strife. It causes the person who's being defensive to go into "attack-mode" and become angry at his or her spouse at the slightest provocation. If this is a habit you're accustomed to giving place to, I encourage you to quickly admit when you've misunderstood something your spouse has communicated. Instead of arguing, be peaceable. Instead, you could say, "I'm so sorry. Let's pray about this."

Defensiveness can also cause a person to spiral downward into feelings of worthlessness. The enemy wants this husband or wife to believe that there's no hope and that he or she is a complete failure. If he succeeds, in time the spouse will begin to act out what he or she believes.

The enemy is after your marriage, but, really, he's after your mind! He knows that if he can get to your mind and begin to influence your thoughts and emotions, he can destroy your marriage in just a matter of time. So instead of allowing negative voices to play in your head, you need to begin to say some things out loud from the Word of God. You need to "stand down" those thoughts until they become weaker and weaker. Eventually, they will have no more power over you or your marriage. And when your spouse speaks, you will hear him or her correctly instead of through a filter of hopelessness, failure, and defeat.

Usually defensiveness occurs in a relationship in which one spouse is overly critical. In fact, one definition of defensiveness is an attitude that challenges criticism. But if you're the defensive type, don't connect to the criticism. Instead, the next time your spouse criticizes you, recognize it as a trigger point and say, "What is your need, Honey? I want to help you. Let's pray and seek God."

Negative Response Number Four: Contempt

The fourth negative behavior that manifests in conflict is contempt. When you're contemptuous of your spouse because you're disappointed or frustrated, you're disdainful of him or her. Contempt motivates a person to ridicule his or her spouse, especially in public or in front of other people. Someone who's contemptuous of someone shows great disrespect toward him or her. The person who's in contempt keeps a running list of the other person's transgressions and can't wait to let everyone else know what's wrong with that spouse.

Contempt is a manifestation of the most intense lack of respect. Someone's need is not being met, so the offended party creates a sort of rap sheet on the offender and uses the person's "crimes" to insult him or her to others. He or she uses every opportunity to air the faults and failures of the other person to anyone who will listen.

In the Old Testament, we see an example of contempt in Michal's attitude toward her husband, King David, as he danced before the Lord.

> *Now as the ark of the Lord came into the City of David, Michal, Saul's daughter, looked through a window and saw King David leaping and whirling before the Lord; and she despised him in her heart.* (2 Samuel 6:16).

David was praising God and celebrating the arrival of the ark of God's Presence in the city. Afterward, Michal said, "…'How glorious was the king of Israel today, uncovering himself today in the eyes of the maids of his servants, as one of the base fellows shamelessly uncovers himself!'" (v. 20). Her biting remark showed her disgust and contempt for her husband.

Usually people who show contempt for their spouse picked up this attitude early in life. Their contempt is actually disrespect for authority. Perhaps some authority figure let them down in some way. Maybe their parents weren't there for them or didn't connect with them emotionally. So in marriage, they transfer this image to their spouse. They expect that this other person will let them down as well. Then every time something goes wrong in the marriage, that negative image surfaces, and they are seemingly controlled by their response of contempt.

We already talked about the power of thoughts. A person who manifests this negative behavior of contempt must arrest his or her thoughts the moment they begin to surface. This person must invoke the Holy Spirit's help to recognize those negative images from the past when they come. Then he or she must instantly replace those thoughts and images with good ones. But the person must do this aggressively. Those feelings of contempt didn't become ingrained in the person's emotional makeup overnight. This person is going to have to fast, pray, and start asking the hard question as to why he or she has given place to this destructive behavior.

If this behavior describes you, a good place to start after you've prayed is to simply begin imagining your spouse meeting your needs! Be adamant with yourself in refusing to continue your old way of thinking. It hasn't profited you thus far, and that kind of destructive behavior will never profit you and yield you the kind of marriage God desires for you.

It's important to realize that when strong feelings of frustration are present, we will each be tempted to yield to one or more of these negative behaviors. We need to determine which of these behaviors most often describes us, and when we locate ourselves, we need to ask the Holy Spirit, "Why do I do that?" Then we need to repent, give that behavior to the Lord, and press beyond yielding to it every time we're frustrated.

During the "low times" in our marriage, we must recognize that the reason for most of our frustrations is that an important need is not being met. That frustration is also the product of inner conflict due to a lack of communication. We lack the ability to communicate our feelings properly, so we feel frustrated and we manifest one or more of these negative behaviors. We'll criticize our spouse, withdraw from him or her, or become defensive or contemptuous in our interactions.

Some people are so clueless about how to resolve conflict and communicate peaceably that they would rather have things remain the way they are than to step out and confront an issue. But this behavior is unhealthy for the marriage. When conflict isn't resolved, nobody wins, especially the children in the family. Everyone in the family feels it when there's unresolved conflict between the husband and wife.

It's not good for children to hear their parents criticize one another privately or publicly. It's equally unhealthy for them to experience one or both parents giving the other parent "the cold shoulder." It's also very stressful for children to witness one parent picking a fight with the other parent because he or she has become defensive. That's another reason why all of these behaviors need to be identified and removed from our lives.

No matter how many times you've failed in the past, I encourage you to communicate your needs to your spouse without accusing or criticizing. Then invite your spouse to communicate his or her needs and be willing to meet those needs without getting into strife. Guard your words as you speak. For example, instead of saying, "You never take me anywhere anymore," you could say something like, "Honey, I really need a date night or just some alone-time with just you and me."

The Level of Your Desire
Will Determine the Level of Your Success

I heard a minister once say that "wanting to" is half the battle. In other words, your ongoing desire to walk in love and improve your relationship with your spouse is a driving force that will eventually bring forth a successful marriage. In the low seasons, you will not sputter and quit. Instead, you'll rev up your engine, set your face like flint to seek the face of God, and put into practice everything you've learned about building a marriage that's "Heaven on earth." You'll understand that marriage is about building a life with another person, not stopping during the construction phase short of finishing what you began together.

In other words, you're going to be a doer of God's Word (James 1:22) even in the hard times. You'll hunger and thirst for righteousness (Matthew 5:6) — for the truth of God's Word, His will, and His divine order in every area of your life. And you will receive! Your life will be filled and satisfied because of your earnest desire to make things better for you, your spouse, your marriage and family, and generations of family to come.

A marriage can overcome great obstacles when two people work together as a team. That's why it's so important to build each other up — not tear each other down — in the low seasons. We must be mindful to afford our spouse the same grace, forgiveness, and mercy that we would show to anyone else. In fact, the people in our home — our immediate family members — should receive the best treatment from us, not the worst.

The Role of Personal Responsibility

This chapter is not intended to condemn you but to help you face the issues that harm individuals and marriages. If we obey the Lord and His Word in getting rid of these things — in throwing out our baggage — we will be "...a vessel unto honour, sanctified, and meet [profitable] for the master's use, and prepared unto every good work" (2 Timothy 2:21 KJV).

But you can't just "wish" it and automatically receive it. Personal responsibility is involved. And making right choices is a part of that. You have to choose to do the right thing even when "right" is not always easy.

So what do we do in the low seasons of marriage? Do we "tuck and run" — or fight our way through on our own until the relationship is in ruins? No, we need to go to God! This is the time we need to become more rooted and grounded in His love than ever before and to allow those roots to go down deeper in our walk with Him.

Then we need to educate ourselves so we'll recognize those seasons and know how to handle them. We need to be people of prayer, depending upon the Holy Spirit to bring to our minds the wisdom we need to please the Lord and to build our marriage instead of destroy it. We must walk in love and control our thoughts, understanding that where our thoughts continually go, our feelings will follow.

If we want a Kingdom marriage that's Heaven on earth, we can't be asleep at the wheel, especially in the low seasons. If we'll rely on God's love as the one constant in every season, we can survive and even thrive in the low times. We can go to the next level of love in our marriage. No matter how far our relationship with our spouse has strayed from the right path, that love will provide light and lead us to a highway of blessing and success in our marriage. Love will take us to the next level.

1

---

1   Tina Turner, "What's Love Got To Do With It?" Capitol Records, Hollywood, CA, 1984.

.

.

12

Barriers to Intimacy — Obstacles That Can and Must Be Overcome

Dr. Maureen Anderson

A happy, successful marriage is centered around intimacy — both physical and emotional — between a husband and wife. So you can be certain that the enemy doesn't want there to be intimacy in your marriage. In fact, he'd love it if you never touched or talked to each other at all!

Most couples are very affectionate and intimate when they're dating, but after they get married, for many of them, there is very little touching or talking anymore. For some reason, that part of the relationship grows cold.

What happens when a couple grows cold toward each other in marriage? For one, they distance themselves from one another. A separation occurs even if the couple remains married. This isn't the will of God for two people who have become "one flesh" in marriage.

Tom and I have ministered to couples that had been married for years, yet were so disconnected that they slept in separate bedrooms! For years they'd lived in quiet contempt or indifference toward one another instead of resolving their issues. All those years, they weren't even trying to change their situation — and some of them had children still living at home! The enemy had free rein in those marriages, because they were full of inner conflict and strife, and everyone had become affected by it.

The behavior of "disconnecting" in marriage is so abnormal that it sends a message of alarm to our brain, which triggers a flow of adrenaline in our body that can put us in a state of anxiety, uneasiness, and even fear. So a husband and wife who lack intimacy in their marriage must identify the reason why they're disconnecting. The need to connect is a basic human need — and in marriage, it's an absolute necessity if the marriage is to thrive.

Getting to the Heart of the Problem
Before the Problem Gets to Your Heart

The following are the primary contributors to a lack of intimacy in marriage — barriers to intimacy that we are responsible to overcome if we desire to have God's best. We will look at each of these in this and in the following chapters.

- Negative experiences and emotions from the past.
- Conflict with your spouse.
- Unforgiveness, bitterness, and resentment.
- Lack of communication with your spouse.
- Sexual sin or dysfunction.

Imagine a marriage void of intimacy that somehow continued year after year. It would be an unhappy marriage lacking in fulfillment. Many such marriages don't make it that long. They fall apart completely after a time because the couples lack the knowledge and understanding they need to get themselves off the path they've been traveling and back on the right track in the marriage. So much time has passed and so much damage has occurred in the relationship that they lose hope.

But with God, all things are possible (Matthew 19:26; Mark 10:27)! Nothing is too hard for God. He designed marriage, and He has a plan to make it what He wants it to be so that you're blessed, your spouse is blessed, your children are blessed, and others around you are blessed as they observe His blessing on your lives.

In this chapter, we're going to look at intimacy-killers in marriage, and we'll also touch on some intimacy-builders that you can begin to incorporate in your marriage today.

Dealing With Negative Emotions and Conflict

For many, their marriage lacks intimacy because of negative emotions from the past and conflict in the marriage that they lack the skills to deal with properly. Because they don't know what to do, many people "bury" their feelings instead of dealing with them head-on.

If you have a tendency to hide your pain, disappointment, frustration, and anger — look out! "Out of sight" might mean "out of mind" for a season, but if you're constantly internalizing your negative emotions, those issues will not go away; they'll simply remain hidden deep within your heart and soul. And those issues will resurface at some point in your marriage. They're going to come up, and they're going to disconnect you from your partner if you don't resolve them so that you can enjoy an emotionally healthy relationship with your spouse.

Wrongdoings of the past and the negative emotions that accompany them must be faced and dealt with, not buried. And the first step — even if it's something that happened long ago — is to go to God.

Sometimes we need to talk to God about a situation simply to get His perspective. Perhaps the person who wounded us didn't even mean to do it. At other times, we need to go to God in prayer to receive supernatural help and healing — the kind that only He can give. And He will give it! But we must take the first step. We must ask Him for help and seek Him through His Word for the answers we need. (In the following chapter, we'll talk more about dealings with emotional issues from the past.)

What Not To Do in the Heat of Battle

When we're going through a negative situation, the wrong thing to do in the heat of battle is to jump into that conflict with both feet! If we confront conflict in the heat of the moment, we will probably yield destructive results. In fact, when conflict is dealt with based just on emotions, deeper conflict is always the result. We might even say or do something that could destroy a relationship. That is completely counterproductive, because the goal in marriage is to build, not to destroy.

As I said, everything in marriage is centered around intimacy between a husband and wife. So resolving conflict and dealing with issues are important. If a couple doesn't know how to resolve their issues — or they fail to resolve conflict properly — intimacy will be hindered in the relationship.

Confront Your Conflict — Value Your Spouse

No marriage is completely free from conflict, because marriage involves the union of two people and the blending — not the dissolving — of two distinct personalities. So the goal is not to avoid conflict at all costs — but, instead, to resolve it when it arises so that it doesn't produce a wedge of isolation in the marriage.

So the first step to resolving conflict — after a "cooling period" if necessary — is to face the conflict instead of avoiding it. Recognize it for what it is and deal with it. Great good can come out of conflict when it's handled properly, or dealt with according to the principles of God's Word.

> *Finally, all of you be of one mind, having compassion for one another; love as brothers, be tenderhearted, be courteous; not returning evil for evil or reviling for reviling, but on the contrary blessing, knowing that you were called to this, that you may inherit a blessing. For "He who would love life and see good days, Let him refrain his tongue from evil, and his lips from speaking deceit. Let him turn away from evil and do good; Let him seek peace and pursue it.* (1 Peter 3:8-11)

Once you decide to deal with conflict in your marriage, the next step is to pray. Then after you've talked to God about the problem, you must also talk to your spouse. Begin your discussion by telling that other person how much you value him or her and the marriage. In doing this, you're building up your spouse while demonstrating in word and deed the value you have for the relationship. This creates instant feelings of security and an environment where there can be a peaceful discussion without anyone becoming fearful, agitated, or defensive.

Check Your Attitude at the Door

When confronting a conflict, after you've stated your positive feelings for your spouse, begin by stating the problem in gentle, non-accusing tones. The Bible says, "A soft answer turns away wrath, but a harsh word stirs up anger" (Proverbs 15:1). Speaking in soft tones is another intimacy-builder. In other words, instead of stating the issue in a heated manner and firing off accusations at your mate, you should be calm and gentle in your approach.

For example, never use "you" statements that are accusatory, such as, "You always do this" or, "You're always that." Instead, you could phrase the problem with these words: "When this happens, it's probably just me, but it makes me feel...," and then talk about your feelings without condemnation or criticism.

In other words, have a humble attitude that takes responsibility for your own feelings. For example, you could say something such as, "Maybe it's just me, but this is how I felt when…." Don't automatically put the blame on your spouse. You might feel as if your spouse is truly to blame for the problem, but you must be gentle in the way you confront the issue nevertheless. In other words, you need to check your attitude at the door!

Also — and this almost goes without saying — never resort to name-calling when you have a disagreement with your spouse! In fact, if you and your spouse are calling each other names, your marriage isn't headed for trouble — trouble has already "arrived at the station," and you need supernatural help and a determined desire to change if you're going to turn that situation around and send it packing!

What's Your Point?

When you're addressing an issue with your spouse, be careful to stay on point at all times. Don't use that time to air a whole string of complaints or to enumerate your spouse's every fault and failure. And remember not to interrupt your spouse when he or she "has the floor." If you need to, ask politely not to be interrupted when it's your turn to speak.

When you approach conflict with an attitude of gentleness and compassion, you'll get further than you ever would by yelling and speaking hateful, destructive words. Ideally, when you confront a problem, you'll hear the words, "I'm sorry. I didn't mean to do that." Or, "What you're saying is valid. I know there are some things I need to get free of, and I'm committing myself to it, beginning now." And if you're confronted, you'll respond with equal wisdom and a spirit of cooperation.

However, it's important that even if you don't get the response you desire, you must always be willing to do the right thing, anyway. In other words, unfairness on the part of your spouse doesn't give you the right to "return evil for evil" (Romans 12:17; 1 Thessalonians 5:15; 1 Peter 3:9).

In review, the following are basic guidelines for successfully confronting and resolving conflict:

- Take time to cool off if necessary. Ask for a time-out so that you're not emotionally driven but Spirit-led. If necessary, walk off the "adrenaline rush" you may be experiencing. Then be certain to name a specific time when you'd like to address the problem — and then keep that "appointment" to the best of your ability.
- Pray before beginning. Ask God for wisdom, and He will give it to you (James 1:5). James 3:17 says, "…the wisdom that is

from above is first pure, then peaceable, gentle, willing to yield, full of mercy and good fruits, without partiality and without hypocrisy."

- Begin your conversation on a positive note by talking about some of your spouse's positive qualities.
- Always use "I" statements; never use "you" statements. Be careful not to accuse, condemn, or criticize.
- Use gentle tones. The tone of your voice is the important aspect of conflict resolution. A soft tone and a gentle spirit or attitude is a must. Don't yell or call your spouse names!
- Don't interrupt the other person.
- Stay on point and talk about one subject at a time.

Forgiveness Bridges the Distance
Between You and Your Mate

Of course, there are situations in which conflict remains in a marriage over time because the couple refuses to deal with it. In a case like that — or even when one spouse desires the forgiveness of the other — it's so important that we learn to forgive and to refuse to keep score of each other's wrongdoings.

> *It [love] is not conceited (arrogant and inflated with pride); it is not rude (unmannerly) and does not act unbecomingly. Love (God's love in us) does not insist on its own rights or its own way, for it is not self-seeking; it is not touchy or fretful or resentful; it takes no account of the evil done to it [it pays no attention to a suffered wrong].* (1 Corinthians 13:5 Amplified)

If we're going to "take no account" of wrongdoings, we're going to have to make the decision not to be a victim in life. When we hold on to wrongs committed against us, we can fall into that mindset of feeling sorry for ourselves. In fact, we can pay so much attention to the suffered wrongs that we become obsessed with them.

When God says that His mercies are new every morning (Lamentations 3:23), why do we want to keep reminding people of things they've done that they've repented about? When we keep bringing up past problems and areas where our partner has failed, we make intimacy impossible. If we refuse to let go the things of the past that may have hurt our feelings or even the relationship, seeds of bitterness will begin to grow within our heart and will eventually defile that relationship completely if the bitterness is not stopped (see Hebrews 12:15).

The Bible also says that God is love (1 John 4:8). Since He's in us, our new nature is to love others, not to be bitter or resentful. So we need to be true to who we are instead of yielding to wrong thoughts that try to keep us focused and obsessed with a wrong that's been committed.

Often we want to wait until we feel like forgiving others before we'll actually forgive. But forgiveness is not a feeling — it's a commitment! Forgiveness is a commitment to refuse to pay back evil for a wrong that's been committed against us. As long as we want that other person to feel the pain we felt when he or she hurt us, we are creating a gap in that relationship that will tear down, not build, intimacy. Paying back "evil for evil" is a relationship-killer!

Another reason we should desire to forgive others freely is, God said He would not forgive us if we fail to forgive others (Mark 11:25). Even if someone who's wrong us fails to repent or ask for our forgiveness, we are not to be overcome by evil but to overcome evil with good (Romans 12:21).

Talk to Your Mate!

Where couples often miss it in marriage is, they grow dissatisfied over unresolved issues — but instead of drawing near to God about it and communicating with each other, they disconnect or grow distant in the relationship. Perhaps they don't know or believe that God can help them. Maybe they don't believe in the other person or in the marriage as they should. But if that's the case, that is the exact time they need to purposely draw near to God and connect with their mate!

There is no substitute in marriage for spending quality time communicating with your spouse. In other words, talk to your mate!

Intimacy happens when the heart opens.

Many couples have no problem talking about superficial topics, such as the weather or the news. They can even engage in conversation about the kids' school or something that happened at work with relative ease. That kind of communication is valuable; it has its place because it involves sharing life together, and this kind of sharing is an intimacy-builder.

However, there is a deeper level of communication that needs to take place between a husband and wife. They must talk openly and often about their love for one another, their value for the relationship (this includes resolving conflict when it arises), and their future goals and dreams. And at times, they need to talk about the past by engaging in occasional walks down memory lane!

Reflecting on the past — on the things that brought you together and on the fun moments you've shared — can be a tremendous bonding tool in your marriage. So often when two people have been married for a while, they forget those early days in the relationship when they were first attracted to each other and fell so deeply in love. The only way to keep those memories alive is to talk about them.

Although it's important for a couple to reflect on pleasant memories from the past, a couple must also talk regularly about their future. One thing that keeps many couples from growing together emotionally and spiritually is a lack of communication concerning their future plans and goals. Every couple needs to have a vision for tomorrow — for the seasons of life ahead. They need to know where they're going in life and then have a well laid-out plan for getting there, depending on God and His Word to guide, direct, and bless them — and to even tweak those plans from time to time if need be!

Vision is created with words, so I encourage you to talk to your spouse about the future. You can keep your vision for a beautiful future alive by communicating on a daily basis with your spouse.

The Power of Communication

Never underestimate the value and the power of communication. Without enough of it, misunderstandings and speculations can give rise to suspicion, distrust, and attitudes of cold indifference. The devil is a liar and a thief, who thrives in the dark places where communication is absent. In fact, he often uses a lack of communication and information to supply misinformation — to "fill the in the blanks" with his lies so that a couple drifts further and further apart and the marriage is eventually destroyed.

But when a husband and wife are talking regularly to each other, the enemy's accusations and schemes can be exposed in the light of their open and honest communication. So it's important to talk to your spouse — and then listen to him or her talk back!

We know that communication is a major issue in marriage, and listening is a vital part of communication. We must seek to understand our spouse and then seek to be understood. So, actually, the first part of communication is listening; the second part is speaking.

Four Techniques To Improve Your Hearing

A wise man will hear and increase in learning... (Proverbs 1:5)

Did you know that one of our deepest needs in relationships is to be heard? We want our heart to be heard and understood. So when we're really listening to our spouse when he or she speaks, we are meeting a deep spiritual and emotional need.

The following are four simple things you can do to improve your listening skills so that you can truly hear what your spouse is saying.

- First, respond to what your spouse has said. Attempt to assimilate or understand the message and then paraphrase what you heard or think you heard to clarify the intended message.
- Second, ask follow-up questions to obtain a fuller picture of the speaker's intended meaning. In other words, if you're not sure you understand, it's okay to ask questions. In fact, unless you're putting the speaker on the defensive by taking a wrong attitude or tone, asking questions shows that you're interested in what's being said.
- Third, communicate your desire to understand your spouse's feelings. A big key to effective communication and a great marriage is understanding the other person's feelings. Doing this can be as simple as saying, "I want to understand your feelings."

When you're attempting to understand your mate's feelings, it's important to listen with your heart as well as with your ears. In other words, you may feel lost in terms of what the other person is really feeling, but you can ask the Holy Spirit to help you because He knows exactly what's going on in that person's heart.

Actually, the speaker may not even understand his or her own feelings. But as you communicate your desire to understand, and you ask guiding questions, the heart can begin to open up because that person will perceive that the environment is safe for communicating. When a person feels safe and loved, he or she will be more willing to open up and share from the heart. Intimacy happens when the heart opens.

Fourth, when listening to a speaker, maintain good eye contact and body language. It's amazing the level of comfort and care that eye contact can provide in a conversation. When you're looking the speaker directly in the eyes, it communicates that you care about the person and that you're interested in what he or she has to say. It says that you're stopping everything and putting all of your focus on that person. On the other hand, if your eyes are darting around the room or you're looking in another direction while the person is talking, it communicates that you don't really care about the speaker's feelings or what he or she has to say.

Body language says a lot about how well you're listening to someone who's sharing his or her thoughts and feelings with you. When your spouse is speaking to you, if you'll lean slightly forward in his or her direction, it communicates interest and a certain level of respect.

It's also a good idea to nod occasionally as the other person speaks, because nodding communicates affirmation — you're affirming not only what's being said, but also the person who's doing the speaking! Without words, you're communicating to him or her, You're valuable. You're important. And what you have to say is important.

The last big key to effective listening is to ask how you can best help the speaker. In other words, don't just automatically volunteer counsel or advice. Perhaps that other person just wants you to listen, not try to solve a problem. So if you immediately start in on the speaker about what he or she should do, it could push that person further away.

It's okay to politely ask, "Would you like me to try to provide some solutions to this problem?" Most of the time, the speaker just wants someone to listen and understand his or her feelings.

Steps to Greater Intimacy

Whether or not you and your spouse have experienced problems with intimacy or "staying connected" in your marriage, there are things you must do consistently as a couple if you desire to maintain intimacy in your marriage.

'The Family That Prays Together...'

First, you and your spouse must commit to praying together on a regular basis. We've heard the saying, "The family that prays together stays together." Many have thought that was just a cute saying, but there's more truth to it than they've perhaps realized.

I'm not saying that all of your praying must be done with your spouse. Certainly, every believer must have his or her own time of prayer and fellowship with the Father. Actually, the Bible commands us to "pray always" — with all kinds, or types, of prayer (see Ephesians 6:18). So we're never to be out of fellowship with God; we're to be in constant communion with Him and ready to connect in prayer at a moment's notice for ourselves or for others.

However, besides our own prayer time, we need to create a special time to pray together just with our spouse. We can pray together about matters that concern our family, for wisdom and direction for our future, for each other, or for others.

Every morning, Tom and I pray, make confessions from the Word, and then pray for a time in the Spirit (see Acts 2:4; First Corinthians 14:14-15; Jude 20). In doing this, not only are we building ourselves up and setting the tone for our day and our future, we're also bonding in our marriage. And Tom doesn't just pray with me — he also prays for me.

In His relationship with the Church, Jesus sets the example for husbands and wives. Jesus is our Intercessor. Hebrews 7:25 says that He ever lives to make intercession for His Bride, the Church. Similarly, a husband must cover his wife in prayer. He is in a tremendous position of authority to pray protection and blessing over her and to pray for the fulfillment of her destiny. It doesn't have to be a long prayer; he simply needs to make sure the devil knows whose wife she is and that she's covered with the blood of Jesus!

I'm not saying that a wife has no responsibility to pray for herself or for her husband and family, because she is responsible to do her own praying. But just as Christ loves the Church, the husband must also love his wife and lay down his life, or give of himself, for her (see Ephesians 5:25). That includes laying down his life for her in prayer.

Ways To Draw Closer to Your Spouse

Besides spending time praying with your spouse, it's important that you bond with your mate by making time alone together a priority. Remember we've seen that love gives. So you sow and minister love to your spouse when you give to him or her, and that includes giving that person your time. Whether the two of you are enjoying an activity together or talking about future dreams and goals, spending quality time together creates an emotional bond and contributes to greater intimacy in the marriage.

Another way to bond and create intimacy with your spouse is to show him or her affection. In other words, hold hands with your spouse every chance you get. Hug your spouse often. Touch is very crucial in a marriage. Your mate needs to be touched by you every day! (We'll talk more about affection in a later chapter, which deals with sex in marriage.)

Other ways to develop intimacy in your marriage include:
- Flirt with each other often.
- Show appreciation, even for the little things.
- Express your love for each other several times per day. This can include verbal and non-verbal communication. For example, you can tell your spouse you love him or her — you can also write your spouse a note expressing your feelings of love and admiration.
- Laugh together. A cheerful heart is like medicine (Proverbs 17:22).
- Play together. Plan activities that you can enjoy together.
- Encourage one another regularly and support each other's goals.

A happy marriage in which both parties are enriched and fulfilled doesn't happen by chance. Intimacy is fostered and nurtured in a happy marriage — both physical and emotional intimacy. And it is up to each couple to keep the fires of intimacy burning brightly and to deal with those issues that threaten closeness in the marriage.

As I said, the need to connect is a basic human need — and in marriage, it's an absolute necessity. As a husband and wife, you owe it to yourselves and to God to root out every obstacle that would distance you and your spouse and prevent intimacy in your marriage.

13

Is Your Marriage Overweight? How To Rid Your Relationship of Emotional Baggage

Drs. Tom and Maureen Anderson

Almost everyone enters marriage with some kind of "baggage" — issues resulting from negative experiences or associations from the past. But when you're married, your issues become your spouse's issues and vice versa. So it's the responsibility of you both to help each other get rid of the baggage so that it doesn't harm the marriage.

In other words, it's not important who has the baggage! You both must decide that whatever it takes — fasting, praying, and seeking the Lord together — you're not going to let emotional baggage remain in your marriage.

In a marriage, each spouse is responsible to help the other work through behaviors that don't line up with the Word of God. It's your responsibility to pray for each other and not to criticize that other person as he or she owns up to bad attitudes or behavior.

Facing the Facts

Many people are in denial about certain characteristics in their life that cause great stress on their relationships. For some reason, they're not willing to face the facts and own up to their failures and mistakes. They haven't realized the great benefits that await them on the other side of doing away with the baggage and the behavior.

It won't profit us if we resist God's dealings and refuse to acknowledge that we have issues or problems that we need to work on in our marriage. The Bible says that God resists the proud but gives grace to the humble (see James 4:6; First Peter 5:5). If we refuse to deal with issues in our life that keep coming up, we're simply going to have to keep going "around that same mountain," so to speak, until we finally get to the root of the problem. The out of sight, out of mind solution doesn't work! In fact, we could say concerning these issues: "Deal now or pay later."

We have observed that people who choose divorce over dealing with emotional baggage from the past often find themselves going around the same mountain again and again in their new marriages. They never deal with certain issues, so those issues just keep coming up. The names change, but the problems largely remain the same. So it's important to deal with the issues that prevent you and your spouse from enjoying the physical and emotional intimacy that God intends for your lives.

MAUREEN:

'Naked and Not Ashamed'

One reason why people don't face their issues from the past is, they don't feel unconditionally loved and accepted. Therefore, they're unwilling to open up and make themselves vulnerable to another person. The concept of working through things together — as "one flesh" and as a team — is foreign to their thinking.

> *And they were both naked, the man and his wife, and were not ashamed.* (Genesis 2:25)

When God created Adam and Eve, it says they were "naked and not ashamed." This verse is talking about their physical nakedness, but in marriage, we must also be able to reveal or make bare our feelings to one another without feeling afraid or embarrassed.

Tom and I always felt comfortable and safe making ourselves vulnerable to one another. Early in our marriage, I would ask Tom from time to time, "Do you think I have a problem in such-and-such area?" And he'd often say, "Yes, Honey, you do"! But he didn't abandon me in the midst of my problems, leaving me to figure out how to fix them on my own. He never took the attitude, Good luck with that. Instead, he'd say, "Let's fast and pray and get to the root of this so we can deal with it. I will help you get through this."

With Tom standing with me as he did, I'd always get free from whatever it was that had me troubled or bound. Well, every level of freedom I obtained made our marriage better. So as Tom and I committed to stand together and work through each other's problems together, our marriage kept improving because we both kept getting free from the baggage of the past. Freer people make better marriages!

When two people enter marriage, they each bring with them issues from their upbringing — past associations and experiences, good or

---
Freer people make better marriages!

---

bad. And we were no exception. There were times early in our marriage when we experienced some real low points. We were frustrated and had no idea what to do. But we didn't abandon the marriage. Because we both were committed to the marriage, Tom would say, "Let's get to the bottom of this. Let's fast and pray for a couple of days and find out what God is saying."

That sounds simple, but that's truthfully how we dealt with our issues. We never buried issues; we faced them and dealt with them head-on. We did it together, and we worked them out by the help of the Holy Spirit.

A Real Identity Crisis

Some Christians won't admit they have issues because they're too embarrassed or ashamed to face them. They identify more closely with the issue than with their identity as a new creation in Christ. In other words, they've allowed their baggage to define who they are — and the way they deal with that is to "bury" it and refuse to acknowledge it.

> *Therefore, if anyone is in Christ, he is a new creation; old things have passed away; behold, all things have become new.*
> (2 Corinthians 5:17)

If you're a Christian, you are a new creature in Christ. Your spirit has been reborn; it is completely new. But in your mind and emotions, all things aren't new. That's why Romans 12:2 tells us to renew our mind with the Word of God. The power of the Gospel can change and shape our thinking until we produce the right kind of emotions.

It's also important to understand that your baggage is not you! It's the stuff that in you — in your soul. For example, you might have some garbage in your house, but the garbage isn't the house — the garbage is simply inside the house.

How can you remove garbage from your home — or from your life — if you're not aware that it's present? To be successful in life, especially if you're married, you need to have some self-awareness. You need to be able to step outside of yourself, so to speak, and say, "Okay, this behavior is not godly. I've seen it in my mother, my brother, and my grandfather — and now I'm doing the same behavior. It's time to stop this. It's time to get the garbage out."

You can face your issues and identify them without identifying with them. You have to acknowledge the baggage before you can get rid of it. If you fail to acknowledge and deal with issues from the past, those things are going to start stinking — just as garbage will begin to stink if you leave it inside long enough! And when "garbage" is allowed to remain in a couple's life long enough — when the stench of their issues becomes almost unbearable — one or both parties is usually ready to throw in the towel and quit.

Your 'Baggage' Can Weaken
Your Gifts and Hinder Your Success

We saw that whatever "baggage" your spouse may be carrying from past experiences is actually your baggage too. In a marriage, the two become one. That means that your victories are your spouse's victories — and vice versa; your spouse's victories are your victories. So we should want our mate to be successful and happy in life, and we should work to build up that other person, not tear him or her down!

What happens when a couple lacks this understanding and fails to work together as a team to rid the marriage of issues that cling to the relationship and weigh it down? One or both parties in that marriage has gifts and strengths that will never get developed.

To illustrate this point, let's suppose a man and woman enter their marriage with the following issues:

THE HUSBAND

- His mother was bossy and controlling. She manipulated the entire family and never allowed him to step up and become the man that he should be.
- He feels betrayed and rejected by his mother and as a young man makes an inward vow never to let a woman boss him around again.

THE WIFE

- She came from a home filled with physical and emotional abuse.
- She became very unsure of herself and her place in the world.
- She reverts to emotional passivity in order to keep the peace and minimize her pain.

These two people with two very different backgrounds are now married. Now they're supposed to join forces and combine their strengths. He's at a loss as to how to initiate vision for his new family or provide the driving force that propels them forward in life. And she doesn't even know she has any strengths! They're married and in the same boat, all right. But this couple isn't going anywhere on the sea of life. They're just sitting in their boat in a state of inertia — paralyzed by their issues from the past.

But now suppose the wife begins dealing with her issues and is renewing her mind with the Word of God. She begins to realize some of her gifts and strengths. And instead of being passive, she attempts to utilize these gifts in the marriage. But then suppose that the husband hasn't overcome his sensitivity to his overbearing mother. The minute his wife tries to contribute something in that marriage, he's trying to throw her overboard! He wants her out of his boat!

Why? She's only making suggestions that she feels will benefit them both, but he sees her actions through the clouded lenses of his past. He feels his wife is being controlling and manipulative and that it's "Mom" all over again. He doesn't exactly want to take the helm in the marriage, and when he feels pressured in the least way, he's ready to cry, "Mutiny!" or abandon ship himself!

When two people can't seem to combine their strengths as one, they need to ask themselves why and then deal with that situation at its root. If you don't understand the behavior, ask the Lord. He understands it perfectly, and the Holy Spirit will reveal the answer to you.

Some married couples live their whole lives never really experiencing the best life possible because they're not fully utilizing their strengths. Things are standing in their way, and they've allowed those things to continue for years. That is a sad situation.

On the other hand, there's nothing more promising or exciting than to see a husband and wife cheering each other on. Together in the same boat, they're working together to navigate the sea of life successfully. Yet they want each other, individually, to be the best he or she can be.

Tom:

Relationship Dynamics and Dysfunctions

Just as there are dysfunctional relationships in marriage, there are also dysfunctional relationships in churches — between a pastor and his congregation. Just as dysfunctional marriages don't grow, dysfunctional churches don't grow, either. They generally stop growing at about eighty to a hundred people or so. That's about as big as they can grow, and there are usually three reasons for this, which I will share with you.

There is a connection in the dysfunctional attitudes that exist in marriages and those that can be found in some churches. Just as a dysfunctional church won't grow, dysfunctional attitudes — emotional baggage — that are allowed to remain in a marriage will stifle the growth of that marriage.

- Church scenario number one: The pastor is a victim. He or she has an entire congregation of enablers or "rescuers" that attend that church to take care of the pastor. The pastor always seems to need help, so they're always ministering to the pastor, bailing him out of situation after situation. In return, these enablers are deriving their sense of value and worth from helping him. It's a very unhealthy relationship that produces a stagnant, sickly church.

- Church scenario number two: The pastor is an enabler. In constantly helping his congregation, he has all kinds of victims — and he is "saving" them all! He has become almost like Jesus to his congregation. They are trained to look to the pastor instead of to the Lord. Instead of cultivating a living relationship with Jesus, the people look to the pastor as the solver of problems. He is usually available for counseling at all hours of the day, every day of the week. His church never grows any larger than what he and his wife can take care of.

"Oh, pastor, you're the only one who can help me!" This is the mantra of the enabling pastor's sheep. They eat up all of his time so that he never prays, runs his race, or accomplishes anything in terms of his calling. And the people are hindered in their own race.

- How this relates in marriage: One spouse is constantly needy and "under-acts" in the relationship while the other party continually "over-acts," or over-compensates, to make up for the lack of participation from the needy spouse. The enabling party is not completely altruistic or self-sacrificing: By continually meeting their needy spouse's requirements and demands, the enabling spouse derives feelings of worth from his or her repeated "rescuing" of the other person.

Unless this cycle is broken, these "over-actions" will become exhausting and — in the end — unfruitful. Besides encouraging unhealthy dependence on another and crippling the needy person emotionally and spiritually, the enabler is hindered in his or her own personal growth. This kind of marriage might continue to exist, but it will never thrive unless changes are made by both people in the marriage.

- Church scenario number three: The pastor is a persecutor or abuser. He has a church full of victims, and he "beats them up" every time they go to church. Every Sunday, he's calling them (in so many words), "You low-life, mud-crawling worms. Get your lives straight, you bunch of sinners!" And people respond to that, repenting, getting saved, and crying, bawling, and squalling. They get "saved" every week, and then he beats them up again. Yet they keep coming back for more. It's a very abusive, dysfunctional relationship that halts church growth.

- How this relates in marriage: One spouse continually abuses the other spouse, attempting to control that other person by beating him or her up physically and/or emotionally. Because the abuser isn't dealing with his or her insecurities and fears, the abuser can only be assuaged by inflicting damage on the spouse in order to "break" that person's spirit. Once the victim is broken, the person doubts his or her self-worth and becomes the compliant party who yields to the persecutor's manipulative demands. A marriage in which one or both spouses is devalued dishonors God and will not flourish. Until both parties learn to value what God values — people — the marriage will remain sick and weak.

**Responsibility and Accountability in Marriage —
'And the Two Grownups Shall Become One Flesh'!**

*'And the two shall become one flesh'; so then they are no
longer two, but one flesh.* (Mark 10:8)

I showed you examples of dysfunctional relationships in the church and
in marriage. Now let me show you "functional." In a healthy relationship,
there are times when one party will under-perform while the other party over-
performs, such as in the case of a sickness, injury, stringent work deadlines
or requirements, and so forth. So a helper mentality can be prominent for a
season, as it should be, because marriage requires teamwork.

Also, a helper mentality can be prominent simply due to the personalities involved in the marriage. One spouse simply enjoys serving more than
the other spouse. However, in a healthy marriage, there is a scope and limit
to the help each party provides. A healthy helper correctly believes, I am
accountable for me. You are accountable for you. You make me accountable, and I make you accountable. We speak truth in love. I am responsible
TO you; I am not responsible FOR you.

Healthy people enjoy that kind of relationship. Unhealthy people usually seek out dysfunctional, unhealthy relationships. For example, people
sometimes leave our church — a very large, thriving church — for no other
reason than they want to attend a small church that remains small. What
many of them are saying is, "I need to be beat up regularly" or, "I need to
have a close relationship with my pastor so I can help him."

Have you ever wondered why some people are so "on again-off
again" concerning their church membership or their personal relationships?
Emotionally and spiritually unhealthy people cannot maintain healthy
relationships — whether at church, on the job, or at home. They try for a
while, but soon they either bail out of or bring some kind of destruction to
the relationship. They often sabotage their own opportunities for change
and happiness — as well as the happiness and well-being of others.

A Surefire Solution for an Overweight Marriage —
Let the Baggage Go!

Just as there is a dynamic that exists between every pastor and his or
her congregation, there is a dynamic that exists between every husband
and wife. And it needs to be a healthy dynamic or the marriage itself will
not be healthy.

With all the extra weight emotional baggage brings to a marriage, who wouldn't want to get free of the things that are a burden to the marriage, not a blessing? I encourage you, no matter how shocked, dismayed, or discouraged you are at the baggage that's in your life, don't deny it but be willing to let go of those things that hinder you as an individual and that hinder your marriage.

What are your issues? It may be painful to acknowledge, but it's important to know specifically what it is you're dealing with. Do you have abandonment or rejection issues? You may have a deep-seated fear of loss that has paralyzed you and kept you "stuck" in one place for years. Perhaps that fear has kept you as a husband from affirming or complimenting your wife, because you're afraid she's going to leave you.

Did you know that cases of physical and emotional abuse can stem from this kind of fear? The person isn't trusting God, so he or she is yielding to that fear and trying to control and beat the other party into submission — all of this just so the abuser can have a temporary moment of "peace" without having to permanently deal with the very painful issue at hand.

Hurting people hurt others. And hurting people are not joyful, peaceful, fulfilled individuals. So why would they avoid being delivered and healed from what's causing them so much continued pain and fear? We need to know and understand the driving force behind the things we do to tear down our marriages. Then we can stop those forces dead in their tracks and begin to build the kind of life and marriage that brings us true happiness and that pleases the Father God.

True Romance: A Marriage Beyond the Dream

14

When Sex Has Been Abused —
Righting the Wrongs of the Past

Drs. Tom and Maureen Anderson

We've been looking at some of the barriers between husbands and wives that make physical and emotional intimacy impossible: negative emotions, or "baggage," from the past; conflict; unforgiveness; and lack of communication. However, we couldn't do justice to this subject without looking at a huge barrier to marital intimacy, and that is sexual dysfunction.

Sexual dysfunction in a marriage can range from sexual sin and abuse to issues with sexual health and even sheer ignorance about sex and what it means to your partner! In this chapter and the following chapter, we're going to discuss these topics in some detail, but we encourage you to continually educate yourself regarding the important subject of sex, a subject that's been overlooked by the Church at large for too long.

God created the institution of marriage, and that means that God created sex! Ignorance concerning sex is not bliss and it won't bless your marriage — but we don't have to be ignorant. God has given us the means to grow in every area of married life, including the area of physical intimacy with our spouse.

Your Body Is the Lord's

God intended that sex be enjoyed in the context of marriage. However, outside of the marriage union, sex is considered to be immoral. This isn't just our opinion. This is what the Lord says; Scripture bears this out.

"Food for the stomach and the stomach for food" — but God will destroy them both. The body is not meant for sexual immorality, but for the Lord, and the Lord for the body.
(1 Corinthians 6:13 NIV)

Please read carefully the rest of this passage in First Corinthians 6.

Do you not know that your bodies are members of Christ himself? Shall I then take the members of Christ and unite them with a prostitute? Never! Do you not know that he who unites himself with a prostitute is one with her in body? For it is said, "The two will become one flesh." But he who unites himself with the Lord is one with him in spirit. Flee from sexual immorality. All other sins a man commits are outside his body, but he who sins sexually sins against his own body. Do you not know that your body is a temple of the Holy Spirit, who is in you, whom you have received from God? You are not your own; you were bought at a price. Therefore honour God with your body.
(1 Corinthians 6:15-20 NIV)

According to the Word of God, sexual immorality is the only sin committed in the body. All other sins are committed outside of the body. And the one who participates in sexual immorality is sinning against his own body, which is God's (vv. 19-20).

We are the temple of the Holy Ghost. We are not our own, but we've been bought, spirit, soul, and body, with the precious blood of Jesus. When we are born again, we become His — yet we must yield ourselves to Him instead of doing with our body what it desires or dictates.

It is possible to avoid sexual immorality. God wouldn't command us concerning this very thing if it were not possible for us to obey Him. He plainly tells us, "Flee sexual immorality" (v. 18). In other words, if that's what it takes, we must flee or run from it!

That denotes a very serious, purposeful, determined action on our part! We're not supposed to hang around the wrong people or get ourselves into precarious situations with those of the opposite sex just to see how close to the creek we can get without falling in!

We're not saying this to criticize or condemn anyone who has been involved in a sexual relationship outside of marriage. Through faith in the same precious blood of Christ that saved you, you can be free from the sin and guilt of your past. And you don't have to let the things of the past come between you and your spouse today.

MAUREEN:

Forgetting and Forsaking Your Past

There are intimacy issues in so many marriages today because of sexual sin and baggage from the past that have never been dealt with. Some people were sexually abused as children and young people. Now they struggle with godly intimacy in marriage as a result.

There are also various kinds of sexual sin that have seemingly been "passed down" from generation to generation. For example, in some families, adultery is a widespread problem. In other families, pornography is rampant.

But God wants you to be free from the sins and addictions of your forefathers. He not only wants you to be forgiven, He wants you to forget and to forsake your past. Too many hold on to the things of the past instead of "closing the book"

Too many hold on to the things of the past instead of "closing the book" on what happened yesterday.

on what happened yesterday. You may be tempted in certain areas, but it's time to start a new book based on your new life in Christ! You have the power to withstand every single temptation through the blood of Jesus, the Word of God, and prayer.

Until people are free from the effects of past sins and wrongdoing — even those trespasses committed against them — true intimacy with their spouse will not be possible.

Pray and Don't Give Up!

Then Jesus told his disciples a parable to show them that they should always pray and not give up. (Luke 18:1 NIV)

I encourage you to read this passage in Luke 18 about the widow's petition to the unjust judge. Many people use this parable as an analogy, comparing God to the unjust judge. But God is not unjust, and that's not the lesson Jesus is teaching here. He's talking about the "importunity" of faith — the persistence of faith — or, in other words, faith that won't give up!

God has called you to be one with your spouse — to enjoy physical and emotional intimacy with your mate. So if you're struggling in this area, you can go to God and expect answers. If it's a sin from the past that you're dealing with, He forgives and washes away the past, so no matter what has happened or what you've been through, today can be a new day for you! God by His grace can restore you to a condition that's even better than before or better than you could ever imagine. There's power in the blood of Jesus — more than enough power to wash every sin, and every memory associated with sin, away from your life!

In talking about physical intimacy, or sex, in marriage, we're not talking about something that's dirty or perverted. God created sex, but the enemy, Satan, attempts to pervert everything God has created, including sex. Sex has been perverted in the world, where many people — sadly, even many from the Church — have exchanged the beauty of sex and intimacy in marriage for something twisted, filthy, and destructive.

Keep Pornography in Its Place — Out of Your Life and Your Marriage!

Pornography is a perversion of the sexual relationship God gave to a man and a woman in marriage. And pornography in marriage in an intimacy-killer; it's a thief of the physical and emotional intimacy that God desires between a husband and wife. If you have a problem with pornography, you must get free of that. When you engage in pornography, you're tainting the gift of sex that God has given you for marriage. You must face this bondage squarely and get free of it through prayer and fasting and, if necessary, through professional counseling.

Any kind of sexual act outside of engaging in sex with your spouse is wrong behavior. Being interested in someone other than your spouse is wrong and needs to be dealt with. I'm not saying this to condemn you if this is a problem in your life. I'm saying it because with God, there is an answer — if you truly desire God's highest and best.

Whether it be abuse, pornography, or some other kind of dysfunction, if you feel there are situations in your marriage that prevent intimacy and the sense that the two of you are truly one, you need to face those things and refuse to allow them to continue. Encourage your spouse that you're a team and that you'd like to fast and pray together about the situation. Tell him or her, "Let's get to the bottom of this. Let's get free from whatever hinders us from being what God has called us to be in marriage."

What Is a 'Generational Curse'?

Sometimes sexual sin, such as pornography, is a result of a generational issue coming down the family line from generation to generation. In other words, it's a stronghold a person struggles with — seemingly more than anything else he or she has to deal with in life.

Reclaiming God's Property

As a Christian, you belong to God. Your spirit and your body are His (1 Corinthians 6:20). And, certainly, a Christian has the power of choice to say no to these spirits that come to tempt, harass, and try to lay claim to God's property. But many don't fully realize or understand that fact, and they struggle needlessly for years when, instead, they should be "cutting off the giant's head" (see First Samuel 17:51). In other words, they can get free from that "curse" through the yoke-destroying, delivering power of God!

Please understand me. God does not curse people. In fact, He has redeemed us from the curse of the Law (Galatians 3:13). You can't curse what God has blessed! But the enemy will try to tempt people to give place to things that will stop the blessings of God and hinder or completely cut off what God wants to do in their life. So, you see, if a person yields to the temptation, he or she can open the door to a curse.

Generational sins cannot force themselves on you! They keep getting passed down from one generation to the next because of people's wrong choices. The enemy wants to perpetuate sin and iniquity, but he can be stopped when someone simply says, "Enough!" In other words, someone must take a strong stand on the Word of God and on the redemption that is his or hers in Christ. That person can give place to the Holy Spirit and the blood of Jesus Christ and break the power of that stronghold, preventing it from traveling to future generations.

If you've been plagued with sins and things in your life that you recognize as being a pattern in your family's history, you can break free of that! Whether it's pornography, adultery, divorce, or even poverty or disease, Jesus has paid the price for your freedom, and He says you're free (see John 8:36: Romans 6:14; Galatians 3:13: Galatians 5:1; Hebrews 2:14; 1 John 3:8)!

So what will you say about it? I encourage you to pray the following prayer from your heart.

> *Father God, there have been 'generational curses' in my family in the area of sexual sin — of temptations that were yielded to from generation to generation. I call it sin, Lord, and I renounce it where my life and my children's lives are concerned. I love my forefathers, but I hate their sin. I love what You love, and I hate what You hate. I want the fear of the Lord in my life — that attitude of reverence toward you that guards us from evil and gives us life [Proverbs 14:27; 19:23; 22:4].*

So right now, Lord, where there's been pornography, adultery, fornication, or anything that's sexually impure, I want that out of my life. Forgive me for yielding to those temptations. I haven't taken my place of authority as I should have. I haven't hated that sin as I should have. But I hate it, Lord, and I see it as nailed to the Cross because Jesus paid the price for my complete freedom.

I let go of that baggage by faith. I cut off all ungodly ties and relationships. I've been washed in the blood of Jesus, and You said that if I confessed my sin, You're faithful and just to forgive me and cleanse me from all unrighteousness [1 John 1:9]. I receive my forgiveness and cleansing. I belong to Christ; my body is Yours, so I consecrate my body to You now as an act of my will. I am not an instrument of sin or a slave to sin, but I am an instrument of righteousness [Romans 6]. I am one with You, and I am one with my spouse. Thank You, Lord, for setting me free. In Jesus' Name, amen.

Tom:

There's a connection that takes place spirit, soul, and body in the act of sex. That's why sex outside of marriage is so dangerous — it does damage to people's lives. This needs to be taken very seriously. There are many reasons why people fall into this sin of adultery; however, the sin against God and against the marriage partner that occurs in adultery finds its roots in issues pertaining to the heart. Certainly, Satan is the tempter, but the best defense against his tactics is a firm decision of the heart to obey the wisdom of God's Word and to commit oneself wholeheartedly to pleasing Him in marriage and in life.

You Are Not Your Own — You Really Do Belong to God and to Each Other

The husband should fulfil his marital duty to his wife, and likewise the wife to her husband. The wife's body does not belong to her alone but also to her husband. In the same way, the husband's body does not belong to him alone but also to his wife. Do not deprive each other except by mutual consent and for a time, so that you may devote yourselves to prayer. Then come together again so that Satan will not tempt you because of your lack of self-control. (1 Corinthians 7:3-5 NIV)

First Corinthians 7:5 says, "Do not deprive each other except by mutual consent and for a time, so that you may devote yourselves to prayer. Then come together again so that Satan will not tempt you because of your lack of self-control." As I said, Satan is the tempter, but we can avert his plans and schemes simply by knowing what the Word says, walking in its wisdom, and obeying God at every turn in the road. So when we read First Corinthians 7:5, we're going to have to obey that. If we're not obeying that verse, we're putting our marriage in harm's way.

Simply put, if you're married, you belong to your partner in marriage. You have a duty, then, to understand sexuality in marriage and to do your part to protect your sex life from outside influences that will try to undermine that relationship.

Sexuality and Health

In this chapter, we're talking about dysfunction in the marriage as it pertains to sex and intimacy, and Maureen has covered several spiritual aspects of overcoming dysfunction due to abuse and mistakes of the past.

I'm going to cover some natural aspects of dysfunction that have been overlooked, largely because people have not known where to look! In other words, they know there's a problem, but they don't have a clue where to begin looking for answers. The Lord gives wisdom — we know that's true. Sometimes His wisdom dictates that we fast and pray and root out the "curses" and sins that have plagued generation after generation in our family line. At other times, His wisdom reveals other hidden causes for our problems, and some of these causes are very practical in nature.

What is dysfunction? Briefly and simply, it's the failure to function normally! And, of course, for the believer, "normal" is nothing other than the standard of God's Word and His will. So when a husband and wife aren't physically and emotionally intimate, we know that some dysfunction is occurring in that marriage, and that couple needs to find out why.

Sex and Hormones

I believe that so many problems in marriages, including emotional problems, are directly associated with hormone levels in the individual — and I'm talking about women and men. The good news is, it's a problem that can be easily corrected. With the use of natural hormones, you can bring every hormone level into balance and see drastic changes in your physical health, your outlook on life, and your family relationships.

I can't even begin to count how many people we've counseled who had tried everything and couldn't seem to resolve longstanding emotional issues, both personally and in their marriage. Once they were tested and realized how imbalanced their hormones were, they were able to immediately correct the problem. Their lives completely turned around for the better!

Help for Those Who Struggle

The body is absolutely amazingly put together by God. And who better than our Creator to give us the wisdom we need to function at our very highest and best? I've said it before, but it bears repeating: If you're having problems you can't seem to resolve, check your hormone levels before you do anything else (after you've read this book, of course). You could save yourself months and even years of frustration and agony if you'll follow this simple nugget of wisdom and counsel.

Remember we read First Corinthians 7:5, which says, "Do not deprive each other except by mutual consent and for a time, so that you may devote yourselves to prayer. Then come together again so that Satan will not tempt you because of your lack of self-control."

Let's suppose, for example, that a husband is experiencing a rise in his testosterone levels, but his wife is experiencing a deficiency in her levels of progesterone and other hormones that affect her libido — and she rejects her husband's sexual advances. That husband is placed in a vulnerable position that could potentially undermine and destroy his marriage. His hormones are at unusually high levels, and he's now dealing with issues of self-control. If a seductress — a wayward woman (Proverbs 6:20-35; 7:1-5) — crosses his path to tempt him, he could give in to the temptation to have sex with another woman.

Now, I am by no means suggesting that a husband have an affair — nor would I ever justify or condone that kind of behavior. "Two wrongs don't make a right," as the saying goes. We each must answer to God for our own obedience or disobedience to His Word.

Even if you find yourself in a position of agonizing temptation, you have the responsibility to say, "No, I don't mess around; I'm not going to do that." But you also have the responsibility to talk to your spouse about your sexual needs. Marriage — including the physical or sexual aspect of marriage — requires communication in order to work. In other words, sexual problems are not issues that one party in the marriage should simply resolve on his or her own.

When you're in the throes of temptation, that's not the time to withdraw and go silent. That's where the enemy thrives — when one partner in a marriage isolates himself or herself from the other person. You need to set a standard of openness in your marriage and refuse to allow the enemy to come between you and your spouse on any level.

However, the Word of God warns you that if you deny your spouse sexual intimacy, you're giving the devil a foothold in your marriage. We have counseled couples that had not been sexually intimate in years. It was by God's grace that the marriages survived to the point of our being able to help them. The first thing we always endeavor to do is to get to the root of the problem. For example, is it just that sex is not a very high priority in the marriage? Are hormone levels low or off-balance? Is some other sickness present? Are there negative emotions, such as unforgiveness, that one or both people in the marriage have failed to deal with? Is there a problem with pornography? Are both parties faithful to their partner in the marriage?

There are any number of reasons why couples struggle in this area. But the issue must be dealt with, because sexual intimacy is crucial to the vitality and success of a marriage.

The Road to Restoration and Recovery

Maureen and I have seen so many turnarounds in marriages by exposing the hidden problem of hormone deficiencies and imbalances in people's lives. I am convinced that hormones are at the root of many of the problems couples face in marriage. In one of our recent marriage seminars, we provided a means for those in attendance to have their hormone levels checked, and many of them tested low on certain hormones that affect their sex-drive. Once the problem was discovered, the couples could work on repairing the problem.

The study of hormones has been somewhat of a mystery for years. But now researchers are discovering that hormones are life-givers to the body, having the capability to keep disease at bay when those hormones are in the proper balance. Usually, hormone levels drop significantly when a person reaches his or her mid-forties. I don't think it's a coincidence that people usually begin dealing with greater occurrences of disease at that stage of life.

Many Christians are sick due to a lack of knowledge and education about how to take care of their body. However, I don't believe any amount of education or treatment should take the place of a genuine heart faith in God's Word. Yet some have gotten out of balance in the area of healing, because they've chosen to ignore the care of their body. They've violated certain natural laws under the guise of "just walking by faith."

Two Schools of Thought

There are two schools of thought concerning correcting the problem of hormonal imbalances. One is the belief that these imbalances should be controlled by pharmaceuticals. The other is the belief espoused by naturalists, who believe that the natural forms of these depleted hormones can remedy the problem by helping the body regain its own ability to correct these imbalances.

Medical doctors are trained to prescribe pharmaceuticals, and very few of those doctors embrace the "natural" view of balancing hormones. I'm not doling out medical advice, but I do know that there are published warnings regarding most hormone replacement medications. Even labels warn that these drugs can cause certain cancers, such as breast or cervical cancer, as well as heart attack and stroke.

I personally take a more natural view and believe that the bioidentical hormones are very powerful and effective with little or no side effects. I also believe that maintaining the proper balance of hormones can prevent virtually all serious illnesses. God put those hormones in our body and balanced them perfectly. If we keep them balanced through diet, exercise, and, if necessary, bioidentical hormone replacement therapy, our body has everything it needs to fight disease, maintain the proper weight, and slow down the aging process.

A good doctor can test you and discover if you're suffering from a hormone imbalance severe enough to affect your health and lifestyle. We know of people in their twenties and thirties who were tested and found that they were seriously imbalanced and in need of bioidentical HRT. Had they not received this type of intervention, I have no doubt that many of these people were destined for disease early in life.

In many of the cases involving these young people, they had lost all sexual desire prior to being diagnosed and treated. They were simply co-existing with their spouse, hoping that maybe what they were experiencing was normal.

But it isn't normal to lose interest in sex with your spouse! A diminished libido causes so many problems in marriage, including emotional hurts and problems with self-worth — because the sexually healthy spouse usually has to battle thoughts, such as, Is it me?

Couples in this predicament need to talk to each other and be very open and honest in their communication. But they also need to seek medical advice, and the first step I recommend is hormone testing. Addressing a physiological problem can be as simple as taking replacement hormones — and it can make all the difference in your relationship with your spouse.

Exposing the Lies and the Shame
of the 'Mid-Life Crisis'

Women often lose interest in sex during menopause. Men go through what's called a "mid-life crisis," but that stage of life for men is actually similar to menopause in women: It's a symptom of an underlying hormone imbalance.

Problems occur when a man doesn't understand why he is losing interest in sex with his wife. Often, instead of seeking help, he may turn to something else to fill this void in his life, such as pornography, another woman, or some other radical behavior — spending unreasonable amounts of money, buying a sports car, changing out his wardrobe, and so forth.

When a man resorts to sinful behavior, he often alienates those closest to him. They are hurt and confused by his actions; usually, even he is confused by his actions. He may try to blame his wife or other people in his life for his feelings of frustration, insecurity, and inadequacy. Instead, he should be talking to his pastor and his doctor — and his wife! Those are critical times that must be worked through, but that becomes difficult, if not impossible, when the lines of communication are closed.

I received hormone testing years ago, and it was discovered that I needed to undergo bioidentical HRT. Within four or five months of the therapy, I felt like a thirty-year-old man again! I still feel that way today, and I don't plan to change!

Where Do We Go From Here?

Because men are generally more emotionally guarded than women, it's easier to identify that a hormone problem is possible in a woman. For example, if she's an emotional yo-yo — crying one minute and laughing the next two or three times a day — or if she seems depressed for long periods, that's usually a sign of a problem with hormones.

DHEA, melatonin, and pregnenolone are three over-the-counter hormone supplements that can help a woman who's experiencing the negative effects of menopause or even perimenopause. However, there are other considerations, such as the need for thyroid, estrogen, progesterone, or growth hormones. That's why I recommend that women — especially those who are menopausal or perimenopausal — see a good doctor or qualified practitioner in naturopathy that can prescribe certain therapies that are natural but that may require a prescription to obtain.

For men, I recommend DHEA, melatonin, and pregnenolone, which can be purchased over-the-counter — and thyroid, testosterone, and growth hormones, which must be prescribed by a health-care practitioner. However, even OTC treatments should be taken under the guidance of a professional. And only a qualified professional can test you and accurately prescribe the more potent supplements you need to restore the proper balance to your endocrine system.

Many people suffer with symptoms of menopause or "mid life," yet they won't discuss it and receive the help they need. They suffer silently and alone, floundering in their personal lives and their marriages through ignorance and feelings of guilt and shame. They could obtain victory and get on with their lives if they would simply open up and seek the help they need.

God is ready! He's a God who delights in healing, delivering, and restoring relationships and lives. He is able and willing to right the wrongs that have occurred in the past and in our marriages, and He will meet a couple where they are as they simply seek Him.

15
Made for Each Other: Sex and the Covenant of Marriage

Dr. Tom Anderson

God created sex for marriage. Sex is a gift from God to you to be enjoyed in marriage beginning on your wedding day. He intended sex for pleasure and pro-creation, but it is also a symbol of the covenant between you and your spouse — a covenant to remain together through life as "one flesh" (Genesis 2:24; Ephesians 5:31).

The world certainly doesn't identify sex as being symbolic of a covenant, and we see that in the promiscuity that's so commonplace today, especially in this country. Young people in general don't place the same value on virginity or abstinence before marriage that they once did. For example, fifty years ago, to see a girl pregnant in high school was almost unheard of. In today's society, it's fairly commonplace.

Focusing on the Future — Forgetting the Past

We've lost sight of the covenant that God designed to be consummated in the marriage union. Biblically, a first-time marriage was intended for a man and a woman, who'd reserved themselves for marriage, to give themselves to each other on their wedding night. That act of giving oneself was to be a powerful symbol of purity, fidelity, and emotional security.

In other words, when a man and a woman are joined in marriage, and they consummate that union in the act of sex, there should be no images from past relationships that have to be "erased" — no memories or imaginations to bring into the marriage from old relationships.

True Romance: A Marriage Beyond the Dream

...I do not count myself to have apprehended; but one thing I do, FORGETTING those things which are behind and reaching forward to those things which are ahead. (Philippians 3:13)

There's grace and power to "forget" and to forge a new life and a new marriage beyond relationships of the past. The Apostle Paul, who had to learn to forget some things himself, wrote those inspired words: "...forgetting...and reaching forward..." (Philippians 3:13).

However, just think of the blessedness of a relationship without any ungodly images and memories from the past. God's original intention was that there be no such images from the past for a new husband and wife to deal with. Certainly, He's the God who causes us to overcome despite our mistakes and sins of the past. But when we follow His will from our youth, there's very little to overcome!

Taking the time to communicate with young people about this subject is a big key to helping them avert the dangers and heartache of sexual promiscuity. If you have children or grandchildren, sharing the truth about sex and marriage from God's Word can encourage them to "save themselves" for marriage.

At our church, one of my sons teaches a class on sexual purity for young high-schoolers. It's a great program in which the students make a heartfelt commitment to remain pure until they're married. These young people aren't just parroting words they heard someone else say. By the time they finish the program, they truly understand God's plan for sex and the incredible importance of the institution of marriage.

We certainly don't condemn you if you've missed it by having sex outside of marriage — and neither does God (see Romans 8:1)! We're simply trying to paint a picture of the value of marriage — and of sex in the context and confines of marriage.

Playing for Keeps

Isn't it wonderful how God designed sex and marriage? But think about what the world has done to that design. The world has perverted it so that the idea of "waiting" until marriage is scorned. Sadly, that mentality has crept into the Church, but it's not biblical.

Marriage is not two people setting up house together for a while to see if everything will work out. No, it's a covenant commitment to build a life together for the rest of your lives. And that commitment should be taken very seriously; it should not be entered into lightly or without a lot of consideration and prayer.

What is a covenant? A covenant is a solemn, binding agreement or compact. God takes covenants very seriously. In the Old Testament, if someone entered into a covenant and then broke that covenant or vow, he could be hunted down and killed. And very often, the curse for breaking a covenant came not only upon the guilty party, but also upon the person's entire family.

A covenant was designed to last forever. It was considered the strongest contract known to God and man. And God considers marriage to be so important that He set it up as a covenant relationship comparable to the one established between Christ and His Church. Just as God and His children share covenant rights, husbands and wives also share covenant rights in the marriage. One of those covenant rights is the right to share physical intimacy with their marriage partner.

Sex is not only a covenant symbol in marriage, it's an act of physical intimacy that God created for husbands and wives, and it was intended for their enjoyment and pleasure. It is God's desire that every Christian couple find sexual fulfillment in marriage.

Don't Be 'in the Dark' About Sex

A couple's attitude toward communication is so critical to the health and vitality of their marriage. And this is never more true than in the area of communicating about sex. Open communication is critical to sexual fulfillment. Traditionally, couples have assented to this truth, but they've only gone so far in communicating about sex. It seems that one or both parties have been unwilling to fully expose their feelings about what they consider to be sexually fulfilling.

That act of giving oneself was to be a powerful symbol of purity, fidelity, and emotional security.

How often do you and your spouse talk about sex? Do you know what your spouse likes or dislikes when it comes to sex? If you can't truthfully answer this question, "Yes, beyond all shadow of a doubt," I encourage you to take the first step to break down those communication barriers in your marriage.

I have a saying that anything "left in the dark" between you and your spouse can hurt you, and it can hurt your marriage. If it should have been said — but it hasn't — then it needs to be communicated! God intended sex to be enjoyable, healthy, and satisfying for both the husband and wife. Yet there are many couples that are languishing in this area because of a lack of knowledge — and because of a lack of willingness to communicate concerning that lack of knowledge.

For example, some wives endure pain during intercourse because they don't want to communicate that with their husband. Some think that if they tell the truth, it's going to offend their spouse and cause bigger problems. They are depriving themselves of sexual fulfillment because of their unwillingness to communicate.

There are many great books about sex available that are educational and not pornographic. They were written to help married couples find the fulfillment in marriage sexually that God intended. But if people won't avail themselves of these kinds of books, or if all they've ever been taught came from a dirty movie or magazine, they are destined to stay on the wrong track in their sex life if they don't make a change.

Married couples should not be afraid of a book about sex and sexual intimacy. Sex in marriage is a covenant act. Our sex life is important to God, and it should be important to us as well.

Feast or Famine?
It's Depends on Who You Ask

He brought me to the banqueting house, and his banner over me was love. (Song of Solomon 2:4)

This verse is talking about a feast of food, a "banqueting house." But just as good food nourishes a person, a good sex life will nourish you as well — your life personally and also your marriage. And a person can be full or famished in this area of sex!

What a husband and wife consider as "famine" in the area of sex can mean two different things altogether. If a woman describes her sex life as a famine, she may not be talking about the number of times she's having sex but about the quality of her experience. Quality is more important to women, whereas quantity tends to be more important to men.

Then what constitutes quality sex to a woman? We've heard it said that for a woman, sex begins long before the physical act. That's absolutely true. A sense of security is essential for a woman in order for her to enjoy a satisfying sex life. She must feel loved, cherished, secure, and protected in order to freely give herself sexually to her husband. Those things are absolutely critical if a woman's sexual experience is to be a feast instead of a famine.

On the other hand, a man gains greater connection with his own emotions after he enjoys physical intimacy with his wife. After making himself more vulnerable and more open to her physically, he reconnects with her emotionally. And his ego is greatly influenced by how well he performs.

About That Male Ego

We've already seen that men are very strong by nature. They're tough, protector types, and that's a good thing. A man is a macho, "can-do," knight in shining armor. But criticize him sexually, and he's a mess. It is absolutely necessary that a husband have the assurance from his wife — the one person who he trusts — that he is a great lover.

A man's ego is a very fragile thing. Studies show that most impotence is not caused by physical or physiological conditions but by too much criticism! A man's ego is greatly influenced by how well he performs and how well he's encouraged. Men have been graced and equipped to take on great responsibility in marriage. A man may be looked at as a pillar of strength, but his ego is fragile; it's his greatest weakness.

So famine for a man where sex is concerned can occur because of a wounded ego. When a man's ego has been wounded, it affects him sexually. For example, if he has been made to feel incompetent on his job, those feelings of insecurity could affect his desire for sex.

Wrong Words, Right Words — The Cause and the Cure

A man can be rendered sexually impotent by speaking the wrong words to him. Words are the cause, and words can be the cure! With all the television advertisements we see for cures for Erectile Dysfunction, or ED, I promise you that a majority of cases can be cured simply with words — the right words.

If you're a wife, tell your husband often that he's a good man — a good lover and provider. Find things you can compliment him about. And then look your best for him. Taking care of yourself for your husband communicates love and respect to him without words. If you don't take care of yourself, it communicates just the opposite; he will feel that you don't respect him.

We live in an image-based society, and I'm not saying that we as Christians should allow ourselves to be conformed to that mindset. But we must not throw the baby out with the bathwater, either! In other words, we need to look our best. And since men are predominantly visually oriented, a wife especially needs to boost her husband's ego by being the best she can be. (We'll talk more about "desirability" in marriage later in the chapter.)

Whether he's been incessantly criticized or his wife simply loses interest in him, if a husband feels unloved, unworthy, disrespected, or ill esteemed by the woman in his life, it will affect him sexually. And if he feels that way over a prolonged period of time, he may grow cold and indifferent toward his wife if he doesn't communicate his feelings.

One of the reasons many marriages suffer from this "famine syndrome" is the lack of understanding that exists within the Christian community regarding sex. There simply aren't a lot of people talking about it. The first time I taught on the subject of sex at our church, I announced it in advance and forbade anyone under 21 in the sanctuary that Sunday. Once we made sure we had an adults-only audience, we closed the doors and had a closed meeting.

I was very candid as I taught on this subject that day, and the congregation gasped! But that's okay; I don't apologize. God created sex, and church leadership needs to talk about it.

Satan, sin, and the world have perverted the gift of sex, and people's lives have been messed up over what they've been taught about the purpose of this experience. They've portrayed it as a meaningless experience designed purely for one's own gratification. Believers must stand up and tell the truth about God's gift of sex in marriage.

Just Sex — Or Sexual Fulfillment?

Without sexual fulfillment in your marriage, you're not receiving God's best for your marriage. It's God's will for you to prosper and be abundantly blessed and fulfilled in every area of your life. Satan is the author of mediocre and dull. And he doesn't want you to have God's best in any area, including in your marriage — including in your sex life!

It's not often you'll hear someone tell you that Satan's will for your life is a mediocre, unsatisfying sex life — but that's exactly what I'm telling you. He deceives people, and that's how he's able to steal, kill, and destroy (see John 10:10). Whether it be your health, your finances, your relationships, and so forth, the enemy is a thief and a destroyer. So the wise person will arm himself with the truth of God's Word, because it's the truth that a person knows and embraces that will set him or her completely free (John 8:32).

It's also important to be wise concerning the differences between the genders. The Bible says, "Husbands, likewise, dwell with them [their wife] with understanding…" (1 Peter 3:7). And by the same token, it will only profit a wife to have an understanding of the male gender. Ignorance is not bliss in marriage! Knowledge is power. The more you know, and the more you put into practice what you know, the happier and healthier your marriage will be.

Getting Sex in Perspective

We've already covered the fact that men are primarily planters, and women are primarily "receivers," or incubators, of that which is planted. So in the context of sex, we could say that men tend to be ready to "plant" at a moment's notice! On the other hand, women are not always ready to receive; they are more seasonal when it comes to sex. In other words, like the soil in a garden, the wife must be properly prepared and cared for — cultivated — prior to enjoying physical intimacy.

Whether it's "feast" or "famine" in a couple's sex life often depends on perspective: the husband's or the wife's. Gaining a clear understanding of what each party needs and wants in the relationship will ensure physical and emotional security and a marriage that's Heaven on earth.

The Real Truth
About Sexual Incompatibility

We know that in marriage, a man's needs and a woman's needs are different. Because our emotional needs are so different, our sexual needs are different too. If we don't understand that, problems will result.

In a previous chapter, we looked at how to overcome certain barriers to emotional intimacy and a satisfying sex life. In this chapter, we're going to look at some problems and issues with sex that aren't nearly as complex. And we'll start with desirability in marriage.

Problems with sex in marriage can relate to a spouse being physically undesirable to his or her spouse. I'm not talking about any physical traits that may be perceived as negative, including being overweight. I'm talking about the way a person takes care of himself or herself.

God intends that each one of us be the best that we can be and to look our best and be attractive for our mate. You don't have to be wealthy enough to afford cosmetic surgeries — or as thin or well-built as an actor, model, or athlete. But you can endeavor to be the best you possibly can be at every season of marriage and life.

Your Spouse Is Looking at You

I'm talking about taking care of yourself and looking your best for your own sake and for the sake of your spouse. For example, what type of clothing does your spouse like? There's a saying for wives that goes something like this: Dress for your man, not for every man. The same could be said for husbands: Dress for your woman, not for every woman.

You don't have to own designer clothing or have a "hair allowance" worked into your monthly budget —but you can make sure your clothes are clean and neat and that your hair is brushed or combed and styled. It isn't fair to woo your mate in courtship looking nice, but then after you're married, you look disheveled and unkempt most of the time!

Just one of the things about Maureen that has always impressed me is that there are no days that she doesn't dress nice, put on makeup, and fix her hair. She dresses well every day. And over the years, that has inspired me to shape up in this area! I have been known to hang around the house on my days off wearing cutoffs, a raggedy T-shirt, and flip-flops. But Maureen has truly motivated me in our marriage to look my best at all times.

We often hear that looks aren't everything or that looks aren't important. But they are very important. I'm not saying we need to look as if we've just stepped out of a Hollywood clothier or salon; I'm simply saying that we each need to try to be the very best we can be for ourselves and for our spouse.

What Women Want

Notoriously, we've said that "looks" or appearances matter more to men than to women. But in the following passage from Song of Solomon, I think it's interesting that the woman is looking at the man's physical features here, beginning with the top, his head, and working her way down!

My lover is radiant and ruddy, outstanding among ten thousand. His head is purest gold; his hair is wavy and black as a raven. His eyes are like doves by the water streams, washed in milk, mounted like jewels. His cheeks are like beds of spice yielding perfume. His lips are like lilies dripping with myrrh. His arms are rods of gold set with chrysolite. His body is like polished ivory decorated with sapphires. His legs are pillars of marble set on bases of pure gold. His appearance is like Lebanon, choice as its cedars. His mouth is sweetness itself; he is altogether lovely. This is my lover, this my friend, O daughters of Jerusalem. (Song of Solomon 5:10-16 NIV)

In this passage, the woman notices the tenderness of her husband's eyes, but she doesn't neglect the strength of his hands and legs. How reflective this passage is of the female gender! She's looking for tenderness and strength, romance and friendship. She finds all of these things in her ideal mate.

This should be incentive enough for a husband to look his best and be his best for his wife!

What Men Want

As I said, men are well-known for being "visual" people. In other words, they are very moved by what they see. Let's look at the following passage at the way Solomon notices his wife.

How beautiful your sandalled feet, O prince's daughter! Your graceful legs are like jewels, the work of a craftsman's hands. Your navel is a rounded goblet that never lacks blended wine. Your waist is a mound of wheat encircled by lilies. Your breasts are like two fawns, twins of a gazelle. Your neck is like an ivory tower. Your eyes are the pools of Heshbon by the gate of Bath Rabbim. Your nose is like the tower of Lebanon looking towards Damascus. Your head crowns you like Mount Carmel. Your hair is like royal tapestry; the king is held captive by its tresses. How beautiful you are and how pleasing, O love, with your delights! Your stature is like that of the palm, and your breasts like clusters of fruit. I said, "I will climb the palm tree; I will take hold of its fruit." May your breasts be like the clusters of the vine, the fragrance of your breath like apples, and your mouth like the best wine. May the wine go straight to my lover, flowing gently over lips and teeth. (Song of Solomon 7:1-9 NIV)

Solomon was obviously very attracted to his woman! He compared her body to a beautiful tree and then communicated his plans to get very close to that tree! There has been so much foolish controversy in the Church about how a woman should look. I'm saying there's nothing wrong with a wife taking care of herself — with decorating the "tree"!

The Difference Between 'Killer Good Looks' and 'Roadkill'!

Beyond looking your best, smelling good is important too! If you're a husband, you especially need to know that your wife is not into sweat! I say this in fun, but if you're in doubt, take a shower. Being clean and fresh is always better!

Do you think smelling good is that important? Even if my nose didn't know, the following verses cause me to believe it is!

> *Pleasing is the fragrance of your perfumes; your name is like perfume poured out. No wonder the maidens love you…. While the king was at his table, my perfume spread its fragrance. My lover is to me a sachet of myrrh resting between my breasts. My lover is to me a cluster of henna blossoms from the vineyards of En Gedi…. Who is this coming up from the desert like a column of smoke, perfumed with myrrh and incense made from all the spices of the merchant?* (Song of Solomon 1:3,12-14; 3:6 NIV)

That sounds to me like a little aftershave or cologne might be beneficial in your relationship with your wife! A pleasant scent or aroma makes a great impression on a woman — just as it makes an impression on a man.

It seems that women are better than men at smelling nice. And the pleasant scent of a woman's cologne or perfume is very attractive to her husband. We will also see from the following verses that pleasant-smelling breath is an important trait to have when it comes to sexual compatibility with your spouse.

> *Your lips drop sweetness as the honeycomb, my bride; milk and honey are under your tongue. The fragrance of your garments is like that of Lebanon. You are a garden locked up, my sister, my bride; you are a spring enclosed, a sealed fountain. Your plants are an orchard of pomegranates with choice fruits, with henna and nard, nard and saffron, calamus and cinnamon, with*

every kind of incense tree, with myrrh and aloes and all the finest spices. (Song of Solomon 4:11-14 NIV)

A Touching Response

We've talked about the importance of looking good and smelling good in regard to sexual compatibility. Appealing to the senses of sight and smell is an attractive quality in a spouse.

Now we're going to look at appealing to your mate's sense of touch — in other words, responding to the sexual advances of your spouse.

When we talk about giving your spouse the appropriate attention during foreplay and sex, it's important to talk about what not to do. For instance, watching television over your mate's shoulder is not conducive to sexual compatibility! Answering the phone while your spouse is flirting with you is another mood-killer that can hurt the relationship because it communicates disinterest or disrespect.

In Song of Solomon 7, where Solomon notices his wife's physical features, it's interesting that he didn't start at her head as she did when she noticed his features. He started somewhere else in beholding the beauty of his ideal girl! He started with her feet for some reason and then worked his way upward toward her curves.

Then he spoke of physically being near. He says, "'…I will go up to the palm tree, I will take hold of its branches.' Let now your breasts be like clusters of the vine…" (vv. 8-9).

Some have said, "This is too explicit to be in the Bible." But, re-member, God created sex; it's a gift from Him for the marriage. It seems that some Christians have a very skewed view of sex. They see it as dirty instead of a gift from God to be enjoyed. They must renew their mind to the truth of God's Word (Romans 12:2) and get rid of those wrong ideas about sex.

Sex is not dirty in the marriage; it's holy. And what Solomon is saying to his wife here in verses 8 and 9 is not dirty or crude. He's simply talking about his anticipation of foreplay and sexual intercourse as acts of love to be enjoyed between the two of them as husband and wife.

In writings from Early Church and Old Testament history, we can find that it was common for married couples to read from the Song of Solomon on the Sabbath and then participate in sexual intercourse. As you know, the Sabbath was a holy day set apart for God's people under the Old Testament just for rest and relaxation. Certain activities were forbidden, yet intercourse was considered as an act to be partaken of on that holy day! What did the patriarchs know back then that perhaps we don't know today?

More Than 'Icing on the Cake'

Sex is not just some benefit of marriage or "the icing on the cake"; it's an integral aspect of the bond of marriage. In fact, sex and the covenant of marriage cannot be separated — anymore than the ingredients in a cake can be separated once they're mixed! So we must never be guilty of downplaying this important function in a marriage relationship.

Sex in marriage plays a big part in how bonded we feel to our spouse. It's a scientific fact that the act of sex creates chemical changes in the brain that bring feelings of euphoria and then great peace and calm. It's at that moment that two people in a marriage feel the most bonded.

Sex promotes and deepens the bond of love between a husband and wife. In fact, the chemical peptide oxytocin that's released during sex actually "encourages" more affectionate behavior between the couple. And, ironically, the more affectionate you are with your spouse, the more peptide oxytocin is released!

When peptide oxytocin is released in the body, it helps block negative memories. Hollywood has made jokes about "makeup sex," but there's a real truth to utilizing sexual intimacy with your spouse to eradicate negative feelings that challenge the relationship. During sexual intercourse, the brain actually releases "memory blockers" that help you focus on the present and on each other again instead of on a fight you may have just had. These brain chemicals promote feelings of well-being, happiness, and "forgetfulness" where an offense is concerned.

> *...Do not let the sun go down while you are still angry, and do not give the devil a foothold.* (Ephesians 4:26-27 NIV)

God has provided us with everything we need so that there wouldn't be any footholds of the enemy in our lives. So when you become angry with your spouse, don't stay mad — get close to him or her and allow your positive feelings for each other to wash over any emotions of anger or frustration.

Engaging in sex as a married couple even has health benefits! A certain study revealed that one sexual encounter burns the same number of calories as running five miles! Endorphins that are released during sex also have anti-aging effects on the body. Endorphins help produce energy, burn fat, and strengthen the immune system. They can also produce an "analgesic" effect that lessens the sensation of pain.

God made no mistake in creating sex to be enjoyed between a husband and wife in the covenant of marriage. In fact, the two — sex and marriage — were made for each other as gifts and the blessing of God.

16
Responsible With Money, Ready for a Bride

Dr. Tom Anderson

We've seen that one of a husband's biggest responsibilities in marriage is to protect and provide. In fulfilling this responsibility, he creates an atmosphere of security and trust for his wife and children. I cannot talk about this subject adequately without specifically addressing the topic of money in marriage — or, more specifically, men and money in marriage.

Some men don't have a clue about how to create or stay on a budget. Often a husband is buying "toys," or the things that he wants, while he can't even pay the rent or mortgage. That is irresponsible, and that lack of taking responsibility creates stress and feelings of insecurity in a man's family.

I know that it's not popular to lay the responsibility for the finances strictly on the husband. I've heard countless times the excuse, "Well, my wife is better at that kind of thing than I am."

That might be true. Many women are more detail-oriented than men. But if you as a husband don't balance the checkbook and pay the bills, you don't know exactly what you're bringing in as income, what you owe, or what you have on hand. And you need to know all of those things! Otherwise, how will you know whether you have enough money or whether you need more money? Often husbands leave it to their wife to make ends meet and to figure out how to stretch their income to meet the family's needs. This is not God's intent. The husband is the head of the home, and it is his responsibility to manage the financial affairs of that home.

If you as a husband haven't taken your place as the leader in your financial affairs, I strongly urge you to take a bookkeeping or basic class on business math so that you can build security and trust in your marriage by properly managing your money.

One thing you need to do is set up a budget, cutting expenses if necessary, to ensure that money is not always "tight" at your house. For example, it's important that a husband pray about making large purchases, such as buying a home. I encourage you not to do it until it's God's will. Don't get ahead of yourself and jump into a large commitment, such as a home purchase, that puts your family in a bind financially.

This happens more often than you might think. A family becomes overcommitted financially, and the wife feels pressured to go out and work. The wife begins taking on responsibility that belongs to her husband. I'm not suggesting that it's wrong for a wife to work outside the home if she desires to do so and if she and her husband are in agreement about it. But if she has to forfeit doing the things that fulfill her as a wife and mother because she's forced to take on outside work, chaos and disorder will eventually set in because the home is operating outside of God's design and order.

Simply put, it is the husband's responsibility to create and manage the household budget so that the family doesn't become overcommitted financially. My son Jason recently bought his wife a nice car. She said to him, "You need a nice car too." He told her, "Not now. I can't buy two cars right now. I will drive the 'junk' car so that you can have a nice one."

In buying his wife a nice car while he drove the older one, Jason showed his wife that he valued her, but he also showed her that she could trust him with their financial future. It's not that Jason doesn't like new cars; he likes them very much! But he understands his responsibility in the home and that he must protect and provide for his family first above all else, including above his own desires.

I have seen husbands spend money frivolously on themselves and then tell their wife there was no money to buy her a new outfit or take her out on a date. If he spends $200 playing golf but she can't have something nice, something is wrong with that!

As a husband, protecting and providing for your family entails taking leadership where the finances are concerned. If your wife is the one who's responsible for knowing what you have and what you owe, you have just added to her a responsibility that belongs squarely with you, not her. You've added stress to her life that shouldn't be there. And the time she's taking to do one of your jobs is time she doesn't have to do the things that are in her heart to do in the home.

A Job First, Then a Wife

Then the Lord God took the man and put him in the garden of Eden to tend and keep it. (Genesis 2:15)

Clearly, God gave the man the responsibility to "tend and keep" the garden. Notice God gave Adam a job before He gave him a wife! Adam had to do the work; it was his assignment from God. And it is no less the husband's assignment and responsibility today.

As I said, I'm not condemning a wife's working outside the home if she desires to do so — or if the husband and wife are in agreement with that arrangement for a season. But the husband is nevertheless responsible for managing the finances in the family and for making sure enough money is coming in to support them.

> *The husband is the head of the home, and it is his responsibility to manage the financial affairs of that home.*

It's very important that the husband accept responsibility as the provider for the home. If the wife's wants to have a profession, that's great. However, if you as a husband have a wife whose heartfelt desire is to stay at home with her children, it's your responsibility to make certain she's able to do it!

When our children were young, there was a season during which I held two and three jobs to make it possible for Maureen to stay home with our children. That's what was in her heart to do. She had a college degree, and she could have had a career. But she desired to stay at home and raise our children. And I'm so thankful and glad that she was able to invest that time in our sons at that stage of their lives.

I realize that some women are doctors, lawyers, and business owners. Maybe you're a husband who earns less money than your wife, and your wife enjoys her career. The responsibility to make sure that the bills are being paid and that the future is being provided for is still yours. Your wife's income isn't what brings her security. It's the way you manage the family's finances that bring her comfort and security in life.

It Boils Down to Trust

Women need two important things from a man: unconditional love and security. In fact, the entire home needs that. This comes down to an issue

221

of trust. In other words, can your wife trust you to look ahead and foresee the future needs of the family? Or is she anxious because she thinks you can't see past the "here and now"?

Sometimes people go to the local church looking for help when they're about to be evicted from their house or lose their car "tomorrow." They should have known they were in trouble long before then. If a husband foresees that his home is in jeopardy, he can get a second job and avert a crisis. Even working at a fast-food restaurant, he can earn enough to make his late car payments.

In my way of thinking, a forty-hour workweek is a lie from the pit of hell! Ask any business owner you know who's successful and doing well, and he or she will tell you that a forty-hour workweek is a myth! I worked seventy to eighty hours a week most of my life. I don't understand the mentality of someone who comes home after eight hours and just sits there while his financial future is in jeopardy.

Most people waste forty hours a week watching TV, anyway. They could make wiser use of their time working to get their family caught up and even ahead. But instead of bringing their budget back in line, they often complain, "My job just doesn't pay enough."

And what about Christmas season? If you as a husband are meeting your budget but don't have extra money for gifts at Christmas, you can get a seasonal job that will pay for your family's Christmas. The same is true concerning vacations. Your family needs at least one vacation together every year. It's your responsibility to make sure the extra money is budgeted or comes into the family somehow for you to able to do that.

Extra money for Christmas gifts and vacations may not seem like absolute necessities in life. But as a leader in the home, when you provide these things for your family, beyond blessing them, you also build trust and security into those relationships — trust that will last a lifetime. You can't put a dollar amount on that in terms of the value it holds.

Your Kids Are Watching You

As a father, you largely influence the relationship your kids will have with God and with their own children when they grown up. My son Scot vividly remembers the time I got laid off when he and Jason were children. I sat the family down and said, "I got laid off from work, and everything is going to be fine. I will do everything I can do, and God will provide for us. So let's go out and eat!"

Scot recalls the emotion of that moment even more than the details of the layoff. He said he learned that day was that no matter what happened, Dad would always take care of it. He also learned to trust God as his Heavenly Father. Now, as a dad himself, Scot instills this same sense of confidence and security in his own wife and children.1

Your children need to feel like you're an immovable, unshakable rock! You may need to go to the Rock, Christ Jesus, to receive the strength you need. But your family needs to see that no matter what the circumstance, Dad won't be crushed by it; he's an overcomer.

Early Lessons and Challenges

In my younger days, finances were a bit of a challenge for me. But I overcame this challenge, and I want to share with you my simple system for getting started on the road to financial responsibility and stability in your life and marriage. I developed this system when I was in college, and it has served me well for many years. In fact, I've taught this very system to businesses, organizations, and families all over the world.

First, there are so many advances in computer software today that make money management easier than when I was young. For example, I now pay bills online so that I don't have to write checks anymore. But the principles I share are practical and useable today. They are simple, yet profound, and you can incorporate them into whatever system of management you choose to use. You simply need to find what works for you and then stick with it as a discipline until it becomes a habit. In other words, the longer you stick with it, the easier it becomes to do.

This system of organizing and managing your finances will give you the means to know where you stand financially twenty-four hours a day, seven days a week, and all year long. You will know in a given situation whether you should spend money or not. And that's the problem with most people — at any given time, they don't know where they are with their budget. So they tend to overspend. They make costly mistakes with their money, and if they keep making too many of those mistakes, it will eventually ruin them financially.

A Simple Assignment

The first part of this system involves an assignment. Get a notebook or loose paper that can be placed in a binder and write down all of your expenses. It's important not to leave anything out, but you don't have to know every bill to the exact cent, because there will be variables each month, especially with utilities.

Begin with your tithes, offerings, and mortgage and automobile payments, if any. Then list your home and/or automobile insurance payment and your utilities (electric, water, phone, and so forth). After that, list any other personal insurance you might carry as well as any medical payments or retail payments you might make besides your car payment. For now, leave off groceries, fuel, and other expenses, such as clothing, eating out, and miscellaneous items.

This is a great program whether you're paid once a week, every other week, every month, or even twice a month, such as on the first and the fifteenth each month. It will even work on commissioned sales, but you'll have to improvise when you don't receive income on a regular, consistent basis.

You Must Know
What You Owe and Earn

Now, add up the expenses you listed on your worksheet. These are your standard, finite expenses because they can readily be defined. Your other expenses, such as groceries, fuel, and so forth can be classified as relative expenses because they can change from month to month. For instance, you could cut your grocery bill by eating different kinds of foods or by buying the store labels at the store instead of the name brands. You could carpool or take the bus or public transportation instead of driving yourself to work every day. You could forego buying clothes for periods at a time, or you could change where you shop for clothes (consignment stores versus the department stores and so forth).

You could also sacrifice eating out for a season — or eating out as often. And you could rent a movie instead of going to the cinema. All of these expenses can fluctuate from month to month as you determine.

After you've listed your standard expenses, total what you earn, or take home, during that same period. For the sake of this teaching, let's just say you figured your monthly standard expenses at $2,750.00 per month. Now let's say that you take home $750.00 per week. With those figures in mind, if you were to multiply your weekly net earning by four (because there are four weeks in an average month), you'd have $3,000.00, and you'd have very little surplus for groceries, fuel, and so forth — only $250.00.

$ 750.00	weekly net pay
x 4	number of weeks in an average month
3,000.00	monthly net pay
- 2,750.00	monthly standard expenses
$ 250.00	disposable income for groceries, fuel, etc.

However, there is an average of four weeks and three days in a month, not just four weeks. So if you get paid every week, you'd need to figure your budget a little differently, because you'd get paid fifty-two times a year, not forty-eight.

$ 750.00	weekly net pay
x 52	number of weeks in the year
39,000.00	annual net pay
÷ 12	number of months in the year
3,250.00	monthly net pay
- 2,750.00	monthly standard expenses
$ 500.00	disposable income for groceries, fuel, etc.

Of course, certain months contain five weeks, but with this system, you'll know in advance what you can and cannot spend each month. In other words, you'll know on June 1, for example, not on June 30, if you're going to be short on money. The important thing is that you always know where you are with your finances.

Using the preceding scenario, just because there are 5 weeks in a month doesn't mean you can make a larger purchase during that fifth week — unless you've based your expenditures on a four-week budget instead of a 4.3-week budget. In the former case, you could then use your "surplus" in that fifth week to buy extra groceries and so forth.

This is not a complicated program, and you can use it at the beginning of each month to plan for the month ahead. People who work for commission often have problems when they receive a large payout and then "blow it" quickly instead of spreading it out over several less profitable months so they can pay their bills on time and meet their monthly budget. That is why knowing exactly what you owe and planning ahead are so vital to a healthy financial picture.

Some people have a separate checking account where they deposit a predetermined amount of money each pay period to meet their monthly set or standard expenses. They don't write any checks on that account except to pay those expenses. Then at the end of the month when it's time to pay the following month's bills, all the money is there. They simply write out the checks and pay each bill. They pay all of their bills on time and even pay most of them early. Besides taking the stress out of bill-paying, it helps their credit score too.

The way some people operate their budget is, as a bill comes in, they write a check for it. Even if it's the bill for their mortgage, they'll write the check, and then they have to borrow from the next pay period to make ends meet. Then they usually have to borrow from the week after that, and so the cycle continues. In time, they are months in arrears, and occasionally, they get caught up because of an extra week in a month. But then the cycle begins again. That's a very stressful way to pay bills. It's not healthy emotionally, and it's not good for a marriage.

When There's 'Month' Left
at the End of Your Money —
A Short-Term Cure for Shortfalls!

"That's all well and good, Reverend Anderson, but what happens if I figure my budget, and I see that I just can't make ends meet?"

Many people avoid creating a budget because they don't want to see on paper what they already know — that they're spending more than they're earning. But avoiding the issue will not repair the situation or make it "go away." That's why I said that knowing what you owe and earn as the leader in the home are the basic, vital steps for bringing health and vitality into your finances and your marriage. Marriage and finances are so intricately linked. So it's important to have your financial affairs in order for your own sake and for the sake of your marriage and your posterity — your children and your children's children.

When you figure your budget — your standard expenses and your standard earnings — what if there's not enough for food, fuel for your car, and so forth? I've been there when that was exactly my situation. I went out and got a second job to ensure we had the money for those things.

If you find that your bills are greater than the income you're taking in, you may need to increase your income until you can decrease your bills. You might need to take a second job. If your wife is not already working, perhaps the two of you will come into agreement about her finding temporary work.

Of course, taking such stopgap measures is not a long-term solution but a temporary fix. Yet it's your responsibility as the leader in the home to ensure that you have enough funds to meet your family's needs. Really, it's simple economics: You must either decrease your outflow — what you owe and spend — or increase your income — what you earn. If you owe more than you earn each month, there's an imbalance, and some kind of action must be taken to return that situation to a condition of stability.

Taking the Next Step: Ensuring
Cash Flow for Your Family

What happens when you figure your budget, and you have enough to pay your standard bills and to cover the cost of food, fuel, and reasonable clothing and entertainment? You need to invest and save. You need to ensure cash flow for the well-being of your family both now and for the future.

Cash flow is an especially critical issue in America right now. Even banks are discovering how vital cash flow is — it will determine whether they stand or fall. So besides doing long-term investing for your retirement years, you need a short-term savings account to ensure cash flow in the event you lose your job or are unable to work for some reason. That account should contain funds to cover three to six months of living expenses.

In other words, if your budget is $5,000.00 a month, you should have a minimum of three months' worth of expenses — or $15,000.00 — in the bank to sustain your family while you find other means of earning an income.

When the Mundane Becomes Dramatic

If you will set yourself up on this program or one like it, it will change your life for the better if you'll stick with it. It hasn't always been easy, but I've utilized this system for forty years. I set our church up using this system, and I've helped many businesses set up their accounting systems with this program. They know what their expenses are, and a predetermined amount gets deposited regularly into a separate account set aside just for meeting those expenses on time. No one touches those accounts until it's time to disburse payments to meet the obligations of those businesses.

These things might not seem fun or exciting, but they will be dramatic and life-changing if you'll put them into practice! When the opportunity is presented for you to buy something on credit, you will know immediately whether you'll be able to pay for it — and whether you'll have to give up eating steak and go back to soup in order to do it!

No matter where you are with your finances, you can use this system to discover by the end of day whether you're in trouble financially or whether you simply need more cash flow for your family's needs in case of an emergency. Whether you need to remedy a bad situation or simply take additional steps to ensure a prosperous future for your family, I encourage you as the leader in your home to implement this plan or devise one of your own.

Also, as you pay down your debt, don't take on new debt. Use that extra money to save and invest in your future. Debt is a very dangerous thing that can ruin an individual, a family and also threaten entire nations. It's a well-known fact that Americans as a whole do not live within their means. Our system of credit has made it easy to spend more than we earn (it's called "living above our means"). Even the Bible says that it's not good to live above our means — in other words, to be "poor," yet try to appear to be rich.

> *Better to be a nobody and yet have a servant than pretend to be somebody and have no food.* (Proverbs 12:9 NIV)

Most of the people I know who are genuinely rich aren't showy and don't appear as rich. And they don't necessarily earn piles of money, either! They simply know how to utilize what they earn and to live within their means. And I promise you, they utilize their money wisely, not because they're "willy-nilly" with money but because they operate according to some kind of budget and financial plan.

Proving the Plan
In My Own Circumstances

Years ago, I was laid off work at one time for seven months. I used my own system during that time, and it worked fantastically. I'd signed up for unemployment, and because I knew all my standard expenses, I knew exactly what it would take to supplement my unemployment pay so that I could meet those expenses. So I took part-time jobs to supplement the unemployment. I did whatever work I could find to make sure I deposited $400.00 per week into an account for meeting standard expenses.

During the time I was laid off from my job, God had given me a word: "Take no thought" (see Matthew 6:25). Yet I understood that I needed to utilize this system, which I believe was the wisdom of God for my life. As a result, I never missed paying my tithe, and I never missed paying a bill. I could go to bed each night and get up each morning without a care — "taking no thought" — because I had a system in place.

During the time I was laid off, I hung wallpaper and I bought and sold cars. I had never hung wallpaper before; I had to learn. But I did so well at it that I was once offered a job hanging sixty double rolls in a brand-new house.

I ended up earning more money during that time period than I would have earned at my old job. And although the hours were long many of those days, I actually had more days off than I would have had where I previously worked.

Just to show you how much God blessed my efforts, I actually had enough money after paying all of our bills to buy a couple of three-wheelers, and I was able to spend a lot of quality time with my children that summer. I'm not saying that to brag. I'm endeavoring to show you what God can do in your life and your family's lives if you will step up to the plate and accept your financial responsibility in the home.

Certainly, I'm not saying that the seven months I was laid off was like a vacation! But because I had a system in place, my finances were in order instead of in chaos and disarray. I had a plan. I worked the plan — and the plan worked for me! It will work for you, too, if you will put it in place in your own life.

When the economy is suffering, there is always work to do. It may not be what you want, and it certainly isn't something you'll likely have to do forever. But there's work to do; you simply have to find it. During those seven months of unemployment, I also did cleanup of construction sites. That was a dirty job and a lot of hard work! But because I always found work to do, at the end of those seven months, I earned more than if I'd continued my old union job making $25.00 an hour. And back then, that was big money!

During those seven months, because I had a financial system in place and knew I needed to deposit $400.00 a week into an account for paying bills, I also could plan special family outings without worry, and we were able to spend quite a bit of time together as a family. We even took a trip to Disneyland during that hiatus! But I knew my bottom line. I knew what I had to accomplish each week.

Be the Best

In tough economic times, corporations are forced to become "lean," and when jobs must be cut, they will generally keep only the best employees on board. That's why it's important as Christians that we always be the best workers anywhere. God expects excellence of us, and He certainly gifts and graces us to be the best. As we walk in that, He can protect our situation when others are vulnerable in tough times.

These are some very practical, yet rich truths that you can learn and apply to secure your family's financial future. Remember, God gave Adam a job first before He ever gave him a bride. If you haven't already done so as the leader in your home, I encourage you to take your place of responsibility in managing the money in your marriage. As you do, new doors of opportunity will open to you because you'll be ready to step through those doors with confidence and skill. Your wife will be exceedingly blessed, your children will be happy, and life will be different for you.

---

1   Read the story of Scot's experiences as a son and a father in More Than a Dad by Scot Anderson.

17

What's Working in You? The Secret to Success in Marriage and in Life

Dr. Tom Anderson

A man was being tailgated by a stressed-out woman on a busy boulevard when, suddenly, the traffic light turned yellow just in front of him. Although he probably could have accelerated and "beat" the light, the man did the right thing in stopping his vehicle at this busy crossroad. The woman tailing him became furious, honking her horn and screaming in frustration.

In a frightening rant, she didn't hear at first the tap on her car window by a very concerned policeman. The officer ordered the woman out of car and escorted her to the police station, where she was fingerprinted, photographed, and placed in a holding cell. After a couple of hours, she was led back to the booking desk, where the arresting officer was waiting with her personal effects.

"I'm very sorry for the mistake," the officer told her. "I pulled up behind you and saw you 'flipping off' the driver in front of you and cursing and yelling. Noticing the 'What Would Jesus Do' and 'Follow Me to Sunday School' bumper stickers on the bumper and the chrome-plated fish emblem on the trunk, I just assumed you'd stolen the car."

This is a humorous commentary on the lack of character that many Christians exhibit today. I used this particular anecdote because it involves a woman — and it seems that men love to blame the women in their lives for their problems!

In this chapter, I'm going to share five secrets for avoiding many of the problems of life that we face as men. And blaming the woman in our life is not one of them! It's unfortunate that it took me so many years to discover these secrets and put them into practice. But if I can share them with you as a husband and leader in your home, life can better for you than you can imagine — and sooner than you think!

How To Measure Success

What is success? We know that success cannot be measured by money alone. All we have to do is look at some of the major corporate failings in recent history and the enormous bonuses paid to chief officers at taxpayers' expense to see that this is true. You can't prosper materially at the expense of your soul and still be truly happy and prosperous. Success is ultimately measured by a man's character — by what's working inside him, in his heart. A man's character often produces outward manifestations of success as we tend to measure success. However, we must never confuse outward, material blessings with true success.

Character is the pathway of true success in life, and there are no shortcuts. The following are five "characteristic" secrets to lasting success in life — for yourself and for your family.

Secret Number One: Commitment

What is commitment? I'll share with you another humorous story to illustrate the characteristic of commitment — this one about a chicken and a pig that ran away from a farm. Traveling all night, they became very hungry. Up ahead, they saw a diner with a sign out front that read, "Bacon and Eggs — 99 Cents."

Excited, the chicken says to the pig, "Eggs and bacon! Let's get something to eat!" Reluctant, the pig says to the chicken, "That's easy for you to say: From you, they just want a donation; from me, they want complete commitment!"

In short, commitment means you put your life on the line. And commitment in marriage means you commit to that other person for life — not just while emotions are high or when things are going smoothly. Marriage is a lifetime commitment from which there is no turning back.

Commitment is the first key to success as a man, husband, father, leader, and provider. Commitment to whom or to what? Number one, commitment to God; number two, commitment to your wife; number three, commitment to your children; number four, commitment to your job; and, number five, commitment to your church.

As a man, you have many responsibilities in life. However, to be truly successful, those responsibilities must all must be kept in order. For example, some pastors and ministers get ministry out of order and begin placing more preeminence — more time and energy — on ministry than on their own family or even on their relationship with God. But if a minister really wants to minister and serve (because ministers are servants), he should minister first to the Lord and then to his wife and family before he ever thinks about ministering to others.

Handling responsibility successfully is about prioritizing your time and commitments. As we've seen, our first commitment is to the Lord; our second commitment is to our wife; our third commitment is to our children; our fourth commitment is to our job or our employer; and our fifth commitment is to our church. If we keep our commitments in this order in terms of our priorities, we will find ourselves on the road to success.

Commitment to God

What does commitment to God — our number-one priority — look like? Commitment implies relationship. That means we don't just "flop" our Bible open and read it. We read God's Word purposefully and we fellowship with Him around His Word. If we don't take this attitude toward the Word and have the sense of purpose that we are committed to the Lord for the rest of our lives, we will never do this consistently.

I encourage you in your reading to pick a subject or topic and look up word meanings. Even if you only begin doing this five minutes a day, you can do a little bit more the following day. If bodybuilder Joe Weider could build a "muscle man" in just a few minutes a day, God can do a whole lot more for you than that in the same amount of time. But you have to have a vital relationship with Him, because apart from Him, you can do nothing (John 15:5).

It's important to realize that without a commitment to God and to self, your commitments to your wife, your children, your job, and your church will not likely stand the test of time. When I talk about commitment to "self," I'm not talking about a commitment to selfishness; I'm talking about a commitment to self-growth and self-improvement. You must constantly commit to being better tomorrow than you were today.

Commitment to Your Wife

In order for marriage to thrive and for a man to be truly successful in his professional and his family life, he must make a one hundred-percent commitment to his wife.

Many marriages hang on and last because of the woman's commitment. But that's not God's highest and best. He doesn't just want your marriage to "hang on" year after empty year. God wants your marriage to thrive and be a source of great happiness and contentment.

Dedication on the wife's part is wonderful and great, but without the husband eventually engaging in the growth of the relationship, the woman will eventually "give out" and give up. That's why we're seeing three out of four marriages end in divorce today. That means that most marriages end in divorce! That sad statistic was never God's intention concerning His institution of marriage.

A woman's emotions can eventually run dry. But a man's commitment can go on and never stop, because he doesn't operate on feelings; rather, he operates on the power of his will and his mental fortitude. So don't ever allow your wife to carry in the marriage what you should be carrying. She wasn't anointed to carry it, and if you don't take your place and fulfill your responsibilities in the marriage, chaos and catastrophe will be the ultimate result.

Commitment to Your Children

Commitment to your children — like commitment to your wife — entails so many areas of responsibility. It's a commitment of your love, your time, your energies, your strength — the very best of you. As husbands and fathers, we simply must be committed to giving our family our very best. And where children are concerned, that commitment also includes the commitment to discipline, teach, and train — and to do it consistently, throughout their young lives.

I've had parents come to me in tears because their children were skipping school, and the mom and dad felt completely helpless about the situation. Some were worried sick that their child wouldn't graduate from high school. If necessary, I would have told my sons as they were growing up, "You will attend school. If you skip a class, I will take time off from work, and I will follow you to every class. I will sit with you in class and in the cafeteria. I will hang with you at recess. And I will follow you to the bathroom. I will sit with you while you do your homework. You will graduate from high school."

In fact, there was a brief season in which one of my sons began hanging around a young man who was a bad influence on my son and on others. This young man drank alcohol and had already been in trouble with the law. He would come to church and then skip out on church — and influence other kids to follow him outside behind one of the church buildings during the service. I made this same "proposition" to my son. I offered to follow him around church and school. He knew I wasn't joking (and I wasn't). Needless to say, I never had a problem with that renegade friend again.

There was another season in which my boys thought they were really tough and began to take a certain attitude with me. I remember one night as they stood in front of me, side by side, I placed one hand on each boy's shoulder and "sat" them both down simultaneously. Don't misunderstand me; I love my sons. It is a well-understood fact that discipline and rules without relationship breed outright rebellion. But that was never an issue in our house. My children knew that I loved them. They still know it. We were always a very close, tight-knit family. But I wasn't about to give up my position as head of my home and let anarchy reign just because two teenagers wanted to see if they could challenge me!

As fathers, we simply need to ask ourselves, How committed am I to my family? We must determine our level of commitment to our God, our family, and the things we value most. We must ask ourselves, Am I going to do whatever it takes to do the right thing and to usher God's blessing into my life and my family's lives? Or am I going to falter and wilt at the first sign of trouble?

You — Dad — must take your position in the house and fulfill your role. Don't allow your wife to carry the weight of matters pertaining to the family. That's your job, so commit yourself to God first and then to your family — that you will be the very best you can be and do the very best you can do for them.

Although your children will "leave and cleave" when they get married (see Genesis 2:24), you will be a parent for the rest of your life. You can still train your grown and married children by your lifestyle and example and provide for them lessons without words that will serve as a support for them as they attempt to navigate their way through life.

If you're walking with the Lord with a teachable heart, you will always have twice the wisdom and experience as your children. You still have something to offer them even as they grow older, but it takes commitment on your part to walk in the truth and to be ready to impart truth when the time is right.

Commitment to Your Job

Being committed to your job or vocation means sticking with it whether you like it or not. You may not like the particular job or season you're in right now. But the attitude you take toward the work that's set before you can make or break your future and your family's future.

Jesus Himself said that He came not to be served, but to serve. He was the consummate Servant-Leader and our Example that we should follow as believers, especially as men. Jesus served because He loved the Father and because He chose to live pleasing to Him. We have that same power of choice today.

There is a great difference between being a servant and a slave. If you're doing something, and you feel as if have to do it, you're a slave to whatever it is you're doing. But if you're doing something because you desire to serve and you have a heart of service — even if it's only for a season — you are truly free.

> *Bondservants, obey in all things your masters according to the flesh, not with eyeservice, as men-pleasers, but in sincerity of heart, fearing God. And whatever you do, do it heartily, as to the Lord and not to men.* (Colossians 3:22-23)

There is true freedom in serving. Even if you're not where you want to be in life right now, you can change your attitude toward your work and, before long, you'll love serving God and others in whatever capacity you're working. Yes, it will take a little bit of death to "self," but in submitting your will to the Lord's will to serve, you'll find great freedom as a servant of Christ.

Commitment to Your Church

Commitment to your church can be closely related to commitment to your children in the sense that your commitment to attend church will serve as the model or example that your children will follow as they grow older.

Volunteer service aside, let's just talk about church attendance for a minute. Studies have shown that almost eighty percent of children whose fathers took them to church will stay in church even as adults! That figure is astounding! Fathers have largely let the mothers provide the spiritual nurturing for the family, yet the same studies reveal that only about half that amount — about forty percent of children — will continue attending church into adulthood when just Mom took them to church.

So a dad has the responsibility to build into his children the importance of church attendance.

I have actually heard fathers say, "Well, my teenager just doesn't want to go to church." My question is, Since when do teenagers make those kinds of decisions for themselves!

I always took the attitude that any teenager living under my roof must attend church! If I had to pick him up, throw him over my shoulders, belt him in the car, and carry him into the sanctuary, church attendance was not an option!

"Well, that's kind of harsh," someone might say. I allowed my sons to make certain decisions for themselves as they grew older. But if they ever began sliding off wisdom's path, I was right there to step in and make the right decision for them until they got their heads straight. If I had to sit with my sons in Sunday School and follow them from the classroom to the sanctuary and then sit with them among all their friends during the main service, then so be it: I was willing to do it. That was my stand, because I was committed. And you're going to have to be just that committed to stand by your own values and ideals.

Secret Number Two: Trust

Commitment is the first godly characteristic of a successful man and the secret to his success. The second secret to success is the characteristic of trust. To be a successful leader in your home, you have to be trustworthy, and your spouse has to be trustworthy. For example, you have to be trustworthy in the way you handle the household's finances, and you have to be able to trust your spouse to handle money too.

A lack of trust causes division and separation. That's why this issue of trust is so serious. You must be cautious and guard yourself in this area of integrity. And you must work to develop trust both ways. Trust doesn't happen just because you make a decision; it is earned over time in a relationship.

In our marriage, this trust issue where money is concerned was a challenge to us at one time. I was always extremely frugal because I was raised without money. But Maureen's father had butlers working for him. She grew up spending money like water, so to speak. In fact, I once asked her, "Don't you ever look at price tags?"

She answered, "No, I've never looked at a price tag a day in my life.

Maureen has always had a knack for selecting the highest-priced item as her favorite when she shops. It's almost uncanny! Without looking at the price, she'll zero in on the highest-priced item. But as a responsible leader in our home, if I ever had to tell her that we couldn't spend that much money at the moment, she was fine with it. She trusted me to take care of our household financially. And she has become extremely faithful and trustworthy in the way she handles finances.

Then when it comes to marital fidelity, Maureen and I made a commitment never to cheat. I trusted her commitment, and she trusted mine. And we've never broken that. I'm not saying that temptation isn't out there. But when you have that level of commitment, temptation can never lead you astray, because commitment keeps you on-track and off a destructive path.

Trust also has to be developed with your children. They have to be able to trust you, and you must raise them to be trustworthy. Trust is earned by the parent even when the child is an infant. For instance, when a baby cries because he's wet, hungry, tired, or sick, trust is built when you respond to his cries. Of course, there's another kind of cry that says, I'm spoiled; pick me up! I'm not saying you should always respond to that, because that goes beyond trust and into manipulation.

A child also learns to trust his or her parents when the child is disciplined consistently. In other words, if we want our children to trust us, we can't have a rule in place and then enforce it inconsistently. If we enforce a rule one day, and then the next day, we fail to follow through on enforcing that same rule, trust is broken down, because our children can't trust that we will do what we say we're going to do.

Whether you're promising some kind of blessing or reward, or you're promising some form of discipline or punishment, it's so important that you keep your word with your children. (I'm not saying you should always follow through on some rash promise you've made in haste or in anger to punish your child in a way that's cruel. We need to make these promises with level heads so that we're firm and resolute, not reckless and harsh.)

Number Three: Service

A third godly trait and secret to success is service. Too often, people equate successful leadership with authority over others in subservient roles. In other words, they think that if you're successful, others will constantly be serving you.

But a true godly leader will serve God, his family, and others because he's a leader, not because he's trying to become one. He's not trying to impress anyone; he's simply motivated by what's working in him: a heart for service.

Number Four: Loyalty

A fourth godly trait that a successful man possesses is loyalty. Loyalty is directly associated with thoughts, words, and actions. In other words, loyalty can be outwardly recognized by one's words and actions, but God knows whether a person is loyal in his or her thoughts.

Loyalty in Your Thoughts

As I've already shared, even your thoughts can affect and impact those around you. So you need to be especially careful about thinking negative thoughts about others, especially your spouse. On the other hand, thinking the right thoughts can be powerful, as those thoughts will positively affect those around you.

The same is true concerning your children. If you're thinking fearful, pessimistic thoughts, those thoughts create a certain energy in the home, and it will affect your children. If you don't believe there's power attached to fear, think about the times you've felt most afraid. In certain cases, every cell in your body can feel the effects of the presence of fear. That's why the Bible teaches us not to give place to fear — or to anything else that comes from the enemy — and that includes giving place to it in our thought life.

Loyalty in Your Words

What about the words we speak? Loyalty can definitely be communicated through speech. And words are powerful! Doesn't it make sense that we should speak only positively to and about our wife? And what about our children? From the time our children were very young — in fact, while they were in the womb — Maureen and I began speaking to them about how intelligent and good-looking they were. We also told them that every day when they were kids. We still do it today, and they're grown and married with families of their own! We realize the power that's manifested with every word, so we're careful to put the right beliefs and attitudes into the lives of our loved ones.

What does that have to do with loyalty? Like trust, feelings of loyalty are built over time. My wife and children understood my loyalty to them because I was always thinking and speaking positive things about them. That built within them a deep sense of security and well-being. They knew I always had their best interests at heart. They could trust that I was looking out for them spiritually and in every area. They depended on me to bear fruit from the Word, and I always did my best not to let them down.

The condition of your family is really the result of your faith — your thoughts, beliefs, and the words you speak. What have you been sowing into them? Do you believe they're a success going somewhere to happen? Do you believe God has a plan and purpose for their lives and that they're going to fulfill it?

Loyalty in Your Actions

Loyalty is expressed in your thoughts and words, but it's also expressed by your actions. For example, what do you do for your wife on her birthday, on Mother's Day, and so forth? Your actions portray loyalty and create feelings of loyalty in others as well.

I try to celebrate Maureen's birthday for a whole week leading up to her special day. That way, on her actual birthday, Maureen is already "filled up" because I've made her feel so special. There are any number of creative ways you can show your wife and children by your actions that you're loyal to them and that they are your number-one priority in life next to your relationship with the Lord.

Number Five: Unconditional Love

A fifth godly trait that successful men possess is unconditional love. Unconditional love is about loving the inside person, and it's based on a decision of your heart. People tend to want to love others because they've earned or deserved it in some way. They'll love someone because of what the person does for them, how that person makes them feel, or even how he or she looks. Very little of their loved is based on the real person on the inside — and on their own heartfelt commitment to love him or her unconditionally.

My wife is beautiful and takes great care of herself. But even if she didn't look the way she looks, I would still love her the same because of my own heart of love and my commitment to her. In other words, loving others unconditionally has more to do with you than with the people you're loving.

240

Unconditional Love and Your Happy Marriage

Marriage is about making a heart connection that's eternal in its commitment and that's based on unconditional love. Marriages last, not because the other person is changing but because you're changing and growing in the love of God, and you're making those commitments in your heart to love forever, not just for a season of fancy or for convenience.

Husbands, love your wives, just as Christ also loved the church and gave Himself for her. (Ephesians 5:25)

Of course, the wife is to love her husband, too, but it's interesting that wives are never directly commanded in the Word to love their husband. Remember, we said that Christ is the picture of the husband — and the Church is the picture of the wife, or the bride. Husbands are to love their wife as Christ loves the Church. When husbands love their wife as Christ loves the Church, wives will automatically respond to that, and they will love their husband fervently and devotedly.

Closeness of heart is very closely connected with the intimacy of sex.

One thing we know about the way Christ loved the Church is, He loved us first before we loved Him (see First John 4:19). Therefore, we as husbands must love our wife first. If we're waiting to be loved by her first, we can forget it. We might enjoy her initiating love for a season, but it won't last. We must ultimately act as the initiator in the relationship; we must be the sowers if we expect to reap on a consistent, long-term basis. We will never receive the love that truly fulfills us and makes us happy until we first give that kind of love away.

He who finds a wife finds a good thing, And obtains favor from the Lord. (Proverbs 18:22)

Think about this. A woman gives up her name to become the wife of her husband. What does he give up? He doesn't give up anything — he gains something: favor with the Lord. That and responsibility to love and care for his wife.

So another aspect of showing unconditional love toward your wife is to take care of her as the gift from God that she is.

Do you see your wife as a gift from God? She could have given herself to someone else, but she chose you. And now that she has entrusted her life to you, what are you going to do with it? She gave you her heart, trusting you to love her unconditionally for the rest of your life.

I have loved Maureen since we were in middle school and she was still in braces. When she later accepted my marriage proposal, my attitude was, I'd better take care of this gift from the Lord. I'd better honor her, provide for her, and serve her. I'm going to give her the best in life that I possibly can. She's trusting me, and I'm not going to let her down!

Love and Sex

Unconditional love is also associated with sex or physical intimacy. And a man needs to know that foreplay begins from the time he wakes up in the morning to the time he goes to bed at night. In other words, he must invest in his wife outside the bedroom. And if he can get past just what he wants out of sex — and get to the place of desiring what his wife wants and needs from the relationship — he and his wife will experience a very rewarding sexual relationship. Closeness of heart is very closely connected with the intimacy of sex.

A man can attempt to blame his failures in life on the people in his life or on the circumstances that surround him. But ultimately, the responsibility for his failure lies squarely with him.

Similarly, the secret to success in life — to a happy marriage, a happy family, and a happy life — is as close as your own heart. When you develop the characteristics of commitment, trust, service, loyalty, and unconditional love in your life, success in every area will ultimately find you and envelop you and your family in the blessings of God.

Salvation Prayer

Throughout this book, I have spoken of God's desire for you to be in control of your emotions. None of that means anything, however, if you haven't taken the first step. You need to make Jesus your Lord and Savior.

It is easy to do that. The Bible says that if you believe in your heart and confess with your mouth, then you will be saved. It is a matter of faith. If you want to have that relationship with Jesus now, just pray this short prayer.

Dear heavenly Father,
forgive me for my sin.
Come into my heart.
Jesus, be my Lord and my Savior.
Thank you for giving me
new life in you.
In Jesus name,
Amen.

Congratulations! You have made the very best decision you have ever made or ever will make. Now you are saved. You are forgiven and you are on your way to heaven. The next step is to grow in this new relationship with God. The best way to do that is to read your Bible every day so that God can speak to you through it, and get involved in a good church so that you can have support and fellowship of other believers.

Now that you are saved, we would love to hear from you! Please call us at (480) 964-4463 so that we can come into agreement with you and bless you with a free Bible.

Taking A Minute - Girl
Jason Anderson

This is a book that makes forming a Biblical attitude in life a bit easier for young girls.

ISBN-13 978-1-58588-166-6
Paperback
Retail $11.00
Devotional//
Self Improvement

Taking A Minute - Guy
Jason Anderson

This is a book that makes forming a Biblical attitude in life a bit easier for young guys.

ISBN-13 978-1-58588-166-3
Paperback
Retail $11.00
Devotional/
Self Improvement

What in Health Do you Want?
Dr. C. Thomas Anderson

In 90 days you can change your life, body, soul and spirit! Diets don't last, but God's plans, promises and purpose will.

ISBN-13 978-1-58588-099-7
Paperback
Retail $10.00
Health and Fitness/
Self Help

Think Like A Billionaire
Scot Anderson

We prepare today for today. Billionaires prepare today for the opportunities of tomorrow.

ISBN-13 978-1-58588-146-8
Hardcover
Retail $20.00
Finance/Business
Self-Improvement

Featured Winword Publishing Books

Confessing God's Word Leather-Bound
Dr. Maureen Anderson

ISBN-13 978-1-58588-150-5
Paperback
Retail $8.00
Self-Improvement/
Christian Living

In *Confessing God's Word*, Dr. Maureen Anderson helps to zero in on the appropriate scripture for any situation.

Confessing God's Word Leather-Bound
Dr. Maureen Anderson

ISBN-13 978-1-58588-155-0
Leather
Retail $13.00
Self-Improvement/
Christian Living

In *Confessing God's Word*, Dr. Maureen Anderson helps to zero in on the appropriate scripture for any situation.

Power of Confession Binder
Dr. Maureen Anderson

ISBN-13 978-1-58588-050-8
Binder
Retail $20.00
Self-Improvement/
Christian Living

In the *Power of Confession*, the promises of God are organized to aid in effective prayer and counsel.

DAD
Scot Anderson

ISBN-13 978-1-58588-025-6
Hardcover
Retail $20.00
Parenting/
Home and Family

A Step-by-Step GUIDE to building a great relationship with your children!

Featured Winword Publishing Books

Damaged DNA
Dr. Maureen Anderson

Dr. Maureen Anderson shares from her own experience and from biblical promises the path to freedom from generational curses and new life in the blessings and promises of God.

ISBN-13 978-1-58588-147-5
Paperback
Retail $11.00
Self-Improvement/
Christian Living

Releasing the Miraculous Through Fasting with Prayer

This book was designed to help you understand how to fast, hear more clearly from God, develop a greater relationship with God, and understand how fasting purifies your faith.

Dr. Maureen Anderson
ISBN-13 978-1-58588-067-6
Paperback
Retail $13.00
Self-Improvement/
Christian Living

Get the Hell Out of the Church
Dr. C. Thomas Anderson

Religion is the hell that needs to get out of the church! We need to get back to the true principles of life.

ISBN-13 978-1-58588-160-4
Paperback
Retail $20.00
Self-Improvement/
Christian Living

Making Marriage A Love Story
Drs. Tom & Maureen Anderson

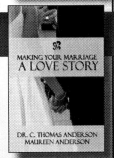

In *Making Marriage a Love Story* Drs. Tom and Maureen Anderson share vital insights about marriage and relationships from the Word of God and from their own personal experience.

ISBN-13 978-1-58588-012-6
Paperback
Retail $15.00
Marriage & Family

Featured Winword Publishing Books

Making Impossibilities Possible
Dr. Maureen Anderson

ISBN-13 978-1-58588-129-1
Paperback
Retail $13.00
Finance/Self Improvement

Dr. Maureen Anderson takes you on a journey into the world of God's best for you as you learn the faith process of *Making Impossibilities Possible*.

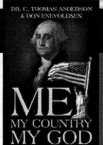

Me, My Country, My God
Dr. C. Thomas Anderson

ISBN-13 978-1-58588-048-5
Hardcover
Retail $20.00
Political Science/
History/Education

It is no small thing to be a citizen of the greatest nation on earth. Living in the freedom and the individual rights that we have also means that we live with the responsibilities of those freedoms.

Becoming A Millionaire God's Way
Dr. C. Thomas Anderson

ISBN-13 978-0-44651-096-7
Paperback
Retail $14.00
Finance/Self Improvement

Dr. Anderson explains the process of experiencing God's blessing through wise investment and the resulting increase of wealth.

Millionaire Habits in 21 Days
Scot Anderson

ISBN-13 978-1-58588-029-4
Hardcover
Retail $20.00
Finance/Self Improvement

Using my proven System of Success, S.O.S., exercise and understanding of the 12 laws that guide your life, in 21 days you will have the habits of a millionaire.

Featured Winword Publishing Books

MOM
Holly Anderson

A Step-by-Step GUIDE to building a great relationship with your children!

ISBN-13 978-1-58588-026-3
Hardcover
Retail $20.00
Parenting/
Home and Family

More Than A DAD
Scot Anderson

This book gives you the practical tools needed to build a great trusting relationship with your children.

ISBN-13 978-1-58588-049-2
Paperback
Retail $15.00
Parenting/
Home and Family

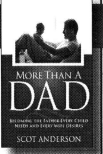

RE:Worship
Jason Anderson

This book will inspire people to let go of all their inhibitions and self-imposed notions of dignity in worship and help them to experience the resounding presence of God as never before.

ISBN-13 978-1-58588-035-5
Paperback
Retail $12.00
Christian Living

Toxic Emotions:
We Have Power Over Our Emotions in God.
Dr. Maureen Anderson

When you don't take control of your emotions, you will then get into toxic emotions which release poisonous chemicals that will eventually kill you. This book will give you the information that will save your LIFE!

ISBN-13 978-1-58588-047-8
Paperback
Retail $20.00
Christian Living

Featured Winword Publishing Books

Wisdom Wins
Dr. C. Thomas Anderson

ISBN-13 978-1-58588-017-1
Paperback
Retail 8.00
Humor

The book, *Wisdom Wins*, is filled with 80 power-packed stories, jokes, anecdotes, and inspirations. It is a teaching aid for pastors and entertainment for the lay person.

Wisdom Wins 2
Dr. C. Thomas Anderson

ISBN-13 978-1-58588-018-8
Paperback
Retail $8.00
Humor

The book, *Wisdom Wins 2,* is filled with 40 power-packed stories, jokes, anecdotes, and inspirations. It is a teaching aid for pastors and entertainment for the lay person.

The How To's On Making Marriage Last Forever
Dr. Maureen Anderson

ISBN-13 978-1-58588-010-2
MP3
Retail: $8.00
Christian Living/
Relationships

Learn about the "love molecule," a chemical released when we become emotionally attached to the opposite sex.

Living the Dream
Dr. Maureen Anderson

ISBN-13 978-1-58588-183-1
CD Series
Retail: $36.00
Christian Living/
Relationships

See into the unseen, and create with God. Your dreams are capable of lifting you to new heights and overcoming self-imposed limitations.